GIANTS
on Ancient Earth

An In-Depth Study of the Nephilim

Jason M. Breshears

THE BOOK TREE
San Diego, California

© 2017, 2024
Jason Breshears
Revised and Updated Second Edition
All rights reserved

No part of this book, in part or in whole, may be produced, transmitted, or utilized, in any form or by any means, electronic or mechanical, including photocopying, recording, or by any information storage or retrieval system, without permission in writing from the author or publisher, except for brief quotations in articles, books or reviews.

ISBN 978-1-58509-158-4

Cover Image
© 2024
The Book Tree
Original image generated
March 15, 2024 via
Shutterstock .AI
all ownership and usage rights
hereby claimed to fullest legal extent

Published by
The Book Tree
San Diego, California
www.thebooktree.com

We provide fascinating and educational products to help awaken the public to new ideas and information that would not be available otherwise.
Call 1 (800) 700-8733 for our FREE BOOK TREE CATALOG.

Table of Contents

Prologue: Vast Gulf of Missing History..........5
1. Some Discoveries of Note..........9
2. Origin of Nephilim Theory..........15
3. Antediluvian Giants and the Flood..........28
4. Post-Diluvian Giants..........42
5. Giants in the Promise Land..........55
6. Conquest of Canaan..........65
7. The Last Bible Giants..........78
8. Giants in Ancient Egypt..........89
9. The Giant of Babylon..........101
10. The Giant Wars..........114
11. Albion...Isle of the Giants..........133
12. Epics of the Giants..........149
13. Relics of the Gods..........161
14. The Bones of Giants..........173
13. Birth of the Great Lie..........181
Epilogue: As in the Days of Noah..........196
Reference Notes..........201
Bibliography..........215

About the Author

Jason M. Breshears is a researcher of occult antiquities and widely known as one of the best chronologists in the world today. Five of his previously published works are nonfiction with extensive bibliographies concerning fascinating information on ancient civilizations, cataclysms and the modern establishment's attempts to suppress these discoveries from the public today. The following works are published by Book Tree in San Diego.

The Lost Scriptures of Giza (2006, updated 2017)

When the Sun Darkens (2009)

Anunnaki Homeworld (2011)

Nostradamus and the Planets of Apocalypse (2013)

Awaken the Immortal Within (2022)

Return of the Fallen Ones (2017, updated 2024)

Jason Breshears' research, articles and discoveries can be found at www.archaix.com

Prologue

Vast Gulf of Missing History

Silently lying in the darkened basements of some of the world's most renowned museums are the skeletal remains of humans measuring seven to nine feet in height. Giants. Because of the explosion of Darwinian thought in the mid-nineteenth century, the anthropological remains and fossils of enormous human giants have been secretly pushed beyond the confines of scientific study because of their apparent defiance of the theory of human development from primate hominids to modern Homo sapiens.

The historic presence of giants is an extremely controversial topic among scholars, historians, scientists, and theologians. So debatable has this subject been that until now almost no one has ventured to publish a book-length study about giants and their truly mysterious history.

What the public is led believe should not contradict what we know. The sum of all human knowledge today is descended from our experiences and records of our distant past. Except for what has been buried or concealed, our beliefs today are little different from our predecessors. Censorship is an old practice.

But what we are taught today is not what we know. The past that we have known for thousands of years has been buried, relegated to myth and replaced with fables of greater magnitude, cleverly cunning tales that serve to alter our memory of true history and origin.

Among these most ancient beliefs held by our forefathers and ignored today is the existence of giants long ago. They believed that in a bygone age now forgotten, the gods gave birth to enormous people before departing from the earth. Our ancestors wrote that the gods were Guardians of the earth. They took human women in exchange for sharing many wonderful secrets concerning the planet's resources. As a result of this unusual union an entire nation of hybrids terrorized the earth for hundreds of years.

Though the guardians departed, their powerful offspring were left behind. These giants ruled over mankind, polluted the earth and provoked their true Creator.

Longing for relief from these huge and violent people, our most distant ancestors yearned for the return of the *gods*. They consulted their astronomers, studied star charts, etched enormous pictures in the surface of the earth and built celestial observatories on stone temples as they faithfully watched the star paths in the night skies. They also recorded their histories and complaints against their giant overlords on stone, clay and metallic plates.

All over the world the unearthed remains of massive structures, unusual artifacts and large relics tell a puzzling story of the activity of giant architects long ago. Fascinating information concerning these giants in antiquity is found in ancient Sumerian libraries, Akkadian, Babylonian and Assyrian writings, Celtic and Irish histories, Hebrew non-canonical works and annals, and is found extensively in Egyptian artistic reliefs, in hieroglyphics, monuments and excavations of unique crypts.

These giants were immortalized within the beliefs of the Greeks, Romans, Chinese, and Indians of the Far East, in the lore of the Olmecs, Aztecs, Mayans and Norse Icelandic, European and Viking folklore.

But no other book among the ancients reveals more about the giants than the Bible. This book reveals the history of the giants, their malignant intentions and mysterious disappearance.

Unearthed from the spades of archaeology, pens of history and labs of science is unveiled an extraordinary portrait of the birth, life and destruction of an advanced race of powerful and enormous people who ruled the earth.

Though thousands of traditions concerning giants are still extant today the *origin* of these people of heroic stature is only detailed in the world's ancient religious texts. Pliny, Homer, Virgil, Ovid, Berosus and many other scholars in antiquity wrote about the giants in their histories, but none of these men reveals to us today the origins of these mysterious people. For this information we will now delve deep in to the penetrating historical archives of our Bibles.

The foundation of evidence supporting the history and origin of civilized giants comes exclusively from over seventy biblical passages; however, hundreds of other pieces of evidence drawn from archaic texts, inscriptions, excavations, fossils and amazing chance discoveries are cited in support of the biblical record of giants.

As the writer and researcher of this work I must warn the reader that this book contains new and disturbing information that defies many orthodox beliefs and common theories about human history and ethnological evolution. This book is primarily about giants in world history, yet I touch upon other relative topics such as creationism, evolution, flood geology, astronomy, catastrophism and even eschatology—subjects that help shed light on the full scope of historic giants and the alarming implications of their past existence and center of origin.

This book is a massive compilation of biblical, extracanonical and ancient traditional research on the origin of the Nephilim. In the course of this author's studies, and since the first publication of this work, it's been realized that the ancients were merely postulating how giants and titans were born into the world. They invented the stories of angels visiting females, but it has been found that the true cause for giantism is from purely environmental conditions, i.e. a vapor canopy world, increased atmospheric pressure, intense volcanism producing ambient radiation and nutrition in the vapor canopy periods. Clear evidence shows that all other animal and plants species were larger during these times than what we have today.

> Here in early times the famous giants were born, a mighty race skilled in war. But God did not choose them to be His people or show them the way of knowledge. They died out because they had neither understanding nor insight. (Baruch 3:26-28)

Chapter One

Some Discoveries of Note

Writing of events before his own time when he finished his monumental book *The Histories* about 440 BC, Herodotus wrote that an excavation of what was believed to be the crypt of a Trojan War hero, Orestes, yielded forth the remains of a giant who had stood 10 feet high.[1] This book of world history was written over 24 centuries ago and, as will be shown in this work, is but only one of the multitudes of ancient texts that mention an historic race of giants.

In 170 AD Athenagoras wrote the book *Of Angels and Giants*. It was the accepted history of the time and had been for two millennia, including the story of wicked angels long ago before the Deluge copulating with human females, who then gave birth to monstrous giants. These angels were gods, djinn, demons, fairies, with each culture painting them with their own brush. Only later did official Christianity stamp out the belief by declaring it *pagan*, similar to how the modern scientific community censors all discoveries concerning giants from the public domain.

After the Romans conquered Jerusalem in 135 AD the rabbi Johnanan ben Zakkai led Hadrian into the deep underground catacombs beneath the Temple. He was shown the bones of enormous men who had stood over nine feet tall and told they were *Amorites*.[2] About the same time...Sertorius in Spain was shown the crypt of a giant named Anteaus, the skeletal remains of a man who stood six cubits high.[3] This measures to a height of 108 inches, or *nine feet*. It was during Hadrian's reign sea waves at Rhoeteum washed open an ancient tomb containing a giant's skeleton. Its kneecaps were the size of a large discus. Hadrian ordered that the bones be reburied.[4] In 240 AD Mani the Persian wrote *The Book of Giants*, a text not to be confused with the Dead Sea Scrolls text of the same name, that is almost three centuries older. Mani was a religious reformer but was killed by the religious authorities of his time. He believed that Christianity had become corrupted by the influence of Judaism.[5] He founded the Gnostic sect of Manichaeism. Mani may have derived much of his material from the various writings in circulation at the time attributed to Enoch. These texts will be explored in this work.

Some of the more unusual information from ancient writings has now been verified in chance finds. In the Babylonian Talmud called the *Berakthoth* we learn that giants before the Flood had double rows of teeth.[6] Such large human skeletons have now been found that prominently exhibit these double rows of teeth. In 1822 at Lompcock Rancho, California, soldiers excavated among carved shells, huge stone axes and blocks of porphyry adorned in an unknown script containing the skeleton of a man who once stood 12 feet tall with a double-row of teeth.[7] Later, more gigantic human skeletons were found with double dentition inside a mound near Clearwater, Minnesota.[8] In 1872 at Seneca Township, Ohio were excavated three human skeletons 8 feet tall with *double-rows of teeth.*[9] In 1880 giant skeletons with double-rows of teeth (hyperdontia) were found in Clearwater, MN.[10] In 1892 a gigantic human skeleton was found with a double row of teeth at Proctorville, Ohio.[11] The ancient race of giants occupying Ireland of old called the Fomorii had a double row of teeth.[12] More will be revealed on the Fomorii later in this work.

A double row of teeth is the result of a genetic mutation. There are people today of average height who have hyperdontia. This genetic increase of anatomical traits is also found in Nephilim studies in the six-fingered and six-toed skeletal remains unique to gigantic human skeletons. In 1891 at Crittenden, Arizona, was discovered a stone sarcophagus of a giant who once stood about 12 feet high having six fingers and toes on his hands and feet according to the carving of the giant on the stone.[13] In 1895 a 12-foot tall fossilized giant was found in County Antrim, Ireland. It had six toes on its right foot.[14] In 1949 in New Zealand it is reported that gigantic human footprints with six toes were discovered in volcanic ash (petrified), giants once standing at least 12 feet tall.[15] At Tiahuanacu in South America were excavated statues of great age with men having six fingers on their hands and six toes on their feet.[16] In the area of Braystown near the headwaters of the Tennessee river were found fossilized footprints of six-toed giants, one being monstrous, the heel impression 13 inches wide.[17] Petroglyphs found near Three Rivers, New Mexico are of hands with *six fingers.*[18] For those wanting more information on actual archaeological discoveries of human skeletons with six digits, see the final Chroicon edition on Podia (1052 pages).[19]

In 1999 a washout unearthed humanoid skeletons about 7 feet tall with six fingers and six toes, with human teeth but *no canines.* Extra large molars and incisors, large skulls, larger than proportional eye-sockets and fingers too long for such small hands. Skeletons had been buried with beautiful pottery and baskets of fine weave. They were unearthed at Arizona's Canyon de Chelly National Monument. All Park Service personnel were pressed into service to box up the artifacts and remains as they were directly overseen by personnel from the Smithsonian Institute and FBI who conducted full body searches. All involved were forced to sign nondisclosure secrecy documents.[20]

Extra teeth, extra fingers and toes and now this: In 1899 near Mexico City was unearthed a human skeleton having two extra ribs—26 ribs in all.[21] The entire human race has 24 ribs... how did that happen?

In 1947 gigantic human skeletons 8-9 feet tall were found in 32 caves bordered by Arizona, California and Nevada along with strange hieroglyphic texts on highly polished granite. Agents of the Smithsonian Institute arrived, confiscated the artifacts and covered up the find.[22] The Smithsonian Institute originally championed archeology in North America but was heavily influenced and then *controlled* by those who would make sure that no new artifacts would surface that opposed the new theory of evolution. In 1884 The Smithsonian Bureau of Ethnology reported the discovery of a stone structure inside a mound in Kanawa County, West Virginia, that yielded the remains of a skeleton measuring 7'6" tall with a 19" chest.[23] Prior to 1890 the Smithsonian was involved actively in the excavation of giant remains. The 1800s brought forth by far the most discoveries of giant remains for the simple fact that it was during this century that most of North America's infrastructure was laid out, lands cleared and hills levelled for roads, towns and farm land.

In 1829 British millionaire James Smithson died, leaving a fund behind for the establishment in America of an organization that became the Smithsonian Institute. Since about 1890 the Institute has become one of the greatest knowledge-filters in the world, actively destroying tens of thousands of ancient artifacts and remains. Hundreds of shipments of strange relics and gigantic human skeletons have vanished at the Institute and there are several good, well-documented books showing how the Smithsonian has succeeded in erasing all evidence of the true past while manufacturing fictions to perpetuate a false history, especially concerning North America.

Censorship is nothing new. In 1881 a prominent and famous display of a fossilized woman who had stood 5'5" in the British Museum was quietly removed because its existence was contrary to the new scientific paradigm being taught—evolution. The female human fossil was embedded in hard limestone and was discovered in 1812 off the French Caribbean coast of Guadeloupe.[24] In 2000 American archeologists excavated the remains of skeletons belonging to gigantic humans in the desert region of northern India, along with tablets bearing ancient script.[25] The Indian government has since sealed off the area. In 2004 at Rab-Ul-Khalee, SE Saudi Arabia, a titan 36 feet tall, a *humanoid* skeleton, was excavated by the company Aramco, but the find was taken over by the Saudi military.[26]

So many interesting finds cannot remain unmentioned.

In 1184 in the reign of King Henry II atop Glastonbury Tor, after excavating 16 feet down, were found the remains of a male skeleton eight feet in length next to a female, shorter with the remains of golden tresses of hair. Gerald of Wales wrote that the male skull was so large and capacious that it seemed a veritable prodigy of nature.[27]

In 1456 AD a 23 foot tall giant human skeleton unearthed at Valence, France[28] and 53 years later, in 1509, was unearthed a 17 foot tall giant skeleton unearthed at Rouen, France.[29]

Near Reyden, Switzerland in 1577 AD a very ancient and decayed oak tree fell and revealed a cave wherein was excavated the bones of a truly gigantic man, a giant that would have stood 16 feet in height. A well-known physician, Felix Plater of Basle, studied the anatomical remains, refashioned them and presented them to the Senate of Luzern. After this the giant skeleton was immortalized upon the Coat of Arms for the town of Luzern and was painted by Johannes Bock.[30]

On December 17th, 1615 Jacob Lemaire was investigating a site at Port Desire in England when to his astonishment he "...unearthed the skeletons of men which measured between 10 and 11 feet." They were discovered underneath several rock-buried graves.[31]

In 1757 AD a 9'6" tall human skeleton unearthed at Fullwell-Hills, Durham, England.[32] The Annual Register of 1790 of Ireland reveals that the sepulcher of an ancient Irish chieftain had been unearthed 17 feet deep in a peat bog at Donnadea. Inside the sepulcher were found a human skeleton 8'2" long with a 7' spear.[33] A similar find was made in the early 19th century at an old Roman Catholic chapel where a huge lead coffin was discovered which was found to contain "...a skeleton of heroic dimension," measuring 8'3".[34] Both Britain and Ireland have rich giant histories as will be reviewed. In Britain ancient swords over 96 inches (8 feet) have been excavated.[35] The historic links between ancient Briton and Ireland and the Danaan, the Aegean, and Crete are well know, so we are not surprised to find that at Knossos on Crete in the Mediterranean was found a gigantic bronze sword longer than any known sword in Europe, gold plated on the hilt and with a crystal-faceted knob.[36] The famous gigantic bat-winged battleaxes found on Crete are also well known. Men would have to stand 9 feet tall or more to wield them.

In 1843 AD farmers in a Moldavian village in the region of ancient Dacia uncovered gigantic human remains, one being an *upright giant*. The military governor examined it and declared that it was the remains of a Roman soldier of unusually gigantic stature.[37] As the Romans were a very short people, it is doubtful that the remains were of a Roman.

Because very detailed material about the giants from the biblical record declares the exact region where they were living in the 15th century BC, the following two books provide proof for the existence of these historic giants. An old book titled *Ancient Bashan and the Cities of Og* (1858) by Cyril Graham, records that the ruins of cities in Syria inhabited by the giants ruled by Og in the Old Testament "...all betoken the workmanship of a race endowed with powers far exceeding those of ordinary men; all giving credibility to the supposition that we have in them the dwellings of the giant race... we find rooms in these houses so large and lofty that many of them would be considered fine rooms in a palace in Europe.[38] In 1873 J. L. Porter in his *The Giant Cities of Bashan* wrote that a single door in Kerioth was "...nine feet high, four and a half feet wide, and ten inches thick—one solid slab of stone."[39] We will explore the topic of the giants of Bashan in this work.

In 1868 AD at Sank Rapids, MN a 10 foot tall petrified giant was discovered when a local water company blasted it out of solid granite.[40] In 1883 at the State Prison in Carson City, Nevada at a depth of 25 feet was discovered, in sandstone, the petrified remains of footprints once belonging to men who stood 18 to 20 feet tall. They were happened upon by men who quarried sandstone blocks for building material. Also found were the fossil prints of cats, deer and elephants.[41] In 1884 a large mound near Gasterville, PA was excavated, and discovered within it was a vault covered with unknown inscriptions containing a huge 7'2" human skeleton.[42] In 1884 six fossilized human bodies were found in a coal mine in Pas de Calais, France, with utensils, petrified wood near eleven *giant human* skeletons in a cave with wall pictures depicting huge men battling enormous beasts.[43] In 1898 Archeologists in Death Valley found the fossilized remains of a giant human female that had stood 7'6" tall.[44]

In 1902 Mount Pelee on the French island of St. Martinique in the Caribbean exploded, and a searing gas cloud incinerated 30,000 people. Shortly after the volcanic eruption, it was noticed that plants and animals returned quickly to the region, but were *much bigger than usual.* Two scientists studying the island also underwent major changes in their own body size and height. Dr. Jules Graveure grew **2.5 inches taller** while on the island and his assistant, Dr. Rouen, aged 59, grew almost two inches.[45] This is a major clue as to the origin of giants in the past. Ambient radiation from intense volcanism on a global scale would cause all life on this planet to grow to larger sizes, however, the preflood world was enshrouded by a thick marine vapor canopy that would have added pressure to this layering of ambient radiation, causing fauna and flora to grow to the astonishing sizes we find in the fossil record. Volcanism thus provides us a natural cause for the existence of historic giants without nullifying the Nephilim-hybrid evidence of genetic mixing in antiquity that resulted in the birth of strange creatures found in ancient texts. Double rows of teeth, extra ribs, six fingers and six toes are Nephilim traits, for there have been unearthed many perfectly normal human skeletons that were gigantic in stature, but shared none of these characteristics.

In 1912 a Mr. Ernest A. Edwards of British Columbia uncovered an enormous human skeleton on the isle of Neskain at a riverbank where many arrowheads had been found. The skeleton was of a man who had stood eight feet tall. He wrote that "...the teeth were of huge size, but in perfect condition—no cavities noticeable. The jawbone was so large that it could span my face easily at the cheek bones."[46]

In 1929 excavations on Catalina Island off the California coast yielded forth amazing finds. A huge human skeleton measuring 7'8" tall was discovered with a spear blade stuck through the ribs on its left side. Of the 3781 skeletons excavated the largest was 9'2" tall.[47] In 1960 at Tura, India was excavated the skeletal remains of a humanoid who had stood 11 feet tall, along with a metal cup.[48]

In the 1970s near Dogubeyazit, Turkey were found the fossilized thumb bones of a human more than twice the size of men today, with enormous human jawbones.[49] Near the Paluxy River close to Glenrose, Texas was discovered the skull of a woman who had stood seven feet in height, found in Panther Cave. This is near the site where giant human footprints were discovered in Glenrose Dinosaur Park.[50] After excavating enormous stone implements, large clubs and knives, gigantic molars and fossilized human footprints over thirty inches in length in 1970, Dr. Rex Gilroy wrote that men of 12 to 20 feet in height once roamed the Australian continent.[51] This is a profound statement for Australia is the *dead* continent. Unique for having the highest concentration of marsupials, proto-mammals and the presence of a Stone Age people, the Aborigines, the Australian continent boasts of *no ancient ruins*. I venture that Australia was once a thriving land full of life that suffered a cataclysm and the deep remains of giants are from a time period long before the Aborigine came to be there.

In 2000 a 15-16 foot tall human skeleton was found in southeast Saudi Arabia.[52] The wastes of Saudi Arabia are little explored, especially the Empty Quarter, where giants have been excavated. It, too, is a region exhibiting many signs of having suffered a disaster.

More discoveries of giants will be revealed in this book. We shall now delve into the ancient texts and mine fossils of knowledge.

Chapter Two

Origin of Nephilim Theory

Sons and Stars of God

The term <u>sons of God</u> is only found five times in the entire Old Testament, and not surprisingly. These five references are located within the two most ancient books: Genesis and Job. Both of these books were originally written upon scrolls, probably composed in the halls of a Babylonian library. The book of Genesis alone details an expanse of time over half of recorded human history within its fifty chapters. In this book the <u>sons of God</u> are mentioned twice.

The other book, Job, is an archaic story of a righteous man who suffered at the hands of Satan himself, who was the lord over the wicked angels. He was once called the <u>son of the morning</u> (Isaiah 14:12). In the book of Job is found the other three references to the <u>sons of God</u>. When questioning God, Job received answers directly from the Lord, and the following example is part of a rebuke from God meant to humble Job:

> ...<u>when the morning stars sang together, and all the sons of God shouted for joy?</u> (Job 38:7)

God had asked Job where he was when the Creation took place, where only the <u>sons of God</u> were present. Satan had long ago been called Lucifer, which translates to <u>daystar</u>, or <u>morning star</u>. His official title in heaven was <u>son of the morning</u>. Another proof as to the identity of the stars is the fact that they do not sing, not literal stars, therefore they are symbolic of <u>sons of God</u>.

Only angels were present at the earth's creation. The fact that angels are often referred to as <u>stars</u> is indisputable. In the apocalyptic book of the Revelation, Jesus tells John that the <u>seven stars are the seven angels</u> (Revelation 1:20), and in the book of Judges (5:20) <u>the stars in their courses fought against Sisera</u>, and also in Revelation (9:1, 12:4) <u>a star has a key to the bottomless pit</u> and that a <u>third part of the stars of heaven fell</u> with Satan, which before was prophesied by Jesus when He foretold that in the last days the <u>stars of heaven shall fall and the powers in heaven shall be shaken</u> (Mark 13:25). To confirm this symbolism, in the Ethiopic Enoch text the prophet wrote:

> I looked in my vision and surveyed heaven; when behold I saw many stars which descended...[and God] seized the first star which fell down from Heaven. And binding it hand and foot He cast it into a valley; a valley narrow, deep, stupendous, and gloomy.

This is found in chapters 85-87. In these writings angels are called stars dozens of times. In Numbers 24:17 a messianic prophecy declares that a star shall come out of Jacob. This is a direct reference to Jesus, the Savior from heaven. Daniel 12:3 is a prophecy promising that the wise and righteous shall be as the stars. This is supported by the promise of Jesus who said that the saved will be equal unto the angels. (Luke 20:36) In several very old texts and translations from the most antiquarian languages like the *Book of Enoch, Secrets of Enoch, Epic of Gilgamesh, Apocalypse of Baruch, Book of Jubilees* and the Dead Sea text called the *War Scroll*, is revealed the ties between the sons of God and the sons of Heaven, with many of the oldest writings directly calling angels stars. At the beginning of the book of Job the sons of God appear before the Almighty to present themselves. This occurred twice in Job (1:6, 2:1). Both times the words present or present themselves are used, which in Hebrew is yâtsab, a word that clearly means to show one's self, to present; however, it has a deeper implication, meaning to be able to withstand, continue. These angels had already committed a trespass against God.

The presence of a tree of evil knowledge in a flawless world is only understandable when reckoning in the fact that evil was already existent. The presence of a deceptive serpent further indicates that the rebellion was relocating from the incorporeal planes of God's heavens to the material planet where He planted His garden.

One of the earliest men recorded in Scripture who knew that the angels committed iniquity was a friend of Job named Bildad.

> How then can man be justified with God? Or how can he be clean that is born of a woman? Behold, even to the moon, and it shineth not; yea, the stars are not pure in his sight. (Job 25:4-5)

Bildad was conveying to Job that nothing was righteous in the sight of God, not men nor angels, stars which are not born of women, like men, which is evident in the next thing Bildad says:

> How much less man, that is a worm? and the son of man which is a worm? (Job 25:6)

The word <u>pure</u> in the Hebrew rendering connotes <u>innocence</u> and refers to <u>purity of conduct</u>, implying that the <u>stars</u> are responsible for their iniquity.

Another friend or contemporary of Job made an astounding statement concerning the angels. This ancient man was named Eliphaz.

> <u>Shall mortal man be more just than God? Shall a man be more pure than his maker? Behold, he put no trust in his servants; and his angels he charged with folly.</u> (Job 4:17-18)

Here again we see a comparison drawn between men and angels and the impurity of both. But what folly did the angels get charged with?

Several chapters later in Job, Eliphaz again speaks to him concerning the unrighteousness of mankind and how the angels are guilty of iniquity as well.

> <u>Behold, he putteth no trust in his saints; yea, the heavens are not clean in his sight. How much more abominable and filthy is man, which drinketh iniquity like water?</u> (Job 15:15-16)

For the third time in Job we discover that people shortly after the flood had a basic knowledge that angels sinned. Here the <u>saints of God</u> are compared to men. <u>Saints,</u> like stars, are a common reference to angels. Eliphaz argues that if saints cannot be righteous, then neither can man who <u>drinks iniquity like water</u>. The translation of saints is <u>holy ones</u>. In Joel 3:11 and Matthew 13:41 the term can be found in direct relation to angels. The <u>heavens</u> are described as unclean. Again we see the ties between celestial bodies and angels. The ancients all believed that the angels were from above, from the realms of stars and space.

Eliphaz told Job these things to illustrate how evil angels were and to comfort him in his own guilt and calamity. Humanity in any way could not have been responsible for any corruption in the <u>heavens,</u> for as he had said earlier, man is <u>mortal</u> (Job 4:17).

Now we have the proof that the <u>sons of God</u> and the <u>stars of heaven</u> are one and the same: angels. Throughout Scripture, stars are emblematic of angels.

Likewise, ancient Sumerian, Akkadian, Chaldean, and many other peoples of distant antiquity linked their gods to certain stars as discovered in their artifacts, art, architecture, and writings on cuneiform, stone, and metallic plates. Interestingly, historians studying ancient Babylonian and Assyrian King-Lists and monuments have discovered that the oldest kings were regarded as gods, their names being preceded by a <u>star</u>, the symbol for a god in early Mesopotamia.[1]

On the other side of the planet, the American Indian traditions of the Maya of Northwest Mexico believed that the children of God were actually stars, and the Jicaque people claim that the ancients were banished from the earth's surface so they flew into the sky and became stars.[2]

The Bible also reveals this in Acts 7:42-43 where it is written ...the star of your god Remphan. Here it also confirms that this star is one of the hosts of heaven that Stephen accuses the Israelites of worshiping. The common denominator between all ancient religions concerning the angels is the universal belief that gods were divinely related to the celestial bodies, by the stars or planets.

Of the five references to sons of God in Scripture, the three in the book of Job have been examined. Now let us search the fourth example and see what we unearth.

Daughters of Men

The only place in Scripture that the term daughters of men can be found is in Genesis 6:2-4, both in direct reference to sons of God. Having mentioned this intriguing fact, we now move on to the fourth example of the sons of God.

> And it came to pass, when men began to multiply on the face
> of the earth, and daughters were born unto them, that the sons
> of God saw the daughters of men that they were fair; and they
> took them wives of all which they chose.

It is unfortunate that so many Bible-believing Christians have fallen prey to the misleading theologians and scholars that have misinterpreted these two verses of history as referring to how ancient men and women married. They contend that the sons of God are a title for those of the righteous bloodline of Seth, while the daughters of men were the women of the evil Cainite lineage. But this is completely untrue and without merit.

Another indication as to the identity of the sons of God is discovered in that all through the Bible the phrase sons of men is used when speaking about large populations of people. Here, daughters of men are not wives of sons of men, but rather they are wives of the sons of God. Scripture differentiates between the sons of God and the sons of Adam (Deuteronomy 32:8). It is not an accident that both of these terms, describing angels and humans, are found within the Torah, the first five books of the Bible.

Other references to sons concerning angels are found in the Jewish apocalyptic literature found among the Dead Sea Scrolls. One reference made is in the War Scroll. It foretells of a last days war in heaven between the <u>sons of light</u> and the <u>sons of darkness</u> (The War Scroll, cited by Russell Chandler in *Doomsday: A View Through Time*). As we learned earlier, Lucifer was called <u>son of the morning</u>, and in Psalm 89 it calls angels of the host of heaven <u>sons of the mighty</u>.

The Hebrew meanings and definitions from which our English translations derive offer us a clearer picture as to the events described in these two verses in Genesis detailed earlier, 6:2 and 6:4. First, the word <u>fair</u> in Genesis 6:2 is <u>tov,</u> which means <u>good, pleasant,</u> andphysically <u>beautiful,</u> while also implying <u>good, right,</u> and <u>beneficial,</u> morally and ethically. The daughters of men could not be described as such if they were truly a reference to the females of the Cainite lineage. Another word in the same verse is "chose." The passage reads: <u>and they took them wives of all which they chose</u>. The word for chose in this Hebrew context is <u>bachar,</u> and it has such a deeper meaning that no word in the English language could have been provided for proper transliteration. <u>Bachar</u> means chose, but more precisely, <u>to select after keenly observing,</u> and is used in Hebrew texts where <u>choices that have eternal consequences are made</u>... and the fact that the angels that sexually trespassed against mankind will suffer eternal consequences is taught all throughout Scripture.

In fact, much of the contention between good and evil in the Bible is focused between the <u>sons of God</u>, former holy angels now fallen, the <u>present sons of God</u> that still remain holy, and the future <u>sons of God</u> they are commanded to protect. Humans are often referred to in the Bible as <u>sons of men</u> until the First Resurrection takes place and when believers receive their <u>sonship</u>. Thus, <u>we shall be like the angels</u> (Luke 20:35-36). This contention will one day end between the fallen <u>sons</u> and <u>holy ones,</u> when the <u>children of the kingdom will be cast out</u> (Matthew 8:12).

In 1 Corinthians we find that Paul retained some knowledge about the former sins of angels and their lusts.

> <u>Neither was man created for the woman, but the woman for the man.</u>
> <u>For this cause ought the woman to have power on her head because of the angels.</u>
> <u>But if a woman have long hair, it is a **glory** to her; for her hair is given her for a covering.</u> (1 Corinthians 11:9-11, 14)

Paul is not suggesting that women have long hair because of the angels, but rather that women should cherish long hair for its serves as a covering.

In these modern days this is difficult to comprehend. Today's culture dictates otherwise by fashions and traditions, but during the days of only a hundred years ago and beyond, through thousands of years, it was universally held that all women have long hair. To view a woman's fleshly beauty was by removing her hair from her body, something only husbands had the right to do. Today this is rarely practiced. By mentioning the angels here, Paul reveals that he was aware that the angels had at one time in history (or still did) lust after human women, and his suggestion is to hinder this by having women grow long hair. His reasoning is sound, though antiquated by today's standards.

In Jude 6-7 the apostle writes that the angels sinned <u>even as Sodom and Gomorrah, giving themselves over to fornication, and going after strange flesh</u>. The Greek phrase <u>strange flesh</u> also translates to <u>sexual abominations</u>; thus, the angels were guilty of sexual relations with women when they were not permitted, just as the people of Sodom and Gomorrah were guilty of homosexual abominations.

<u>He gave me the signs of all the secret things in the book of my great grandfather Enoch</u>. Noah studied Enoch's writings. These texts are prophetic and very informative concerning the geographical, social, spiritual and celestial conditions from Eden to the flood. The Messianic bloodline family, including the ten patriarchs, <u>knew</u> that the world would be destroyed, and this knowledge was preserved through Enoch's books that were inherited by his own son:

> <u>Preserve, my son Mathusalah, the books of the hand of thy father: that thou mayest transmit them to future generations.</u>
> (Enoch 81:2)

Evidence that the *Book of Enoch* was available to the writers of the Bible is unveiled in that a portion of *Enoch* 99:2 is quoted five times by Bible prophets (*The Book of Enoch*, trans. Richard Lawrence, 1821, p. 87) and <u>millions</u> of times by people all around the world. Enoch says, "The apple of my eye," a phrase no doubt connected to the Edenic sin of eating the apple from the accursed <u>tree of knowledge of good and evil</u>. James Kugel in his book *The Bible as It Was* commented that the writings of Enoch <u>seem to be the oldest Jewish writings that have survived outside the Bible itself</u>.

These ancient often debated writings were a part of the universal canon of Scripture, <u>in the Bible for five centuries!</u> [3] Later it was decided that only the book of the Revelation of John would remain canonical. Meetings and disputes raged as the early church selected and deleted various books and writings for the Bible. The writings of Enoch were <u>accepted as Scripture by</u>

Jesus, Paul, and the whole Christian church for several centuries, and quoted by the apostle Jude as well.

The daughters of men in the Enochian text are described as elegant and beautiful. The Enoch writings also make it very clear that there is a difference between sons of God (or of heaven) and sons of men. In this story the sons of heaven assembled and said, "Come, let us select for ourselves wives from the progeny of men, and let us beget children." (Enoch 7:2) In the Hebrew commentary called the *Book of Jasher*, cited twice in the Bible itself (Joshua 10:13, 2 Samuel 1:18), we learn that the rebellious angels shift their authoritative capacities from guardians or Watchers to judges and rulers over men.

> And their judges and rulers went to the daughters of men and took their wives by force from their husbands according to their choice. (Jasher 4:18)

In *Baruch* 56:12-14 it states that the angels descended, and mingled with women. And then those who did so were tormented in chains. But the rest of the multitude of angels, of which there is no number, restrained themselves.

Among all the Dead Sea texts later unveiled in this book is the Lamech Scroll. This pre-flood patriarch had a son so beautiful and radiant that he accused his wife of adultery with the angels![4] This story of Noah's birth is ancient and was not regarded as myth by the Hebrews, nor should it be today. It is evident that Lamech's wife was referring to angels when she said sons of heaven, which is greatly supported by the fact that the Greek version of the Old Testament, the Septuagint, translates "bene Elohim" in the Hebrew as angels of God instead of sons of God like the Masoretic text.

The Greek rendering is not to be regarded lightly; even Jesus and the apostles accepted its authority and quoted from it extensively. Though the Masoretic text was the original version of the Bible, being pure Hebrew, it was the Greek Septuagint that was most widely used by the first century churches and Jewish people.

Concerning the Nephilim, attempts from all avenues of scholarship and theology have attempted to refute the existence of literal giants. Just a few generations ago there existed no proof of the existence of Nephilim. But today the evidence is piling up. Archaeologists are confounded the world over as they dig up artifacts and relics that do not fit into their preconceived beliefs of ancient history. The prophecy of Daniel that knowledge shall be increased in the last days is coming to pass.

Birth of the Nephilim

Of the five instances within the Old Testament where the title <u>sons of God</u> is found, it is this final example here that is the most astounding, presenting undeniable proof that angels had, in ages past, assumed human form and maintained sexual ties with women. This verse also reveals what the result was of these lewd unions of Satan's design.

> <u>There were giants in the earth in those days; and also after that, when the sons of God came in unto the daughters of men, and they bore children to them; the same became mighty men, which were of old, men of renown</u>. (Genesis 6:4)

The Hebrew word for giant here is <u>n'phil</u>, which has its origin in the word <u>n'phal</u>: a <u>bully</u>, <u>tyrant</u>, <u>giant</u>; however, the rendering of this root word synonymously means <u>to fall away</u>, to <u>cast oneself down</u>, but the main idea behind the root of <u>n'phil</u> is of <u>violence</u> or accidental circumstance in the act of <u>falling down</u>. In Aramaic, <u>n'phal</u> means an <u>untimely or premature birth that falls from the womb</u>. N'phal, when plural as the word giants, is translated <u>nephilim</u>: the <u>fallen ones</u>. Thus the giants, mighty men and men of renown that they were, had been brought into this world by the union of disobedient angels and human women, for the translation the <u>fallen ones</u> is an archaic insight as to the nature of the giants' angelic ancestry.

Clearly, the giants and the Nephilim are synonymous; one and the same. In fact, the Jewish Old Testament, referred to as *The Holy Scriptures: According to the Masoretic Text*, does not say in Genesis 6:4 that there were giants in the earth in those days, which is more commonly found. It states, "The Nephilim were in the earth in those days," hence the sub-title of this book (*An In-Depth Study of the Nephilim*).

The terms referring to them as <u>mighty men</u> and <u>men of renown</u> have often been misinterpreted to be ordinary men, tyrants who overran the earth by provoking fear and violence. They are said by many scholars to be the children of the righteous Sethites and wicked Cainites' women; however, this vague interpretation has no Scriptural backing, but some archaeologists have recently declared that they've discovered evidence that <u>tyrants</u> of antiquity were referred to as <u>sons of God</u> and giants long ago. But never, in world history, has the union of a righteous person and a wicked person produced a giant.

The title <u>mighty men</u> in Hebrew is <u>gibborim</u>, which is plural of gibbar. This word means <u>huge</u>, a <u>hero</u>, <u>tyrant</u>, <u>giant</u>, and <u>powerful</u>. But it is the translation of the word men in the phrase men of renown that solidly proves the ancestry of the Nephilim being angelic, rather than mere mortals with diverse moral and ethical beliefs and behavior, as some scholars believe. The phrase mighty men is also used by the Greek epic writer Homer in his famous *Odyssey* to describe a giant cyclops named Polyphemos, a one-eyed giant also called an ogre in the epic. This hideous giant in Greek lore was the son of the sea good Poseidon, a huge beast-like man that will be studied with more scrutiny later in this book. This phrase is found many times in the Hebrew book of *Jasher* where the sons of Jacob battle men of great stature and size, sometimes only able to strike them upon their hips with their swords because of their height.

The fact that gibborim means tyrant does not conflict with the description of their great size, being giants. Tyrants are men who rule over others by their strength and force. This falls completely in line with the contextual description of the Nephilim being mighty men which were of old. Which leads us to the discovery of three words in Hebrew that describe men.

The word for general humanity in the image of God is adam, man. And the word describing men in a masculine sense is ish. These two words for men are used interchangeably about twenty-three times in the first five chapters of Genesis and even in verse one of chapter six where it reads:

> ...and it came to pass, when men began to multiply on the face of the earth...

The men mentioned above are simply human males, adam in Hebrew. It is not until the men of renown are mentioned that we discover that the Bible contains a third word for men. This word is enosh; a very unique word descriptive of mankind in a weakened state, for this word derives directly from ânash, which literally means to be incurable, sick, wicked, and woeful.

The very presence of this strange revelation mentioned in the Bible at the first recording of giants is profoundly demonstrative that these giants were not human, or not entirely so, but were the product of a union between the sons of God and normal Adamic people.

Enosh is not descriptive of the giants' physical natures because they are mighty men, men of renown, called giants and were not sick or weak. The fallen ones could not be giant tyrants, strong and oppressive if they were plagued by weakness. The giants owe their great size and strength to their angelic fathers, where as we will see, the word enosh developed.

Angels are said to be greater in power and might (2 Peter 2:11) than ordinary people, adam. When applied to the fact that human women joined with physically manifested angels, knowing that in purely human sexual relations the child born bears the genetic design of an interwoven pattern of genes contributed from both parents, then it is entirely plausible, if not factual, that the genes contributed to the offspring from the angelic forefathers, being they supernatural in nature, would perfectly explain how the Nephilim became so large and powerful. And evil, being they the children of fallen ones, sometimes considered demons.

Enosh is used for the first time in the Bible in Genesis 6:4 to reveal how the sons of God polluted the pure Adamic bloodline. Though Cain and his lineage were basically ungodly as a people, they were still purely Adamic in bloodline. All Sethites and Cainites are described as being adam (image of God) men until the arrival of the Nephilim.

Woeful, sick, and incurable (ânash) does not contradict the contextual description of the Nephilim, but rather provides us insights as to the weakened natures of these new and terrible beings. Genesis 1:26-27 and 5:3 reveal that God made all men in His own image and then in Genesis 1:24-25 Scripture teaches that all living creatures under heaven were divinely designed by God to mate and reproduce after their own kind. For a *newer* type of human to emerge, an enosh man, then something must have infiltrated the pure Adamic bloodline, contaminating it. This would cause initial sickness. Men were not made enosh; humanity began in perfection. Though the curse of sin was already plaguing earth, God made sure there was sufficient Adamic blood left to carry on... and thus provide a way for the coming seed of Eve. God then flooded earth.

All humans are descendants of Adam (Acts 17:26), so for the daughters of men to produce offspring with polluted blood, weaker, incurable and sick, reveals that the fathers of the giants, and Nephilim themselves, were lesser than human, unable to contribute pure Adamic blood.

As discovered earlier, the word chose is bachar, which means to select after keenly observing and refers to when the sons of God took the daughters of men, all that they chose. However, this particular rendering of the word chose, as read earlier, describes those choices that result in eternal consequences. With this in mind, we can better understand why the Nephilim are described as incurable.

This corruption of the Adamic bloodline is proven in Genesis 6:12 when God was telling Noah why He was going to destroy the entire world. God said, "...all flesh has corrupted his way..." The word flesh is b's'r and is translated as "blood-relation." All blood-relation was corrupt on earth. Giants roamed the earth in the last days before the Flood. Evil and violence increased while earth continued in her daily affairs, unaware that she would soon be reduced to relics of the past and examples for the future. The greatest proofs and facts that giants walked the earth and greatly affected the world of men are yet to be disclosed in this book. These awesome and thought provoking revelations about the Nephilim will be addressed later. First, it is time to once and for all refute the hypocritical teachings of man, found in the majority of the Christian academic community, concerning the identity of the sons of God. The Hebrew and Greek insights into the Scriptures provide many clues and hints as to information concerning the Nephilim, but as for the <u>sons of God</u> themselves, the English we use today will be perfect.

Thousands of scholars, theologians, and learned laymen alike in the recent century are bent on trying to prove that the sons of God are merely righteous men. They affirm this by quoting New Testament verse, so we shall now look into the very New Testament they so revere and shall behold how it in itself disproves their unwarranted conjectures. Most people have never seen angels and could not fathom having sexual relations with them, so these believers all too often rationalize the evidences for such occurrences to be interpreted in another way. But the horror of it all lies in that if one did have intercourse with an angel, that person would probably never know it. <u>Thou shalt not commit adultery</u> was respected by many humans and commanded by God for a reason.

So far, we have already discovered what the term <u>sons of God</u> meant in the Old Testament. Now we will examine a collection of Scriptures and passages used by those respectable people among our seminaries and other theological institutions who refuse to accept the factual history of the Nephilim as being the offspring of giants.

It is noteworthy that the very exegetical principles and guidelines our theological teachers teach us to use when interpreting Scripture are blatantly ignored when the topic of the Nephilim arises. Why is this? How can a man believe that virgin Mary conceived, the dead will resurrect, or the blind can be made to see again, but completely disbelieve that angels, beings he is supposed to already admit exist, can mate and produce offspring? Let's look deeper into this hypocrisy and see what we can find.

The guidelines for accurately interpreting Scripture must be applied to <u>all</u> areas of theology and doctrine. Should any method of interpretation disprove a theory or study, then the information extracted from Scripture must be reevaluated. If other exegetical laws cannot shed some light on the theory or the information is not consistent with the whole of Scripture, then the study must be viewed as mere conjecture and not doctrine.

But when the subject of the Nephilim is brought up among theological debates, literature, or casual conversation, those who disbelieve the biblical account of the giants having been produced from a union of angels and human women disregard these principles and instead rely heavily upon <u>common</u> sense, twisted logic, and <u>sophisticated</u> opinion. Among the more rejected of the exegetical guidelines by these disbelievers are the tools of <u>literal rendering, contextual content, intertestamental relation, multiple reference, comparative symbolism,</u> and the methods of interpretation by use of Hebrew and Greek dictionaries and lexicons.

Although only recorded five times in the Old Testament, the term <u>sons of God</u> is found dozens of times in the New Testament and though they are definitely related in their usage, subjects thus depicted in the texts are not.

> <u>But as many as received him, to them gave he power to become the sons of God, even to them that believe on his name:</u>
>
> <u>Which were born, not of blood, nor of the will of the flesh, nor of the will of man, but of God.</u> (John 1:12-13)

The <u>him</u> refers to Jesus, who saves those who believe in Him, granting them power to become <u>sons of God</u>. However, though this passage speaks of humans becoming righteous, assuming the title of sons of God, the passage here proclaims that despite their humanity they were not born of the flesh and not of blood, but of God. When a believer is <u>reborn</u> in spirit he becomes a son and God becomes his Father.

Likewise was true of the Old Testament <u>sons of God</u>, for they were not born through procreation, but of God. Power to become sons of God was never granted to the angels long ago because they were already sons, born of God.

Even the old prophet Hosea who lived about five hundred years before the arrival of the Messiah, Jesus, foretold of the time when believers would become righteous in the eyes of God and assume the title that some of the angels once exclusively had for themselves.

> <u>...and it shall come to pass, that in the place where it was said, Ye are not my people, there it shall be said unto them, Ye are the sons of the living God.</u> (Hosea 1:1

Hosea was the first to foresee that believers in the Messiah would assume the title that the angels had lost, but he was not the only prophet or holy man to receive this revelation from God. Paul wrote that we <u>wait for the adoption</u>

of sons (Galatians 4:5, Romans 8:23), and that Jesus came to bring many sons unto glory (Hebrews 2:10). John wrote that we as believers are called the sons of God (1 John 1:3), and in the book of the Revelation he also recorded the words of Jesus when He proclaimed that I will be his God and he shall be my son (Revelation 21:7). The him refers to Jesus, who saves those who believe in Him, granting them power to become sons of God. However, though this passage speaks of humans becoming righteous, assuming the title of sons of God, the passage here proclaims that despite their humanity they were not born of the flesh and not of blood, but of God. When a believer is reborn in spirit he becomes a son and God becomes his Father.

But despite the righteousness of any given individual, this transformation has yet to take place and it is claimed will not transpire until the First Resurrection. John confirmed this by writing, it doth not yet appear what we shall be (1 John 3:2), and Paul wrote that we waiteth for the manifestation of the sons of God (Romans 8:19). The resurrection of Jesus by his own power was an example of His promise to those who believe in Him, that one day we shall be like the angels (Luke 20:35-36).

So, if we presently await the appearance of the sons of God today, the transformation of ourselves into holy and immortal bodies, then who could the sons of God have been that took the daughters of men during the days of Noah? Were they unresurrected holy men who God allowed to receive their gloried bodies before the First Resurrection began? Is God partial? Of course not—that is a ridiculous notion. The following from Scripture should clear this and other arguments up.

> But they which shall be accounted worthy to obtain that world, and the resurrection of the dead, neither marry, nor are given in marriage:
>
> Neither can they die anymore: for they are equal unto the angels; and are the children of God, being the children of the resurrection. (Luke 20:35-36)

The Old Testament sons of God did not marry wives, they took them, and probably with violence. Since they were not worthy to obtain that world, the spiritual heaven in which they formerly resided, they enjoyed the pleasures of the flesh with the daughters of men. The phrase equal unto the angels only applies to death, or the absence of it. The promise of a resurrection is the believer's insurance that he will someday be like the angels (Matthew 22:30).

Chapter Three

Antediluvian Giants and the Flood

The phrase <u>all flesh had corrupted his way</u> is much better understood by knowing the translation of <u>flesh</u> in this passage. The word in Hebrew is <u>b's'r</u> and specifically means <u>blood-relation</u>. God was explaining to Noah that all blood-relation was corrupt on earth.

In Charles A. Weisman's book, *Facts and Fictions Regarding Noah's Flood*, we read that Noah was <u>perfect</u> in his generations in Genesis 6:9. The word <u>generations</u> here in Hebrew is <u>toledah</u>, and means descent. <u>Noah was perfect in his descent from Adam, meaning his lineage had not mixed with any other races.</u>[1] These races include the angelic ones ruling over men.

It is interesting to note that nowhere in the Genesis account does God command or even suggest that Noah warn others that the flood was coming. God warned Sodom and Gomorrah, Ninevah, Tyre, Jerusalem, Pharaoh, and even the wretchedly deplorable kings of Babylon. All of these and many more were warned before God visited judgment upon their peoples. They were given space to repent, and sometimes did, prolonging the judgment for a later time. But not the Old World. Why? The answer to this lies in the word <u>b's'r</u>: blood-relation. Polluted flesh corrupted all earth because the angels <u>took</u> the daughters of men, accepting the <u>eternal consequence</u> of being incurable: <u>enosh (anâsh)</u>.

In the previous chapter we learned that Lamech, father of Noah, believed that his wife had sexual relations with an angel. Here, in the Dead Sea Scrolls collection called *Tales of the Patriarchs*, the story is continued:

> ...Then I decided that the conception was at the hands of the Watchers, that the seed had been planted by the holy ones or Nephilim. I was in a turmoil because of this infant.
>
> Then I, Lamech, hurriedly went in to my wife Bitenosh and said to her, "I adjure you by the Most High, by the Lord, the Great One, by the King of all eternity... have you conceived by one of the sons of heaven?"

Bitenosh replied to Lamech:

> "I swear to you by the Great Holy One, by the King of Heaven... that this seed comes from you, this conception was by you, the planting of this fruit is yours... it was not by any stranger, neither by any of the Watchers, nor yet by any of the sons of heaven."[2]

If this ancient story is to be taken seriously, as it was by the Hebrews of old who hid it near the Qumran settlement, then the accusation of Lamech and suspicions he harbored greatly contribute to the biblical knowledge of pre-flood giants being born from unions of human women and <u>sons of heaven</u>. The title attributed to some of the angels, <u>Watchers</u>, will be seen more and more as this book progresses, in both biblical and non-biblical passages where Watchers are found.

One of the greatest early church fathers, Justin Martyr (A.D. 110-165) wrote: <u>"Angels transgressed, and were captivated by love for women and begat children."</u>[3]

As respected as he was in antiquity, Justin Martyr is quoted extensively by writers, scholars, and theologians who praise his doctrines and theology, faith and willingness to die for the truth (martyrdom derives from his name), but despite his intellectual merits, these same people discredit Justin Martyr's belief in the pre-flood sins of angels. They pass it off as a lapse of judgment on the part of this early church father by using Hebrew mysticism and myth.

It cannot be contested, however, that during the times of Justin Martyr, Greek mythology was rampant with tales of gods and giants, with some describing sexual orgies between the goes and mortals. In fact, the primal roots of Greek mythology can be exclusively traced back to Genesis 6, with the lust of the <u>gods</u> for the daughters of men.

<u>Giant</u> in Greek is translated as "sons of Gaea." Gaea was the Greek earth goddess and mother of the Titans, fearsome giants that ruled over mankind by brute strength, incomparable intelligence, and paranormal abilities. Today, Gaia worship, which has its origins in the Greek historical belief of ancient giants of <u>earth</u>, is a global environmental religion bolstered by elemental witches, environmental resource organizations and support groups, and governmental agencies. Today, Gaia is the name of the spirit of Mother Earth and can be found in abundance throughout the toy industries, comics, cartoons, and literary markets. It is <u>not</u> a coincidence that in this last century Gaia worship has appeared, being a resurrection of the belief in ancient Gaea, the goddess of the giants.

Gaea was worshiped in pre-Hellenic times with the center of her cult being in Attica.[4]

Her consort Uranus (Ouranos) is the primordial god of heaven. Originally, Gaea was regarded as a mere mortal woman of exquisite beauty. The union between Gaea (earth) and Uranus (heaven) displays how the pagan version of the parentage of the mighty Titans is ultimately found in the Genesis 6 account of the earthly daughters of men being taken by the heavenly sons of God. The Greeks called the Nephilim Titans, and beginning with the siblings (according to Greek pantheon), Ouranos and Gaea, these giants were involved in an explicit history of incestuous affairs. Other sources that Justin Martyr could have learned from concerning the giants and trespasses of the angels were the old works of *First Enoch, Apocalypse of Baruch, Jubilees*, and various other works of ancient literature that were uncovered within the Dead Sea texts. Other books of antiquity may have been available two thousand years ago as well, such as the *Book of the Wars of the Lord* mentioned in Numbers 24:14, and the *Book of Samuel the Seer* referred to in 1 Chronicles 29:29. Samuel was alive during the days of David when the young boy slew the giant Goliath, a Philistine ancestor of the Nephilim. Justin Martyr could have learned much from these two extinct works of history.

But one of the greatest non-biblical sources that Justin Martyr could have acquired his belief in giants is from the famous and still existent works of Flavius Josephus, a first century Jewish historian commissioned by his Roman masters to write a complete history of the Jews after their almost total destruction by Rome. In *Antiquities of the Jews*, Josephus wrote:

> Many angels of God accompanied with women, and begat sons that proved unjust, and despises of all that was good, on account of their strength... These men did what resembled the acts of those the Grecians called giants.
>
> ...There was till then left the race of giants, who had bodies so large, and countenances so entirely different from other men, that they were surprising to the sign, and terrible to the hearing.... The bones of these men are still shown to this very day.[5]

The bones of Nephilim people were exhibited in the past as evidence of their existence. Today these bones are discovered frequently; however, the archaeologists and scientists who unearth these remains mistakenly attribute them to prehistoric fossils of non-human creatures or Neanderthalic or Cro-Magnon humans. These two ancient races never existed in this giant size (Neanderthals were shorter than us), but are categorized as such to appease the evolutionary-thinking communities that ordinarily fund these expeditions.

Among the artifacts of literature found near the Qumran caves is an old sermon about the flood and those it drowned. Although only partially translated from its fragments, it reads as follows:

> So were they destroyed by the flood, every one of them perishing in the water–for they had disobeyed the commandments of the Lord. Therefore, all on dry land were blotted out, man and beast, bird and winged creature–all died; not even the giants escaped[6]

In the *Jubilees* (second century B.C.) the writer reveals that the flood was a direct result of the sins of angels and their giant offspring.

> For on account of these three the flood came upon the earth. For it was because of the fornication which the Watchers, apart from the mandate of their authority, fornicated with the daughters of men and took for themselves wives from all whom they chose and made a beginning of impurity. And they begot sons, the Naphidim, and all of them were dissimilar. And each one ate his fellow. (Jubilees 7:14-25)

When the Torah was written, Hebrew was in its purest form. From the time that Moses began putting the Scriptures into writing until *Jubilees* was written, almost thirteen hundred years had passed, enough time for the original Hebrew to become polluted from the many exiles of the Jews. The seventy-year captivity of Israel in Babylon ultimately caused the corruption of Hebrew. The name Naphidim in the *Jubilees* account is no different than Nephilim of the biblical text; it is only an alteration of the pure Hebrew, with possibly Babylonian or Aramaic influence.

The final statement, each one ate his fellow, implies that the Nephilim indulged in cannibalism. This strange practice is further detailed in the *Book of Enoch*, also extracted from the Dead Sea texts where is found the title Watchers, the angels that originally sinned.

> So the giants turned against the people in order to eat them. And they began to sin against birds, wild beasts, reptiles, and fish. And their flesh was devoured the one by the other, and they drank blood. And then the earth brought an accusation against the oppressors. (Enoch 7:11-15)

The writers of *Enoch* and those of the *Jubilees* and *Jasher* accounts support the biblical texts concerning the impregnation of earthly women by angels. The Enochian text says:

> And they conceiving brought forth giants... these devoured all which the labor of men produced; until it became impossible to feed them; when they turned themselves against men, in order to devour them. (Enoch 7:11-13)

From these and other old traditions we gather that the Nephilim had enslaved men and that mankind sought deliverance from other men (large and different) rather than the Creator. Enoch is shown in *Jasher* to be a mighty ruler, highly esteemed by both men and angels. He said, "The Watchers called me Enoch the scribe." (Enoch 12:4)

In the *Book of Giants* the Nephilim assembled and begged Enoch to make intercession between them and God. So many women began having giant children that the angels themselves knew their judgment was impending. To counter the advances of the sexually oppressive angels it is revealed in the *Book of Jasher* that some of the sons of men caused their wives to drink a draught to render them barren. (Jasher 2:20)

In the writings of Enoch God declares that the giants shall hope for eternal life, and that they may live, each of them five hundred years. (Enoch 10:14) This futile hope of the giants is deeply reflected in the *Epic of Gilgamesh*, where the mysterious and very physically powerful king of Uruk is a giant, part god. He strives throughout the epic to gain immortality, but in the end he dies just as the other giants. In fact, Gilgamesh is named in the Enochian *Book of Giants*, discovered among the Dead Sea texts.

There are many sources being uncovered today by which Justin Martyr and others could have learned about the Nephilim; many of them probably do not exist today. The Greek term *sons of Gaea* appears in many ancient writings in various forms.

According to *Halley's Bible Handbook* the cities of Eridu, Obeid, Kish, and Ur had been built before the flood, with Ur of the Chaldees being excavated by ancient pre-Babylonian people and rebuilt. In this Chaldean city were discovered golden plates that read:

Gods in the form of men came down...[7]

Turning now to extra-canonical books of the Dead Sea texts we will peer into the *Damascus Document*. Originally found at the beginning of the century by a Jewish scholar in Geniza, it was originally published under the title *Zadokite fragment*; however, this ancient text was later discovered again in caves 4 and 5 by the Dead Sea. It was then retitle to the *Damascus Document*. It reads:

> When they went about in their willful heart, the Guardian Angels of Heaven fell and were ensnared by it, for they did not observe the commandments of God. Their sons, who were as tall as cedars, and whose bodies were as big as mountains, fell by it. Everything mortal on dry land expired and became as if they had never existed.

The *Damascus Document* provides us further support in our endeavor here to understand the pre-flood giants, but the most incredible text ever discovered concerning the original Nephilim that plagued earth before the flood, was likewise excavated among the Dead Sea site and is simply entitled *The Book of Giants*.

Formerly only found in the Ethiopic language, the *Book of Enoch* was also discovered in the Aramaic language among the Dead Sea Scrolls, but also discovered with Enoch was a previously unknown section called *The Book of Giants*.

This badly preserved text is severely fragmented, but it is not difficult to understand that it tells of the dark archangel Azazel and the descent of fallen angels. They knew great and wondrous secrets, murdered many people, corrupted the animal kingdoms, created monsters and giants, polluted earth, and sinned against God and men.

The giants left behind by the disobedient angels began having dreams and nightmares of impending calamity until they sent one of their own to inquire of the holy mortal Enoch, who interpreted their dreams as meaning that a great flood would come and drown the giants and the evil works their angelic fathers performed.

Though copies of the *Book of Enoch* exist in the Ethiopic language outside the Dead Sea discoveries, the Enochian *Book of Giants* is a formerly unknown section of these ancient writings, exclusively found at the Qumran site. A portion of the *Book of Giants* reads:

> ...Ohya declared and said to the giants, "I too had a dream this night, O giants, and behold, the Ruler of Heaven came down to earth... and such is the end of the dream..." All the giants and monsters grew afraid and called Mahway. He came to them and the giants pleaded with him and sent him to Enoch... how long the giants have to live.

Another Dead Sea text entitled the *Book of Wisdom* reads that: For even in the beginning when arrogant giants were perishing, the hope of the world took refuge on a raft.[8]

In another widely disregarded text is the Apocryphal Book of 3 Maccabees, where in 2:4 we read that giants were long ago destroyed in a flood. Another often overlooked detail in the flood account is the fact that the ancient people and giants of Noah's time before the flood would not have comprehended any warnings about a global flood because there was no such thing as <u>rain</u> (explained below). The flood would have been disregarded by many in those days because it would have required something unknown to make such a large and unexpected increase of water.

When God originally created the earth, the planet was watered every morning by a dew, a fine mist that covered the earth and arose forth from the ground (Gen. 2:5-6).

Josephus called this marine sky a <u>Crystalline Firmament</u>.[9] In the book of *Jubilees* we discover that in the beginning, one half of the waters <u>went up above, and one half of them went down beneath the firmament which is in the middle, over the surface of all the earth</u>. (Jubilees 2)

James Kugel, in his thought-provoking research of ancient texts relating to the Scriptures, cited in this book, *The Bible As It Was*, exhibits yet another archaic reference to this watery atmosphere: <u>God, who stretched out the heavens like a curtain, roofed His upper chambers with the waters</u>.[10]

The sky before the flood *never produced rain clouds* because a watery firmament was layered above, containing a vast amount of water that protected the earth from harmful solar radiation and heat. Unlike our atmosphere today, the heavens of the antediluvian world during the daytime was always bright, nothing obscuring the sun's shining (Gen. 1:6-8).

In the Apocryphal apocalyptic writings of 2 *Esdras* 6:41 is discovered that in the beginning there existed a gulf between the waters above and those below.

> <u>On the second day you created the angel of the sky and commanded him to separate the water, so that part of it would move up above the dome of the sky and part remain below</u>.

The writer of 2 *Esdras* is allegedly the priest-prophet Ezra of the Bible, which is not difficult to believe, considering the abundance of eschatological revelations in his writing. Like Enoch's writings, Esdras often associated natural phenomenon and disasters with angels.

The *Book of Enoch* reveals much about this marine pre-flood sky:

> <u>In those days shall punishment go forth from the Lord of spirits; and the receptacles of water which are above the</u>

<u>heavens shall be opened, and the foundations likewise, which are under the heavens and under the earth. All the waters, which are under the heavens and above them, shall be mixed together.</u> (Enoch 53:7-8)

This unusual atmosphere is mentioned in several archaic and once-lost texts that will be examined throughout the book, from the Egyptian archives that record that long ago, mighty beings sailed the sky firmament in boats,[11] all the way to the seventh century A.D. epic writings of *Beowulf.*

Although far removed from eastern civilization, the numerous Mesoamerican cultures remembered the history of their forebears, likely being direct descendants of Mesopotamia. The ancient Mazatecs believed that long ago the stars were so close <u>that people could throw stones at them</u>.[12] According to the sixteenth-century Aztec records, the *Annals of Cuauhtitlan,* the First Age before a great flood was called the Water Sun, reflecting other traditions of a watery atmosphere long ago. After this age, a time came when giants oppressed mankind which in turn was followed by the age called Rain Sun.[13] Not only did the Aztecs remember the deluge, but amazingly, they believed that <u>during the final flood of the ancient time, the sky itself fell to the earth</u> and two people survived on a watertight boat![14] The Yucatec hold that before the flood people were great builders of ruined temples and abandoned cities. Along with the Yucatec Indians, the Bribri, Tarahumara, and Quichè all believed that after the great flood the world <u>was soft</u>, but the sun burned hot and dried the earth, hardening the ground.[15]

The antediluvian aquatic sky to the ancients was referred to as heaven. Long ago, heaven and paradise were hidden in the ocean above and hell was below, under the primordial waters beneath the earth called the abyss. The fall of the atmosphere was poetically prophetic of the Creator. The angels that rebelled were of heaven, and when they fell from the sky (Nephilim means <u>the fallen ones</u>), then it was only suitable that God would cause the <u>worldly</u> conception of heaven to fall upon those who lived among the sea of earth, atop those who regarded this atmosphere as unreachable and upheld with the might of the gods of heaven. Just as the giants were of <u>mixed</u> lineages, both heavenly angelic and earthly human, God Almighty mixed the waters above and below.

In a vision of the flood, Enoch saw <u>falling to the earth... the Great Abyss</u> that <u>absorbed</u> the earth. This abyss being <u>heaven... snatched away</u>. (Enoch 82:5)

In the ancient *Epic of Gilgamesh* story that will be examined throughout this book, the hero, King of Uruk (biblical Erech), goes to an old man named

Utnapishtim who is positively identified as Noah. The Sumerian version of pre-flood history has Noah telling Gilgamesh about life before the flood.

> You know the city of Shurrupak, it stands on the banks of the Euphrates? That city grew old and the gods that were in it were old. There was Anu, lord of the Firmament.[16]

Anu in the old Mesopotamian pantheon was god of heaven, of the waters above. When he fell he married the goddess Ki, mother of earth. Their union, embodied in the symbols of heaven and earth, gave birth to the powerful Anunnaki, men who became great rulers and judges over men. Who exactly the Sumerians were is an historical enigma, their veiled past hardly penetrated by the historian or archaeologist. However, their beliefs were adopted by all of their successors, including their historical traditions, be they mythical or historical:

> The Sumerian view of their own alien past is expressed in their "Poem of the Supersage" in which the great flood marked the end of mythical time and the inauguration of historical time.[17]

In fact, the oldest Sumerian King-Lists (Southern Babylonian) are divided between Antediluvian and post-Diluvian kings.

The belief in giants and floods is a popular one among the ancient Native Americans. The Ixil Indians of Guatemala believed that the ancients were angels who eavesdropped on God. To punish them He sent a flood.[18] The pre-Columbian Indians called the Tarascans believed that a race of giants once lived but God blessed earth and these enormous people disappeared. The Bribri Indians claim the god Sibu tried without success to drown them in the ocean.[19] The Aztec calendar is most unique though, based upon ages of time, similar to dispensations in Bible reckoning; the Jaguar Age long ago had giants stalking the earth in search of men until it happened that the sky collapsed...[20] All of these and hundreds of other flood traditions, many cited in this book, are all borne out of truth.

This thick atmosphere of water was responsible for the incredible longevity of the antediluvian people. Before the flood the genealogies in the Bible specifically recorded the ages of the ten patriarchs of the Messianic bloodline, the seed of Eve. Ancient King-Lists from Mesopotamia mentioned in this book as well, state that the most archaic of kings lived unusually long lives, Gilgamesh being one. Many of the biblical patriarchs lived as long as nine hundred years, Methuselah living to nine hundred and sixty-nine years of age, outliving anyone who has ever lived. The layers of the firmament of water above filtered out the damaging ultraviolet rays and solar radiation that both greatly contribute to aging. Vegetation grew to sizes unparalleled today, enriched with vitamins in mineral-laden soils because the <u>mists</u> that watered the earth every morning described in the Bible, coupled with the unbroken presence of sunlight during the days that was magnified by the aquatic atmosphere, allowed humans to consume a perfect diet that we are incapable of obtaining today.

This very fact is confirmed in the two thousand year-old writings of Flavius Josephus, who wrote that one reason longevity was prolonged before the flood was because <u>their food was then fitter for the prolongation of life</u>. [21]

Fossilized remains of prehistoric animals and people are found buried or excavated in various levels of strata because when the waters of the flood began rising, the heavier and larger beasts were buried first by sediments that settled quicker because of their weight and density. Lighter and smaller animals are found in higher strata because of their ability to get to higher ground as the waters of the flood increased, and because of the buoyancy of their bodies as compared to the larger reptiles and giant mammals such as the ancient mastodons and mammoths. People are discovered fossilized in the highest strata because of their ability to get to the highest ground before the flood drowned them, too, and covered them in the lightest of sediments that settled to the bottom last.

The second century A.D. Christian theologian Tertullian <u>was convinced that sea creatures had been carried to the mountaintops by the flood and left stranded there when it withdrew</u>. [22]

The flood drowned hundreds of millions of animals and people and created a global ocean of churning sediments of various soil materials, hundreds of billions of tons of earth mixed with the bodies of countless creatures. When the waters calmed and the storms abated, the heaviest of creatures were lying all over the planet underneath the planetary ocean deep on the lowest surfaces. The denser soil material caught in the torrents and streams of the flood settled <u>over</u> these huge bodies. The drowned carcasses of pre-flood earth accordingly sunk to the bottom with soil materials of different densities that <u>layered,</u> forming strata.

Humans are discovered at the uppermost strata because they lived longer during the cataclysm than the other creatures. Floating debris from the destroyed buildings of antediluvian civilization sustained many people for a while before their bodies drowned, succumbed to the intense hunger of starvation.

Once the flood waters dried and accumulated to the poles because of the climactic cooling of earth, the world became a planet with many layered skins, each containing myriads of creatures fossilized, almost in perfect states of preservation. Today when animals die they are eaten by other creatures and their bones become dust in a few hundred years. Carcasses do not fossilize in the way that we discover prehistoric creatures today. The large majority of fossils show no indication that the creatures found petrified suffered from anything, and almost all are found in near perfect totality, no bones missing, as predators would carry off. Our fossil record conveys that the majority of life on this planet drowned.

The Angels Judged

Peter had obviously studied the Old Testament closely and even received further revelations from the Spirit concerning the sons of God and their sins in early history, for he provides us today a wealth of information about these subjects in his New Testament writings.

> For if God spared not the angels that sinned, but cast them down to hell, and delivered them into chains of darkness, to be reserved unto judgment; and spared not the old world, but saved Noah, the eighth person, a preacher of righteousness, bringing in the flood upon the world of the ungodly... (2 Peter 2:4-5)

The angels that sinned are the sons of God in the days of Noah. They took the daughters of men who in turn begat giants that wreaked havoc on man and introduced unprecedented evils, which resulted in a flood upon the world of the ungodly.

The word hell in verse 4. above, should read Tartarus. This is the only place in the Bible where Tartarus is found in its verbal form. This spiritual prison is completely separated from Gehenna, Sheol, Hades, or hell. It could very well be a reference to the Abyss; the bottomless pit.

Even the silent apostle, Jude, concedes with Peter concerning the dark history of the Nephilim, even identifying their angelic fathers as wandering stars, to whom is reserved the blackness of darkness forever... (Jude 13)

But Jude's most startling revelation of the past confirms the fact that angels are innately able to enter and exit our physical world at will.

> And the angels which kept not their first estate, but left their own habitation, he hath reserved in everlasting chains under darkness unto the judgment of the great day. (Jude 6)

Jude further exposes the angels' sins by saying that they <u>left their own habitation</u> by going after <u>strange flesh</u>, even as Sodom and Gomorrah. "<u>Strange</u>" in Greek is likewise translated as <u>foreign</u>, or <u>different</u>. "Flesh" in Greek means <u>body</u>, while also being akin to the Hebrew word <u>b_s_r</u>, which we know means <u>blood-relation</u>. Applied to the angels, this verse means blood-relation, but when in reference to Sodom and Gomorrah it refers to homosexual conduct and other sexual sins.

In 2 Peter 2:10-11 the phrase <u>walk after the flesh</u> refers to angels as well as people. Verses 4 and 11 of the same chapter mentions angels in detail, thus exhibiting that by context, the entire passage refers to guilt of both angels and humans. Peter also claims they both have <u>eyes full of adultery</u>. This brings to memory the fact that the Hebrew word for <u>chose</u> (bachar) in Genesis 6:2 meant to <u>select after keenly observing</u>...

The everlasting <u>chains of darkness</u> mentioned by both Peter and Jude were greatly feared by the demons of Jesus' day. In the gospel according to Luke, chapter 8 we read:

> <u>And they besought him that he would not command them to go out into the deep</u> (Luke 8:31).

The translation of <u>deep</u> is Abyss, the bottomless pit God opens during the Great Tribulation, freeing the entrapped demons so they can plunge the world into spiritual darkness.

In *First Enoch*, Watchers are disobedient angels that begat <u>giants</u>.

> <u>Go, say to the Watchers of heaven, who have sent thee to intercede for them: "Ye should intercede for men, and not men for you. Wherefore have ye left high, holy and eternal heaven, and lain with women and defiled yourselves, and done like the children of earth and begotten giants as sons."</u>

In the book of Daniel the order of the Watchers is alluded to.

> <u>I saw in the visions of my head upon my bed, and, behold, a watcher and a holy one came down from heaven.</u> (Daniel 4:13)

Here is drawn a distinct separation from a <u>watcher</u> and a <u>holy one</u>.

According to the Dead Sea findings, Enoch was called by God to deliver judgment to the Watchers of heaven.

> <u>Enoch, scribe of righteousness, go and make known to the Watchers of heaven who have abandoned the high heaven,</u>

> the holy eternal place and have defiled themselves with women, as their deeds move the children of the world, and have taken unto them wives: they have defiled themselves with great defilement upon the earth; neither will there be peace unto them nor the forgiveness of sin. (*Book of Enoch*)

The Dead Sea text entitled *Ages of the World* provides more information concerning the trespasses of angels.

> ...Azazel and the angels who went in to the daughters of men so that they bore mighty men to them. And certainly Azazel who taught them to love iniquity and caused them to inherit wickedness...[23]

In the *Book of Enoch* the old prophet in a vision witnessed the torment of the rebellious angels in Tartarus. Mystified, he asked an angel what he was looking at and received this astonishing answer:

> These are the angels who have descended from heaven to earth, and have revealed secrets to the sons of men, and have seduced the sons of men to the commission of sin. (Enoch 63:1)

Enoch also wrote that because of the Watchers the women likewise have brought forth giants. (Enoch 9:8) Although the women are the mothers of the giants, they themselves are not blamed, accused or judged in any capacity whatsoever in the biblical records, nor in any extant non-canonical texts. This revelation lends more credit to the fact expounded upon earlier in this book— that the daughters of men were abducted; they were taken by force from men, men who are accused for allowing angels to choose their fairest daughters. The ancient accounts hold the sons of men responsible for the sins committed.

In the *Jubilees* account, the Watchers were assigned to earth to instruct men (Jub. 4:15), but they soon lusted after human women, maintained sexual relations, and fathered giants (Jub. 4:17-23, 7:21).

> And he called his name Jared, for in his days the angels of the Lord descended on the earth, those so named the Watchers. (Jub. 4:15)

The statement in *Jubilees* claims that Enoch's father was specifically called Jared because of the appearance of the Watchers. Concerning these physically present angelic beings, the first thirty-six chapters of today's *Book of Enoch* was once an independently circulated text entitled the *Book of the Watchers*.[24] Of this book the text of *Jubilees* states:

> And he [Enoch] wrote everything and bore witness to the Watchers, the ones who sinned with the daughters of men because they began to mingle themselves with the daughters of men so that they might be polluted... and they bore children to them; and they were the giants. And injustice increased upon the earth. (Jubilees 4:11,5)

The very translation of the name of Jared in Hebrew strengthens the veracity of the accounts provided in the works of Enoch and *Jubilees*, for his name means descended, and is evidently an ancient reference of the descending of the Watchers.

Enoch was aware of the coming flood, and said:

> For all the earth shall perish; the waters of a deluge shall come over the whole earth, and all things which are in it shall be destroyed. (Enoch 10:4)

The *Book of Jasher* explains that in the end, Enoch was taken from earth to reign over the angelic sons of God.

Chapter Four

Post-Diluvian Giants

One of the most difficult bridges to cross for the Nephilim researcher is explaining to others how the giants appeared after the flood. Although post-diluvial history is filled with indirect and solid information concerning the giants, the reason for their appearance again after God completely destroyed their <u>seed</u> upon the earth is explained in only one area of Scripture as ascertained by this researcher. Ordinarily, this would be disturbing, but when viewed from a distance, the Biblical evidence of post-flood giant activity can be likened to a pyramid, or family tree, with the apex being the first hint of Nephilim after the flood. Then below this, the previous birth of five different Nephilim races is evidenced, as the pyramid within our mind broadens toward the foundation. At the bottom of the pyramid lies the dead bodies of these giants scattered throughout ancient Canaan and northern Africa, as we will learn in later chapters. But first, let's look at the apex of our Nephilim pyramid.

> <u>There were giants in the earth in those days; and also after that, when the sons of God came in unto the daughters of men...</u> (Genesis 6:4).

As we discovered earlier, this union between the sons of God and daughters of men brought forth <u>mighty men, men of renown</u>, the giants. In the present-tense context of Genesis, this transpired <u>before</u> the flood; therefore, the phrase <u>and also after that</u> refers to a second outbreak of giants *after the flood*, caused again by unions between the sons of God and human women. Both times the results were the appearance of giants, first <u>in those days,</u> and then a second time <u>also after that</u>.

With the wealth of information detailing the existence of pre-flood giants in the numerous texts of the Dead Sea Scrolls, it would indeed be surprising to discover nothing in these old books about post-flood giants. And as Nephilim-hunters, researchers were not at all taken aback, for there is far more information about giants after the flood than before it. But before we search through these ancient books, let us translate a recently discovered cuneiform inscription dug up by archeologists. It is written in Sumerian, the oldest written language known to man today. It reads:

> "And then came the flood, and after the flood kingship came down from heaven once again."[1]

This early Mesopotamian inscription was discovered in an ancient buried library in the Sumerian city of Nippur.[2]

The phrase <u>once again</u> is profound in that it reveals that there was a history concerning the flood and former kingship that the Sumerians knew of. Later in this chapter we will see just what these Sumerian people knew.

In Isaiah 45:14 the Sabeans are called <u>men of stature</u>, thus revealing their unusual height. These people were descendants of Ham through Seba, son of Cush, and they wandered around in tribal bands in the southern Canaan and Arabian desert reaches, sometimes in North Africa. They were sexually linked to the ancient Nephilim as seen in their unusual <u>stature</u>. Also, the word men in <u>men of stature</u> is not <u>ish</u> of <u>adam</u>, but <u>enosh</u>, unveiling their polluted ancestry. In reference to the Sabeans, both the historians Herodotus and Josephus claimed that <u>the great stature and beauty of this people was a theme of the ancients</u>.[3]

Further proof of Job's knowledge toward the existence of Nephilim is Job saying that God's judgment is like a <u>giant</u> running over him (Job 16:14).

Ham's descendants in Canaan were evidently maintaining sexual ties with the Nephilim that lived with them, for in Deuteronomy 9:2 these Canaanite peoples are called the <u>children of the Anakim,</u> and are physically described as <u>great and tall</u>.

All nations and peoples detailed in Scripture can find their ancestors within the genealogical records, and it is intriguing to discover that the giant nations have no ancestral ties to anyone in Scripture. The Anakim, Rephaim, Zuzims, Zamzummims, and Emims are not located in any of the Old or New Testament genealogies. However, those nations that interbred with the giants and are described as physically larger or different than other Adamic races are all solely linked with the genealogy of Ham. These are the children of the Nephilim: The Avims, Horims, Sabeans, Amorites, Hivites, Girgashites, Canaanites, Hittites, Perizzites, and the Jebusites. These nations were completely eradicated by the descendants of Abraham and Lot. Moabites, Edomites, and Ammonites utterly defeated the Avims, Horims, and even the Emims and Zamzummims. Israel <u>almost</u> completely destroyed the seven Canaanite nations, but the Bible is silent concerning the fate of the Sabeans. Unless the sons of God and daughters of men are the parents of the five giant nations, then we will have the only five cultures and peoples in Scripture completely separated from genealogical history.

All of these peoples were the offspring of Ham, whom Noah cursed. To be mentioned in Scripture, Ham's sexual immorality was a prophetic foreshadowing of the unrestraint his descendants would have in their sexual relations with others, namely the giants. The five Nephilim races lived <u>only</u> within the geographical confines of Canaan's descendants, Ham's son who was the ultimate bearer of Noah's curse. This curse was uttered by Noah because of sexual corruption.

The <u>daughters of men</u> after the flood were Canaanite women. These Canaanite women were having sexual relations with giants of contaminated blood. This is greatly supported also by the fact that Abraham would not allow his son Isaac to marry a <u>daughter of the Canaanites</u>, but instead chose a woman from the homeland of his father in Chaldea (Genesis 24:37). The only possible conclusion we can make for Abraham's strict order against Canaanite women, when all through Old Testament history we read about Hebrews taking heathen wives like Moses, who had an Ethiopian wife, is that the Canaanites were <u>enosh</u>, polluted.

The sins of the angels were passed on to their offspring. The Nephilim practiced all sorts of ritual magic, child sacrifice, polygamy, incest, brutality, and many other abominations. One of these trespasses was the creation of <u>hybrids</u>.

> <u>They taught the mixture of animals of one species with the other.</u> (Jasher 4:18)

The angels taught men how to create hybrids among the animal kingdoms, causing men to be guilty of the <u>same</u> sins the Watchers were judged for... hybridization. But this mixing between animals is only one shade of a much darker reality.

The angels taught men the secrets of extracting metallic ores from the earth. Regarding metallurgy, Enoch wrote that:

> <u>They know every secret of the angels, every oppressive and secret power of the Satan [wicked angels] and every power of those who commit sorcery, as well as those who make molten images in the whole earth.</u>
>
> <u>They know how silver is produced from the dust of the earth, and how on the earth the metallic drop exists; for lead and tin are not produced from earth as the primary foundation.</u> (Enoch 64:7)

These metals are <u>alloys</u>, mixed metals not naturally produced from the earth. These materials require men to smelt and forge. The dross must be removed and the ores mixed. The <u>metallic drop</u> is mercury, a fluidic-solid alloy, extremely poisonous. The metallurgical practice of producing alloys comes from beings that were also <u>mixed</u>, half human and half angelic. The *Book of Jasher* confirms the practice of pre-flood metallurgy, revealing that those ancient people made <u>images of brass and iron</u>. (Jasher 2:4)

These giants intermingled with the lesser nations around them and ruled by strength and intimidation. As centuries passed, the offspring of both giants and the Canaanites became more and more alike physically, in height and strangeness, as well as in knowledge. The angels taught their progeny many arts and sciences and ultimately these arcane secrets were adopted by the powerful Canaanite nations.

God's judgment upon His angelic rebels is severe, but fortunately He has exercised mercy with men.

> <u>All the sons of men shall not perish in consequence of every secret, by which the Watchers have destroyed, and which they have taught, their offspring</u>. (Enoch 10:11)

This passage was taken from the Enochian text where giants are expounded upon with detail and dread. However, the focus in Enoch's writings are not directed toward the giants, but to those that fathered them, the angels.

But concerning the giants, the Greeks by far preserved the remembrance of these ancient events far more extensively than any other people of antiquity. But just as any story passed through many generations, the information becomes tainted and the truthfulness is darkened. Legends of the giants were told around the campsites of battle-weary soldiers, by traveling bards and singing minstrels that went from village to village, entertaining people with the histories of their people and ancestors. Recorded within ancient archives are discovered accounts of mortals battling giants and hills fraught with the weight of hordes of man-monsters and great beasts. When these stories are retold to the modern ear, they are reduced immediately to antiquated superstition and fables.

But the regularity of the accounts and their parallels defy coincidence. Every major culture of the ancient past and civilization were left with the remaining evidence of giants in their architecture, sculptures, paintings or writings. It cannot be contested by the serious archaeologists that sexual relations between the gods and mortal women was a common historical belief respected by many ancient peoples, especially by the Greeks. Though they are the foundation of Greek and Roman legends and mythic lore, these sexual gods are found in the archaic writings of the Egyptians, Sumerians, Chaldeans, as well as in Babylonian traditions, Vedic writings of India, in Mesopotamian artifacts, Aztec and Incan engravings, the Norse legends, other European beliefs, and many more.

An excellent example of the distortion of surviving verbal tradition is the story of Hercules. This superhuman man was the son of a god, Zeus, and a beautiful mortal woman named Alcmene. This union of a god and a woman would have made the person of Hercules to be <u>Nephilim</u>, a giant, rather than a normal-sized (but strong and brave) human, which is how he appears in the stories passed down.

Other Greek beliefs in history involve a strange race of giants they called Titans. These giants were born exclusively from the god Ouranos (Uranus) and a woman named Gaea, who was later deified as the personality of the earth. Remember, the Greek word for giant is translated <u>sons of Gaea</u>. The Titans, according to Greek belief, ruled the entire world and everything in it until their influence began affecting the gods above and when they assembled and rebelled against Uranus. Their insurgency was met with a full onslaught by the Olympian gods that ultimately defeated them.

One of these gods was Mars, the Roman god of war. This son of Jupiter is detailed in Virgil's *Aeneid* and was greatly revered by Roman soldiers. Before human history began, Mars was a valiant warrior in the violent battle between the gods and the giants.[4] In the older Greek pantheon Mars is called Ares, son of Zeus. His battle chariot is pulled by Phobos (fear) and Deimos (terror), which happen to be the names of Mars' only two moons orbiting the red planet today. Both of these moons are irregularly shaped and crater-laden, being asteroid and not true moons.

Tartarus is also found in the *Aeneid*. Like many old Greek beliefs, the Nephilim themselves are discovered in rich symbolism and detail.

> <u>Here those ancient sons of earth, Titans of youthful strength, cast down by a thunder stroke, are writhing in the lowest depth. And here I saw the two sons of Aloeus, giants in stature, who had assaulted the vast heaven in an attempt to tear it down</u>...

These two sons of Aloeus were giants named Otus and Ephialtes. Much of Virgil's writings were spawned from more ancient sources such as the *Odyssey* and *Iliad* by Homer. This writer/historian lived seven hundred years before Virgil and knew more about Tartarus and the Titans than anyone in Greek history.

In Homer's poetic epic *The Iliad*, we find Zeus very angry at the other Olympian gods because of their partiality and involvements in the Trojan war. The supreme god said,

> <u>I will hurl him down into dark Tartarus far into the deepest pit under the earth, where the gates are iron and the floor bronze, as far beneath Hades as heaven is high above the earth</u>...

Evidently the threat of being imprisoned in this strange netherworld <u>pit</u> was powerful enough to dissuade the gods from any more direct involvement in the war between the Greeks and Trojans. In his writings, Homer used many phrases such as <u>lower than the Titans,</u> bits and pieces of clues that he used to convey that there was a distant history left unsaid.

Among those Titans cast into Tartarus was Hyperion, regarded in prehistoric times as a god of light, and Iapetos, a giant who fathered Atlas. Kronos was another Titan who defied the Olympian gods and was cast into Tartaros by Zeus himself. Strangely akin to the Biblical account, the Titans were confined in <u>chains of darkness</u>. Like hell, Tartaros was believed to be beneath the surface of the earth.

Other races of giants and <u>children</u> of the Greek gods were the Tritons and Cyclops. The god of the sea was Poseidon, brother of Zeus, who took the sea and became its god. Zeus took the dry land and ruled as god over it, while Hades became the god of the underworld. Poseidon on occasion would sink hapless vessels in search of beautiful women. Through relations with these women he fathered a race of marine giants who had the lower bodies of fish. These strange people were called Tritons, the sons of Poseidon. These were regarded as demigods of the deep who fathered sea nymphs, mermaids, and other faerie folk creatures of the sea. The coastal-dwelling Philistines worshiped a god called Dagon. This god was half man and half fish and resembled perfectly a Triton. The Philistines built temples to this deity in Canaan and Philistia over five hundred years before the Greeks became a national power. Being a maritime race of huge people themselves, there is evidence that the Philistines fled Canaan from the armies of Joshua, spreading their influence as far as the British Isles, as we'll see in coming chapters.

The other sons of Poseidon were the gigantic Cyclops.

In the *Aeneid* the race of Cyclopes was said by Virgil to be <u>monsters of the stones</u>. This is not a formal title of these giants, but merely Virgil's own description used in such a way as to maintain his poetic flow, which also calls to mind the irregularly set stone walls still called <u>Cyclops walls</u> today. The famous Cyclops that was blinded by Ulysses was named Polyphemus. In his first century B.C. story, Virgil wrote:

> The Cyclops is a giant... he feeds on the inner parts and dark blood of his poor victims. I myself have seen him grasp two of our number in that huge hand, and, still lying prone in the centre of his cave, smash them on a rock.

In a few Dead Sea texts it is discovered that the giants were known for cannibalism and drinking blood. Since the giants and Cyclops are anthropomorphic, feeding on humans would be cannibalism. The Bible adamantly warns us not to eat blood; it is an abomination to God.

Virgil also describes the Cyclops as intellectually human, having the mental capacity to communicate verbally, think for itself, express anger, hate, and many more emotions. More revelations concerning cannibalism practiced by the giants is revealed throughout this book, much of it is cited in the earlier chapters, where giants ate men before the flood. Virgil also described the Cyclops as a horrible and hideous ogre of a giant. The word ogre describes a giant race of mutant giants found richly in Celtic and Irish lore. They are club-wielding battle mongers and predators that stood at heights up to ten feet tall. The shadiest tendrils of Irish and British history extend beyond the rise of the Greeks into the second millennium B.C., far into the coastal reaches of Ionia and the no longer legendary states of the Trojan empire. The dark history of the ogres, along with Britain's ancient past, will be unveiled in coming chapters.

Among the nations greatly affected in their lore by memories and actual encounters with giants were ancient Norse Vikings, the Celtic people. In the *Annals of Clonmacnois* it is recorded that long ago Ireland was invaded by the Formorians, a strange race of barbaric people descended from Ham, who lived by piracy. Their pirate ships were known all over the world, primarily the coasts of Europe. Modern occultic history describes the Formorians as a race of misshapen giants that suffered a variety of physical deformities caused by incestual relations. These giants were defeated around 1100 B.C.

A clue as to the identity of these giants can be discerned from the Irish legend of Cuchulain, which claims that an ancient race inhabited Ireland called the Tuatha de Danaan around 1150 B.C. Historians today refer to them as the Nemedians, people who migrated to Europe from the Irish mainland and later returned to fight and defeat the Firbolgs, their distant warlike cousins. Celtic traditions regarded the Tuatha de Danaan as Irish gods, and these foreign Danaanites could very well be former Canaanites.

The *Legend of Cuchulain* also records that the Tuatha de Danaan were powerful, fierce, and capable of godlike abilities. Cuchulain was a valiant Irish warrior, the son of a chieftain of the Tuath de Danaan named Lugh.

Cuchulain himself was prone to fits of battle rage when he would mutate horribly into a hideous humanoid beast in the middle of battle, exhibiting unnatural fighting prowess. So terrible was his visage that he soon became known throughout Ireland as the Warped One.[5]

The early Britons, according to the *Annals of Clonmacnois*, migrated to Britain and drove out a particularly violent race of giants (probably Formorian pirate clans). Note, this is recorded history, not myth. Cuchulain was a legend that possibly derived from an actual person. Though the story could very well be mythical, the Tuatha de Danaan were not.

The old British word for giant is gawr, which is strangely akin to gibbor, the Hebrew word for giant, huge person, tyrant, that we initially discovered in Genesis 6. The *Annals of Clonmacnois* specifically name Ham and Noah as ancestors of the Formorians.[6] Like the seven nations of Canaan, these Tuatha de Danaan might not have been Nephilim, but rather they could have been larger than the ancient Britons due to Nephilim ancestral ties maintained before they migrated away from the Mediterranean area.

The exodus of Israel led by Moses is commonly dated at 1447 B.C. The Formorians were mariners, very likely they were Canaanite or Philistines who fled Canaan and inhabited the isles of Britain, Ireland, Scotland, Iceland, and North America, preying on the coasts of Europe as pirates until the ancient Celts migrated into the isles. A great many artifacts, myths and megalithic edifices within the areas of northern Europe, the present day United Kingdom, Iceland, and North America, cannot be adequately explained without acknowledging the historic presence of giants in these regions. The famous dolmens such as Stonehenge and many rock pyramids in Britain are just a couple of examples.

In the *Books of Invasions* and *Cycles of Kings* the Tuatha de Danaan are the Irish gods, a pantheon of ancient hero-warriors who in prehistoric times of Ireland fought the Firbolgs and Fomorians in the legendary battles of Moytura.[7] Tuatha de Danaan is translated peoples of the goddess Danu. This ancient Celtic goddess was the primordial mother of the Tuatha de Danaan. Twin hills in Munster called the Paps of Anu reflect the old belief in this deity. The father of the Tuatha de Danaan was Dagda, a possible giant from Irish antiquity. He led the ancients against the Firbolgs in the first battle of Moytura, defeating the bearded giants. Dagda, though deified, is described as possessing supernatural strength and an insatiable appetite. He maintained sexual relations with several goddesses. In battle he could slay nine men with the stroke of his club. Later in this book is detailed an historical relic, an earth drawing of a giant called the Cerne Giant that could very well have been designed in remembrance of this deity.

Further proof that Dagda was most likely a giant lies in that he was only acknowledged by the Irish. The continental Celts of Europe did not recognize him in their pantheon.

A local deity among the Welsh Celts was Morvran, a hideous warrior of great stature and ferocity when in battle. Later to become a god of war, Morvran was thought to actually be a personified demon.[8] Although gawr (giant) is distantly related etymologically to the Hebrew gibbor, we find in the Norse mythology another fascinating revelation. The legends of Iceland tell of a giant named Ymir who was created by a melting glacier or mountain of ice, a dying ice age. Ymir fathered a race of Frost Giants that were unusually evil and made continuous war with the Norse gods.[9] The ice melted between the fiery domains of Muspell and the icy realms of Niflheim, the land of the dead. Note the etymological structure of Niflheim and its comparative similarity to Nephilim. Could this be Niflheim, the land of the dead (Rephaim?), meaning giants?

Icelandic Vikings and Celts religiously maintained genealogies that dated back to Babel and the Flood, with some even giving the names of antediluvian patriarchs. William Cooper states in *After the Flood* that The Flood caused global cooling that resulted in an ice age that their predecessors remembered and, through oral transmission over many generations, associated this icy epoch of history with the giants they recalled from their distant past. It is therefore no wonder that we discover in the Norse beliefs that traces of Hebrew-Chaldee still existed, as evidenced in the word Niflheim.

Further proof of their knowledge of biblical-related history is found in their mythology of Odin, the most powerful of the Norse gods who slew Ymir the Frost giant, causing so much blood to flow from the slain giant that the whole earth flooded and everything was destroyed. Only the Frost giant Bergelmir and his wife escaped the deluge in a boat[10] (sound like Noah?). Going even further back in Norse memory we find Yggdrasil, the colossal tree of life that overshadows the entire world. Yggdrasil had three giant roots. One reached Asgard, fortress city of the gods, the second was buried in Jotunheim, the land of the giants, and the third root was in Niflheim, the abode of the dead.

The Norse gods are divided between two deified races called the Vanir and the Aesir. Previously at war with each other, these families of gods had united in an effort to defeat the Frost Giants, their enemies in the world of men. One of the most widely known deities was Freyja, a Vanir goddess of Asgard. She was extremely beautiful and suspected of sexual liaisons with strange gods and elves, spirits of the woodlands often believed to be demonic. Freyja is greatly detailed by Snorri in *Prose Edda*. She was also the desire of many giants who sought to possess her.[11]

The twin brother of Freyja was also a Vanir god named Freyr who was married to a giantess named Gerd. Another Nordic deity was the goddess Gefjon, an Aesir goddess detailed also in *Prose Edda* who bore four giant sons.

In relation to giants, the Norse god Heimdall is by far the most intriguing. He is a guardian deity of Asgard, a sentry for the Norse gods against the Frost Giants and for Yggdrasil, the tree of life. The translation of his name is earth watcher, mirroring the Hebrew title given to certain angels, the Watchers. In Iceland he was also called Rig. This means the White God. [12] This description of Heimdall brings to mind the Egyptian descriptions at Karnak of the Anakim and the Amorites being whitish. Heimdall was also said to have been born from a giantess.

Concerning Asgard, Odin caught the shape-changing Frost Giant Thiassi in the paradise city while in eagle form, and slew him in a fire. Odin removed the giant's eyes and cast them into the night sky as a sign to the other giants that the gods would someday deal with them in like manner. Contention between the Norse gods and the Frost Giants was often bitter, but this strife will be at its greatest in the last days.[13]

The Viking prophecy of the end of the world is called Ragnarok. A stone relic depicting the Ragnarok prophecies is displayed today on the Isle of Man and shows vividly how the earth will be engulfed in flames, the Norse gods and the Frost Giants will engage in a final global battle, the sun will burn out, the moon will plunge into the sea, cold will engulf the earth, and the stars will fall from the sky.[14]

The Midgard Serpent that encircles the whole world, offspring of a half-giant and giantess, will spew poison, destroying everything alive.

Much of the Viking mythology and Ragnarok prophecy contain elements that parallel the biblical stories and Book of Revelation. In fact, Thor was the son of Odin, the most powerful Norse god, and one day Thor will slay the Midgard Serpent just as Jesus will slay and destroy Satan, the dragon of chaos in the lake of fire and by the will of the father.

So profound were the beliefs in the Norse gods and son of Odin in antiquity that the Roman Christian church sacrificed four days of the week to honor the Viking and Celtic gods. Tuesday derives from Tyr, Norse god of war. Wednesday is from Wodin's-day, Odin's name known by Germans and Anglo-Saxons. Thursday comes from none other than Thor's-day. And Friday is named in remembrance of Frigg, Norse goddess of childbirth.[21] The other three days of the week were adopted by the early Christian empire of the Romans in honor of other pagan beliefs. Sunday is in tribute to the sun, worshiped as deity by Egyptians and many other nations of early Christianity that were lured into its worship under the guise of papal rule. Monday, of course, was named in honor of the moon worshiped in Arabia and as a female celestial divinity by dozens of Middle Eastern nations, and Saturday comes from <u>Saturn</u>-day. Saturn was the Roman god of mysteries, which in turn was a modern shade for Nimrod of old.[15]

    Another interesting relationship between Virgil's *Aeneid*, giants, and the biblical Nephilim is that the historic poet-historian wrote that Vulcan had metalsmiths that were giants themselves. Vulcan is the Roman name for the Greek god Hephaestus, the god of metallurgy and forge fires. In Homer's *Iliad* this god made armor for a mortal in the Trojan war. Ancient Sumerian texts reveal that the Anakim giants were involved in a widespread campaign of mining and the construction of metal objects and buildings. Of the conflicting views of the Greeks concerning the Cyclops, one view held is that they were a race of giant smiths and metal workers long ago who mined ore and forged magic weapons. The other view holds that they were reclusive in nature, unproductive, and bestial. Actually, both are true, one belief being their infamous history long ago and the other view being what they became. Later in this book we'll look into ancient texts such as those in Sumerian and Mesopotamian literature to determine more about these mysterious giants. The popular view is that the Cyclops were solitary hermits, not desirous of the social order the Tritons maintained. These unique giants had only one eye in the center of their head and were lacking in intelligence. The parallel between this strange physical trait and the biblical evidence of Nephilim lies in what one of the sons of Goliath, the Philistine giant who David slew with a sling, had six fingers on both hands and six toes on each foot. To create giants from purely Adamic stock would have only been accomplished by forcing an imbalance in the genetic structure of the unborn, which was done by the angels. They were not human, nor were their offspring. The Cyclops of Greek memory and the abundance of fingers and toes on the Bible giant, which we will learn more about later, suggests that there could be many more comparative parallels drawn between the vast whole of Greek mythology and biblical history. Near Eastern ancient documents from the second millennium B.C. around the time of Sargon I in Babylonia and Assyria tell of a multitude of monstrous births from the <u>official records of the ancient astrologers</u> who studied the heavens for signs relating to these unusual births.[16] These monstrous births grew up to be monstrous giants who Eusebius claimed <u>dwelt in the land of Babylonia</u>.[17]

    James Kugel in his book *The Bible As It Was* cites a passage from the writing of Baruch that reads that <u>the giants were born there [Babylonia] who were famous of old, great in stature, expert in war</u>, citing the Baruch text.

Giants were known in the Far East as well. The Chinese have long had traditions of a gigantic race of people who once lived in some remote part of their country, and there is a legend which dates from the fifteenth century, that a certain emperor had a bodyguard of archers composed of men of immense stature.[18] The countries of India and Ethiopia maintained traditions of a distant race of giant-kin peoples who stood eight feet in height.[19] A people called the Mensa in northeastern Ethiopia believed that long ago a race of giants called the Rom once inhabited their lands. In *A Treasure of African Folklore* by Harold Courlander we read that the Rom were nomadic herdsmen. Old tombs made of stone slabs are believed to have been built by the Rom...[20] (*The Treasury of African Folklore*; Harold Courlander, pg. 550).

Interestingly, this same writer quotes an ancient Ethiopian proverb in his work on African traditions: "Does man dig his tomb like the giants?" According to Mr. Courlander, there still remain stone ruins that the natives associate to the Rom giants.

Going back to the Grecian traditions, we have such creatures as the Titans, who are described as of gigantic stature and enormous strength, who carried on war against the gods. From them sprang the Gigantes, beings of fearful aspect with terrible faces...[21]

The Greeks largely preserved their legends and histories by oral tradition. Much was recorded by old Greek historians long ago, but even more was lost in the silence of history. But over a thousand years before the Grecians emerged on the world scene, the Sumerians had already preserved their history in the oldest written language known today. The hero of these ancient people was much like the Greek's Hercules. His name was Gilgamesh.

In the ninth table of the *Epic of Gilgamesh* the hero happens upon two giant demigods guarding the Gate of the Sun. No one is permitted to pass these giants, but special allowance is given for Gilgamesh because he himself is two-thirds god. He is granted passage solely because of his partial giant ancestry. The Sumerian hero appears to have been believed to be Nephilim. This most archaic Sumerian tradition is incredible in that the epic contains a wealth of Genesis information, though formerly would never be confirmed.

Gilgamesh seeks a man who has all the answers named Utnapishtim. He traverses an ocean and endures a long journey before finding the ancient man, who then reveals his mysterious past. Remarkably, the story told to Gilgamesh is told in the first person. The hero listens intently as Utnapishtim tells him of a great flood in the days of old that drowned out the giants and cities of the Old World. From the astonishing biblical parallels seen in the text of the *Epic of Gilgamesh* we know that the hero listens to Noah (called

Utnapishtim in Old Babylonian), who tells Gilgamesh about his own birth. The hero inquires of Noah about the origin of his people and Noah's reply is almost synonymous with the Torah account of the flood. Here we learn that the ancestors of Gilgamesh were responsible for the destruction of the previous human civilization. The giants. This is further proven in that the Dead Sea findings unearthed a very antiquated book attributed to Enoch called the *Book of Giants*. The names for many of the giants are given in this ancient work, and <u>Gilgamesh</u> himself is mentioned. This suggests that Gilgamesh was regarded as a divine giant by the early Mesopotamians of Sumer, Akkad, and Babylon. We'll soon pore over substantial evidence that proves that Gilgamesh is none other than the biblical <u>Nimrod</u>.

In the epic, Gilgamesh exhibits too much familiarity with Utnapishtim, Noah. Noah lived three hundred and fifty years after the deluge and was still alive when Nimrod ruled in Babylonia. Noah was alive when the tower at Babel was destroyed as well. Nimrod was Noah's great grandson through Ham and knew his great grandfather well, so being Gilgamesh in the epic, gives us the visiting of a great grandson to his great grandfather. Gilgamesh said,

> <u>Oh, father Utnapishtim, you who have entered the assembly of the gods, I wish to question you concerning the living and the dead, how shall I find the life for which I am seeking?</u>

Gilgamesh searched in vain for the one thing God would not grant the giants: life eternal. Being the progeny of the angels, they were cursed to roam the earth as vagabond spirits and demons once their bodies died. In the epic, Gilgamesh is said to be <u>two parts god and one part man</u>, his mother a mortal but his father a priest-god mentioned in the ancient Sumerian King-lists, which is detailed in another chapter.

Still, though old writings are interesting and often unbelievable, it is the Bible that contains the most incontestable proofs. Scripture plainly teaches that the flood was caused by the trespasses of angels and wickedness of mankind and giants. It is the Bible that makes our prime foundation of testing the veracity of myths and old stories. Concerning the *Epic of Gilgamesh* and Utnapishtim, we find that the preservation of many of the most ancient of texts of pre-flood antiquity may be attributed to Noah. The writings of Enoch and *Book of Giants,* along with other works, could have been saved by Noah and later excavated. The site of Noah's cache (or someone of his time) could very well be the ancient Assyrian city of Sepharvaim near Babylon. <u>A tradition affirms that Noah buried near this city the records of the antediluvian world</u>.[30] Incidentally, <u>sepher</u> means <u>writer of chronicles</u> and is also found in the Canaanite city Kirjath-sepher in the Bible, which means <u>city books</u>.

Chapter Five

Giants in the Promise Land

The Anakim were a race of Nephilim feared in the ancient world. All the way in Egypt the Israelites had sometime heard of their existence. When the Israelites heard the spies' report, there was an immediate panic through the twelve tribes and others dwelling with Israel. One of the men sent to search out Canaan was named Caleb. This spy tried to assure the people that they were able to overcome these wicked nations, but the other spies instilled fear into the Hebrews, saying:

> ...all the people that we saw in it are men of a great stature (Numbers 13:32).

The word stature is defined as height, tallness, growth, thus proving that these Canaanite nations were of larger size than normal people, but it wasn't until the spies mentioned the giants themselves and their physical appearance that Israel openly rebelled against the authority of Moses and completely lost faith in the promises God had given them through Abraham and Moses.

> And there we saw the giants, the sons of Anak, which come of the giants: and we were in our own sight as grasshoppers, and so we were in their sight (Numbers 13:33).

The sons of Anak here are the three literal giants in Hebron which the spies saw, but the Deuteronomy account called them sons of the Anakims, referring to the seven Canaanite nations listed earlier. They are said to be greater and taller than the Israelite spies. This indicates that these peoples were not Nephilim, as proven in genealogies that trace them all to Ham and his son Canaan. These large peoples gradually developed into nations of very tall and strong people because of their sexual relations with the Anakim that dwelled in their lands and possibly other Nephilim races such as the Rephaim. The giants of Canaan were maintaining societal relations with these peoples through intermarrying, which caused their offspring to become larger, as the sons of God and daughters of men had done in more distant times. The results of these unions were inhumanly large and fearsome offspring. The Jewish historian Josephus in the first century A.D. wrote that the twelve spies looked upon the posterity of the giants at Hebron.[1]

Josephus also recorded that almost four hundred years after Israel's invasion of Canaan, King Saul led Israel against the Amalekites and prevailed. He also took Agag, the enemies' king, captive; the beauty and tallness of whose body he admired so muchd.²

This is considerable that Saul, a tall man himself, should be taken aback at the height of Agag.

Numbers 13:1-24. After escaping the armies of Pharaoh, who drowned in the Red Sea, Moses sent twelve spies, a man from each of the tribes, to search out the land of Canaan for cities and people, the land promised long ago to Abraham. During the excursion the spies passed the city of Hebron, where three giants lived. Their names were Ahiman, Talmai, and Sheshai. All three were fathered by Anak, a mysterious giant detailed more extensively later. This city was formerly called Mamre, which means strength. It was a city that harbored giants and served as a chief dwelling of the Anakim. In times even more archaic, the city was called Kirjath-Arba, which is translated the city of Arba. Arba was a mighty giant, the father of Anak and grandfather of the three giants dwelling in Hebron when the spies beheld the city from a distance.

Numbers 13:25-33. Forty days later the spies returned with a cluster of grapes so large that it took two of them to bear it upon a staff. The mineral rich, fertile land of Canaan grew fruit and vegetables in abundance, much of it larger than usual. To exhibit the size of Canaan's produce to Moses and the rest of the people, the spies brought back grapes, pomegranates and figs. As for the reports concerning the inhabitants of Canaan who enjoyed these fruits, the news from the spies was foreboding:

> Nevertheless the people be strong that dwell in the land, and the cities are walled, and very great: and moreover we saw the children of Anak there (Numbers 13:28).

In Deuteronomy 1:28 the children of Anak, as seen here in Numbers, are called the sons of the Anakims. These sons are the three giants in Hebron, but the text here has dual application, seeming to indicate also that the sons of the Anakims include:

> The Amalekites dwell in the land of the south: and the Hittites, and the Jebusites, and the Amorites, dwell in the mountains: and the Canaanites dwell by the sea, and by the coast of Jordan (Numbers 13:29).

Numbers 14:1-10. Having heard the giants were near, the insurgent Israelites picked up stones to kill Joshua and Caleb, the only two men who proposed to enter Canaan as God commanded. Before they were to be killed, however, God appeared to Israel and spoke to Moses.

Numbers 14:22-40. Moses is told the disturbing news that Israel will suffer until the present generation is dead. The judgment would last forty years. Only Joshua and Caleb are promised to enter the Land of Promise.

Numbers 14:39-45, Deuteronomy 1:41-44. Israel mourns because of the severity of God's judgment and delaying of the promise of the land for an inheritance, and decides prematurely to attack Canaan as God formerly commanded. But Moses explicitly reveals to the people that it is too late to appease God. But still, despite the words of Moses, Israel enters southern Canaan and is defeated in battle and driven back out of Canaan by the Amalekites and the Amorites of the highlands.

The Amorites and the Anakim comprised the main bodies of power in southern Canaan and were obviously employing a wide program of interbreeding. Both the Anakim and Amorites appear on Egyptian monuments as light-skinned and fair-eyed peoples. On these inscriptions the Anakim are referred to as the Tammahu, from Talmai, one of the sons of Anak that lived in Hebron. Another son of Anak as read earlier is Sheshai. This name means whitish. These Egyptian edifices reveal that the Amorites had blue eyes, a rare trait to the dark-featured Egyptians.[3]

The Anakim were described as men of a great height (stature), greater and taller, and the Amorites are described as the children of the Anakims.

> Yet destroyed I the Amorite before them, whose height was like the height of the cedars, and he was strong as the oaks; yet I destroyed his fruit from above, and his roots from beneath (Amos 1:9).

The Amorites were taller and stronger than ordinary people, which strongly indicates their sexual affiliation with the Anakim. Being originally descended from Ham, this would not at all be contrary to their sexual unrestraint.

The phrase fruit from above has interesting application. Fruit comes from seed, and also means offspring, revealing that the height and strength of the Amorite derived from above. Likely from rebellious and lustful angels, originally from above, that have their root in hell, or below.

In Genesis 15:13-16 Abraham is told by God that his seed shall become a stranger in a land that is not theirs because a delay in judgment was necessary "for the sins of the Amorites is not yet full." The translation of sins here is aw_n, which means a depraved action, perversity, and specifically signifies the sum of past deeds against God. Aw_n derives from awah; to make crooked, act perversely, commit iniquity, turn upside down, and essentially means to deviate from the proper path. The sins of the Amorites were primarily the sexual integration of their people with the Anakim, the giants of southern Canaan.

Numbers 20:14-21. After recuperating from defeat, Israel migrates further eastward. The country of Edom, whose people were the descendants of Esau, Jacob's brother, refuse the Israelites safe passage through their land. Refusing to make war, Moses turns Israel away.

Numbers 21:1, 33:40. King Arad of the southern Canaanites learned that Israel had camped at Mt. Hor at the borderlands of Edom and attacked them, taking many Hebrews as prisoners. Mt. Hor was the dwelling of the ancient Horites, earlier called Horims of strange lineage. They dwelt at the mountain also called Mt. Seir. King Chedorloamer in Abraham's day defeated them, but Esau's descendants ultimately drove them out of the land completely and renamed the region Edom. Today, Mt. Seir is called by its Greek name Petra, a perfectly preserved city hewn out of the solid rock of the mountain and probably the most fortified and impenetrable city of the world, both past and present, accessible only by a very narrow crevasse. Petra is an ancient wonder of the world over 4000 years old. The *Book of Jasher* states that the inhabitants of Petra are described as the mighty men of the children of Seir the Horite. (Jasher 57:9) the Tel-Amarna letters reveal that the Horites were Indo-Aryan and in the later chapters in this book we will discover that their unusual height and traits link them to the Amorites and Anakim giants.

Numbers 21:2-3. Angered by the unexpected attack of the Canaanites of Arad's kingdom, the Israelites seek the permission of God to make war against King Arad and to destroy his people, cities and all. This vengeful request is granted, and the Israelites under Moses assemble for war and then flood the land of Canaan in a storm of blood and ruined structures in their wake. King Arad's realm in southern Canaan was ruined.

Numbers 21:4, 33:41-44, Deuteronomy 2. Israel then travels along the outer edge of Edom and around the wilderness of Moab. The Edomites were the ancestral brothers of the Israelites, both descended from Isaac, son of Abraham. The hate between Jacob and Esau manifested in their peoples hundreds of years later, exhibiting the prophetic fulfillment of one aspect of the Edenic prophecy of enmity in the seed of the woman.

Moses is told by God that Canaan is the land of promise to Jacob's descendants. Yet Moab belongs only to the descendants of Lot, because long before those days the descendants of Lot drove out the giant remnants left behind by the forces of Chedorlaomer.

> The Emims dwelt therein in times past, a people great, and many, and tall, as the Anakim.

> Which also were accounted giants, as the Anakims, but the Moabites called them Emims (Deuteronomy 2:10-11).

Later in this book is the fascinating account of King Chedorlaomer's campaign against these and other giants in Canaan, a war hidden within human history, hardly understood by even the most knowledgeable historians.

The Moabites defeated these ancient giants and took their land. These Emims only appear in Scripture twice, their first appearance being in the days of Abraham. They had been defeated then, too.

Of the five Nephilim races mentioned in Scripture, only the Anakim and the Rephaim remained by the time of the Exodus, which is commonly dated around 1400 B.C. The other three giant nations were probably extinct by this time. The Emims had been slaughtered with many Zuzims and Rephaim in the rebellion against King Chedorlaomer (Genesis 14:5). The Emims were called terrors, but died out with the establishment of Moab as a sovereign nation. The defeat of these three old giant nations is likewise recorded in detail in *Tales of the Patriarchs*, a collection of stories found among the Dead Sea texts. And despite the Moabites ridding the land of these giants, they could not get them out of their blood. This and other disturbing revelations will be revealed in depth in coming chapters.

Numbers 21:21-23, Deuteronomy 2:19-32...Just as Moses had entreated the king of Edom for safe passage through his kingdom, Israel requested the same from King Sihon of the Amorites, but his response was no different. He gathered all the Amorites of the highlands and cities to battle Israel.

Numbers 21:24-32. Israel utterly defeats the Amorites and lays waste their cities and towns all the way through southern Canaan to the borderlands of Ammon, another country protected from Israel by the Lord, as were Moab and Edom. The Moabites destroyed the giant civilization of the Emims, and the Edomites drove out a mysterious race of people called Horis that dwelt long ago in the mountain fortress-city today known as Petra, the city of rock.

Israel slew the Amorites but could not enter Ammon because of God's divine protection. Long ago the Ammonites did God service by eradicating much of the seed of Satan that King Chedorlaomer of Elam did not kill.

> That was also accounted a land of giants dwelt there in old time: and the Ammonites called them Zamzummins; A people great, and many, and tall as the Anakims; but the Lord destroyed them before them; and they succeeded them, and dwelt in their stead. (Deuteronomy 2:20-21)

Deuteronomy 3:1-11. King Og of Bashan heard of the Israelite invasion and their victories over the other Canaanite kings that had tried to stand up against them. Og gathered the armies of his sixty cities and numerous towns and went against the Israelites. But the Hebrews, under the guidance of Moses, systematically conquered every single city of the lands of Argob and Bashan of King Og. Even Og the giant was captured. The giant king attempted to lift an enormous boulder to throw at the Israelites, but Moses himself struck Og on his ankle with the staff of God, which Moses had held up at the division of the Red Sea. Og was killed by the blow from Moses, strengthened by God (Jasher 85:27). Although old Hebrew texts tell this story, it is a valuable confirmation to discover that an ancient Somalian tradition in Africa also affirms that Og the giant was slain by Moses, with a staff on the ankle.[4]

Not only did Flavius Josephus mention the giants, but he also wrote about King Og in his *Antiquities*: Now Og had very few equals, either in the largeness of his body or handsomeness of his appearance. He was also a man of great activity in the use of his hands, so that his actions were not unequal to the vast largeness and handsome appearance of his body; and men could easily guess at his strength and magnitude when they took his bed at Rabbath, the royal city of the Ammonites.[5]

King Og had his capitol at Edrei where he was killed. Archaeologists have recently discovered an old subterranean city, complex in design with chambers, streets, stores, and a trading center. The underground site today is called Edra'ah.[6]

> For only Og, king of Bashan, remained of the remnant of giants; behold his bedstead was a bedstead of iron; is it not in Rabbath of the children of Ammon? Nine cubits was the breadth thereof; and four cubits the breadth of it, after the cubit of a man. (Deuteronomy 3:11)

The archaic Hebrew cubit is measured at eighteen inches. This giant king must have stood between 10 1/2 and 11 1/2 feet tall. His bed measured 13 1/2 feet in length from head to foot and exhibits his great height because the dimensions of his bedstead would never have been recorded by Moses (in Deuteronomy) if Og were not truly a giant. Because of its immense size the Ammonites kept the bed as a trophy and souvenir in remembrance of the giant Zamzummims, that once dwelt in their lands and left behind artifacts of unusual size.

Found among the numerous antiquated writings in the Dead Sea archives is an obscure statement concerning this powerful giant:

> ...all his servants with Og... a spear like a cedar, a shield like a tower...[7]

The kingdom of Og recently leapt out of the pages of biblical history and into the sigh of archaeology. Like western ghost towns visited only by the wind, Og's cities remain with us today in rock edifices hardly touched by time, astonishingly preserved by the arid climactic changes wrought in the past three thousand years in the Middle East.

More than a hundred ruined cities are found—though only deserted, not ruined; for the houses are quite perfect and habitable still, being built of stone, even to the doors and window shutters, hinges and all, and roofs of fine solid stone. Some of the dates are before our era, and it is quite probable that these cities are the very same that Moses described.[8] (See also Deuteronomy 3:5)

The translation of giants in Deuteronomy 3:11 is Rephaim, which means the dead. Rephaim is plural of rapha; dead, tall. In a contextual sense it is clear that many places in Scripture reveal the error of translators who were unsure of the meaning of rapha, and instead inserted the dead instead of giants. The two words are interchangeable when referring to the Nephilim race of giants called the Rephaim. This problem does not arise when the context refers to the Anakim, Emims, Zuzims or Zamzummims, only the Rephaim. Rapha is translated the tall in height and means also the dead. These Nephilim people were so infested with angelic ancestry that little human blood flowed through their veins. The aspect of the dead in rapha portends that the Rephaims were so polluted they would not live, nor see a resurrection. The prophet Isaiah confirms this dark facet of the Rephaim's nature:

> They are dead [Rephaim] they shall not live; they are deceased [rapha], they shall not rise: therefore has thou visited and destroyed them, and made all their memory to perish (Isaiah 26:14).

Rephaim and rapha, as seen in the above brackets, are the Hebrew words that the English translators put in as dead and deceased. Though the translation of "dead" is indeed rephaim (dead; giant) and "deceased" in this context is rapha, which is likewise synonymous with the dead, this verse could have just as well read: they are giants, they shall not live... and still be correct.

The giants here are the other lords, who aside from God had exercised dominion over Israel as read in the preceding verse, Isaiah 26:13. The curse of being rephaim toward the giants in this context is made more profound by one of the most incredible prophecies concerning the resurrection of the body of believers, which is found in verses 19-21. In this same chapter the giants are promised by God that they will not live, while the Hebrews are told that they will resurrect!

The Hebrew implies in verse 26:14 that anything found to be rapha is feeble, flaccid and weak, however, since we already know that these giants called the Rephaim were not at all weak, we understand that the Hebrew inference pointedly refers to the blood-relation (b_s_r) being lesser than human, being <u>weak,</u> as seen coupled in the phrase describing the Nephilim in general as being <u>mighty men</u> (enosh), <u>men of renown</u>.

This implication behind the name Rephaim suggests that these giants were so completely inhuman that they will not be resurrected for judgment day, for they <u>will not rise</u>. Lacking sufficient Adamic lineage it appears that God regards these giants as being too contaminated to be considered human, thus the promise of resurrection does not apply. In reference to the Rephaim the *Jubilees* text reads:

> <u>But formerly the land of Gilead was called the land of the Rephaim because it was the land of the Rephaim. And the Ephraim were born as giants whose height was ten cubits, nine cubits, eight cubits, or down to seven cubits. And their dwelling was from the land of the Ammonites to Mount Hermon and their royal places were in Zarnaim [Karnaim], and Ashtaroth, and Edrei, and Misur, and Beon. But the Lord destroyed them because of their evil deeds since they were very cruel.</u> (Jubilees 29)

<u>Numbers 22-24.</u> Seeing the defeat of the Amorites and Og's empire, Balak, the king of Moab, summoned the famous prophet and diviner of Baal named Balaam. The *Book of Jasher* says Balaam <u>was very wise and understood the art of witchcraft</u> (Jubilees 61:8).

<u>Numbers 25:1-8</u>. Unable to curse Israel, the king of Moab, no doubt influenced by the machinations of Satan, begins to entice the Hebrews with Moabite women. King Balak's intentions were the preservation of his people and throne, because the tribes of Jacob were now greatly feared throughout Canaan.

> <u>And Israel abode in Shittim, and the people began to commit whoredom with the daughters of Moab.</u> (Numbers 25:1).

King Balak reasoned that Israel would not be so great a threat if Hebrew and Moabites intermarried extensively.

The sinister plot is made known to Moses by God who orders the execution of all Hebrews with Moabite or Midianite women. They are beheaded, and God specifically commands Moses <u>to vex the Midianites, and smite them</u>... (Numbers 25:17)

<u>Numbers 31:1-18</u>. One thousand Hebrew warriors from each tribe assemble for war. Moses leads the twelve thousand-man army and destroys five Midianite cities.

> And they burnt all their cities wherein they dwelt, and all their goodly castles, with fire (Numbers 31:10).

All male Midianites were slain, but the Israelites saved alive the women and children to the shock of Moses, who revealed to the Hebrew soldiers that it was by the counsel of Balaam the prophet that the women of Midian were used against them. The Israelites slew the five Midianite kings, found Balaam and killed him, and every female as well, that was not a virgin or infant.

Numbers 32:33. East of the Jordan River, Moses assigns the tribes of Gad, Reuben, and half the tribe of Manasseh their inheritance in the conquered kingdoms of Sihon of the Amorites and the territories of the kingdom of Argob and Bashan, ruled by Og the giant. Moses specifically claims to these tribes that they have inherited a land of giants in Deuteronomy 3:13.

Deuteronomy 7:1-6. Israel is commanded by God to show no mercy to the seven wicked Canaanite nations that were greater and mightier, the Hittites, Girgashites, Amorites, Canaanites, Perizzites, Hivites, and the Jebusites. Also, because of the importance of the purity of their seed, God commanded them:

> Neither shalt thou make marriages with them; thy daughter thou shalt not give unto his son, nor his daughter shalt thou take unto thy son. (Deuteronomy 7:3)

Deuteronomy 20:13-15, 21:10-13. Moses was given many laws by God concerning offensive and defensive warfare. In conquering other peoples, God explicitly permits Israel to save alive the women and the little ones. But this did not pertain to Canaan, only to those nations outside the borders of the lands promised to Abraham.

> Thus shalt thou do unto all the cities which are very far off from thee, which are not of the cities of these nations.
>
> But of the cities of these people, which the Lord thy God doth give thee for an inheritance, thou shalt save alive nothing that breatheth; But thou shalt utterly destroy them... (Deuteronomy 20:15-17)

Why would a loving God command His people to eradicate entire cultures and nations? Why was it necessary that all Canaanite races be unmercifully put to the sword, even slaying the women and children? The answer to this difficult question is discovered in the Hebrew word enosh, which refers to the weakened blood-relation (basar) condition of contaminated peoples, due to sexual relations with angels long ago.

In Genesis 13:13 it is revealed that after the flood mankind had again become enosh, as evidenced in the wicked societies of Sodom and Gomorrah.

Jude wrote that the people of these cities were guilty of going after strange flesh, which was also a trespass of the angels that left their own estate (Jude 6-7).

Obviously, the sins of these nations in ancient Sodom and Gomorrah were fornication and homosexuality, and this revelation was recorded by Jude to exhibit the awareness that both angels and humans are guilty of sexual trespasses. But concerning the killing of the Canaanite women, we discover a clue embedded in the ancient text of the *Book of Jasher*. In the battles for the conquest of Canaan the enemies of Israel were aided because their wives were experienced in battle... and smote the sons of Jacob by showering down stones like rain. (Jasher 39:5, 11)

Interestingly, the Jasher accounts of Israel's forced occupation in Canaan are far more detailed than the biblical texts, and even more interesting is that the Bible only refers to the *Book of Jasher* when concerning the Conquest, and nowhere else in Scripture is Jasher mentioned.

Like *Jasher*, the *Book of Jubilees* also explains the eradication of all the Canaanites, however differently. In *Jubilees 20*, Abraham commanded his children to not take wives from the girls of Canaan because the seed of Canaan will be rooted out of the land. And he told them, the judgment of the giants and the judgments of the Sodomites, how they had been judged on account of their wickedness.

Deuteronomy 9:1-4. Israel is now commanded to cross the Jordan River and infiltrate the heart of Canaan, no longer skirting the borders.

> Hear O Israel: Thou art to pass over Jordan this day, to go in to possess nations greater and mightier than thyself, cities great and fenced up to heaven,
>
> A people great and tall, the children of the Anakims, whom thou knowest, and of whom thou hast heard say, Who can stand before the children of Anak? (Deuteronomy 9:1-2)

These very giants, called the Anakim, were the cause of Israel's fear forty years previously when the spies brought back word of their presence in Canaan. Though Og of Bashan was the last to die of the remnant of the giants (Rephaims), there is little known about the race of Rephaim in Scripture. But not so concerning the Anakim.

Chapter Six

Conquest of Canaan

For fear of the Anakim, Israel remained in the barren wilderness at the edges of Canaan for forty years, in a hostile and wild land so uncultivated that God Himself had to feed His people with manna, angel's food. Moses had initially sent in twelve spies to search out Canaan, but now Joshua, the high priest and military leader of all Israel, selected only two spies, the number of those who had faith forty years earlier to bring back a positive report to Moses. These two spies searched out the borderlands of Canaan where they would soon traverse.

Joshua 2:1-21. The two spies infiltrate the city of Jericho and meet a strange Canaanite woman, a prostitute who exhibits more faith in God than most of Israel. She hides the spies on her roof in the city from the servants of the king who had received reports that they were there.

This woman, Rahab by named, deceived her own people, the hunting parties, into believing the spies had already departed. As reward, by her own request, Rahab was promised that she and her family would be spared from death when the armies of Israel returned to destroy Jericho.

Joshua 2:22-24. The spies waited three days for the hunting parties to return to the city where they remained hidden in the harlot's house. Upon returning to Israel's camp they tell Joshua everything about Jericho and its people. The spies report what Rahab had told them; that all the nations of Canaan fear Israel, for they have heard of the utter defeat of Egypt's army, and two kings of the Amorites, being King Sihon and Og, the giant king of Bashan and Argob.

Joshua 3:14-17. Priests cross the banks of the Jordan River holding the ark of the covenant that Moses built by divine instruction. This contained both stone tablets of the Ten Commandments written by the finger of God. They also carried manna and a copy of the Torah. This wide and dangerous river divided, just as the Red Sea did when Moses raised his staff. Israel crossed this river and camped at Gilgal, where twelve giant stones were erected as a monument unto God.

Joshua 5:1, 6:1. The Jordan River in those ancient times was regarded as an impregnable boundary, especially during the harvest season when it overflowed its banks. And it was at this precise time of the year, according to the biblical narrative, that God miraculously stopped the river's flow so that Israel could pass into Canaan. This feat of impossibility stunned the kings of the Amorites and Canaanites who thought they were protected from Israel's war campaigns. In fact, fear and dread permeated through these regions of Canaan, causing the gates of Jericho to be shut and sealed from opening because of Israel's presence on their side of the Jordan River. Geologists assert that this was likely less than a miracle, because the Jordan River lies precisely on a fault line and a slight earthquake could have temporarily altered the flow of the Jordan, especially in light of the fact that the Jordan's course has been altered in just such a way in recent history.

Archaeologists have discovered many ancient letters, with pleas from various Canaanite kings to their Egyptian overlords, asking for military aid against the invading Hebrews. They encircled Jericho's walls for seven days, marching around the city and blowing trumpets, and on the seventh day the walls of the city fell down. Israeli soldiers stormed the city, slaying everything that hath breath, all humans and animals. In Jericho was saved only the faithful prostitute Rahab and her household, while the rest of the Canaanite city flowed with the blood of men, women, and children at the commandment of God. The biblical reasoning to justify this genocide is hidden in this passage.

> And the Lord said unto Joshua, See, I have given into thine hand Jericho, and the king thereof, and the mighty men of valour, (Joshua 6:2)

The men of Jericho were Canaanites, men of great stature (Numbers 13:29, 32), associated to the dreaded Anakim. Since the Canaanites are definitely included in the lineage of Ham, it is evident that they were not Nephilim, but only guilty of sexual ties with these giants. Their description from the mouth of God to Joshua was mighty men of valour. Mighty men is gibborim, which is located first in Genesis 6:4 and is translated giants, heroes, tyrants, huge, and powerful. The word valour is very unique in that in Hebrew it is chayil, which describes strength and power. It etymologically derives from ch_l, a rare word that is descriptive of a painful birth, twisting in labor pains. This is exactly the same as the root for Nephilim; a painful birth that falls from the womb.

God commanded the execution of the sexually defiant people of Canaan because of their contaminated bloodlines that strayed farther and farther with each passing generation from the pure Adamic blood. This is proven in that in the days of Abraham, God told him that the sins of the Amorites are not yet full. The Lord raised Israel in Egypt and kept them there until the Amorites and their Canaanite brothers were ripe for judgment.

Though Rahab was saved by faith, even she was of polluted ancestry. The translation of the harlot's name, Rahab, is large, broad, exhibiting that she was considered to be larger than ordinary women.

Joshua 7:1-5. Israel then prepared to destroy another city. Ai was a major fortified city of the Amorites, but little inhabited. Joshua was told by the spies that a few thousand men would be sufficient, but when they were dispatched to Ai to destroy it, the Amorites defeated and chased them away. In their retreat were slain 36 Hebrews because a greedy Israelite took some of the forbidden spoil of Jericho:

> "A goodly Babylonish garment, and two hundred shekels of silver, and a wedge of gold of fifty shekels weight." (Joshua 7:21)

Jericho was spiritually regarded as the first fruits of Canaan, a sacrifice to God. Nothing was taken by the soldiers from the city but Rahab and her family. All gold, treasures, flocks, and foods remained. When the thief and his family were executed for stealing from God and burned along with everything they owned, as an addition and trespass offering to the first fruits of God did the Lord command Joshua to destroy the city of Ai.

Joshua 8:1-29. The high priest chose thirty thousand mighty men of valour from among Israel's tribes to go take the city of Ai. The terminology here is significant because earlier we read how the inhabitants of Jericho were called mighty men of valour. However, this must be understood as a discrepancy in the transliteration of Hebrew into English. Though in English these are alike, in Hebrew they differ. The men of Jericho in Joshua 6:2 are gibborim, mighty men, giants, tyrants, etc., but in the above passage of 8:2 they are mighty men, the word men being ish, which signifies men in a masculine sense. Also note that enosh is not used. The mighty men of Jericho were nothing etymologically comparable to the mighty men of Israel.

After an elaborate ambush, the Israelites sacked Ai and destroyed its army and people in the fields, twelve thousand altogether. Joshua had the king of Ai hung on a tree. Ai was not like Jericho being the first fruits sacrifice to God, a gift offering for, by the word of the Lord, the Israelites were permitted to take alive all the animals, treasures, supplies, and furnishings of the city.

Joshua 9:1-27, 10:1-5. Certain Hivites of the Canaanites deceived Joshua into believing that they were from a far away country, sojourners like themselves. Unfortunately, their deception was discovered only after the high priest gave them an oath of allegiance not to slay them. But for their trickery, Joshua enslaved them to serve Israel by chopping wood and fetching water for the tribes. But they were given Gibeon as their capitol city.

The act of judgment by Joshua has profound implications. To make the Hivites (which were descendants of Ham through Canaan) serve the Israelites in such a way, demonstrates this high priest's awareness of the Noahic Curse placed upon Canaan, uttered by Noah himself:

> And he said, Cursed by Canaan; a servant of servants shall he be unto his brethren,
> And he said, Blessed by the Lord God of Shem; and Canaan shall be his servant. (Genesis 9:25-26)

The Israelites were descendants of Shem. This act of enslavement was merely a partial fulfillment of the servitude borne by the Canaanites.

The five Amorite kings of the highlands (Amorite means highlander) assembled their combined forces around Gibeon to destroy them for their defection. In the *Book of Jasher* the city of Hazor of the Amorites is called Chazar. In this exhaustive historical account the Israelites, called sons of Jacob, completely obliterated several cities and villages on their path to the Amorite capitol of Hazor. Once arriving at the city four mighty men, experienced in battle... would not suffer them to enter the city. (Jasher 38:11) How could four warriors stop a military campaign of thousands? These mighty men must have been huge and intimidating. This was likely a ploy by the Amorites to make the Israelites believe that their entire city was populated and protected by men of the same stature and size; however, this was not the case. The giants, though feared and popular, were thinly spread throughout Canaan.

In another Amorite city attacked by the Israelites, we read that a warrior from the tribe of Judah fought against a giant named Arud on the wall of the city. The Amorite giant struck the Hebrew so hard that the giant's sword shattered upon the soldier's shield, and still, defended by the shield, the assault injured the warrior's head: His head pained him from the blow of the powerful man... and he nearly died from it. (Jasher 39:40) The giant lost his balance and fell off the city wall into a crowd of Israelites below, who butchered him before he could get back up.

God commanded Israel to destroy the five Amorite cities and their armies, but the Hebrew warriors were only able to slay less than half of the Amorites because of God's own intervention in raining hailstones down upon the pagan warriors.

> ...the Lord cast down great stones from heaven upon them unto Azekah, and they died: they were more which died with hailstones than they whom the children of Israel slew with the sword. (Joshua 10:11)

This supernatural judgment on the Amorites was because of their sexual relations with Nephilim. Earlier we discovered that these people were as tall as cedars (Amos 2:9-10). Also, these hailstones were not icy, but meteoric rock. The passage reads great stones from heaven. This event occurred after Egypt, forty years earlier, was laid waste by meteor showers as the Israelites prepared to leave from their desert location outside Egypt's communities. Strange celestial events were brewing. One of them depicts Joshua commanding the sun and moon to stand still; however, this was provoked directly from God, the Creator, who alone knew what the planet was going through. The biblical account states:

> And the sun stood still, and the moon stayed, until the people had avenged themselves upon their enemies. Is not this written in the book of Jasher? So the sun stood still in the midst of heaven, and hasted not to go down about a whole day. (Joshua 10:13)

The historic *Book of Jasher* is uniquely cited here by the Bible writer as a credible source, relying on the Jasher account to confirm the biblical record because of the strangeness of the event. The sun was visible in the sky over the city of Gibeon and the moon could be seen over the valley of Ajalon. Therefore, hailstones of an icy nature must be ruled out because there was no overcast sky that day over Canaan. This judgment of the Amorites was of a completely celestial origin. The entire planet ceased to rotate for almost a day; however, the moon continued its orbit around the earth, but was slowed, or appeared to slow down over the valley, until all the Amorites were slain.

Because of the immense project of slaying the multitudes of Amorite warriors left from the stones from heaven, Joshua needed more time to complete the commandment of God. He apparently told the sun itself to stand still, but this was really the action of the Creator working through a human agent.

This astronomical miracle did not pass over the earth unnoticed. In the annals and archives of several ancient nations and cultures it was recorded that a day lasted for a very uncommonly long time. The Greeks and Norse mythologies reveal a belief in an extended twilight and in the *Annals of Cuauhtitlan*, the history of the empire of Culhuacan, we find: <u>it rained not water, but fire and red-hot stones</u>. These records claim that this fire afflicted their ancestors, burning them, and gravel fell from the sky while the earth opened up and lava boiled. This story is preserved in the National Museum of Anthropology in Mexico City on what is called the Aztec Calendar Stone.[1]

Interestingly, the Aztecs believed that their progenitors were a more powerful race who were <u>taller, swifter, and wiser</u> than ordinary humans.[2]

This race was called the Raràmuri, an ancient evil people that God destroyed. The name Raràmuri indicates that the American Indians are truly descendants of Mesopotamia because Raràmuri identifies these archaic people as Amorites, sun-worshipers of second millennium B.C. Sumer, Babylonia, and Canaan, for the God Amurru is found in Rar[Amuri], the word "Ra" being the old Egyptian word for the sun-god. The occultist Lucius Apuleius long ago wrote in his *Metamorphoses, Book I,* <u>That by magical mutterings... the sun stopped in his course, the moon made to drop her foam, the stars plucked from their spheres, the day annihilated, and the night indefinitely prolonged...</u>[3]

In the writings of James Lloyd, cited several times throughout this book called the *Apocalypse Chronicles*, we discover an ancient Native American text called the Codex Chimalpopoca, which says, <u>During a cosmic catastrophe that occurred in the remote past, the night did not end for a long time...</u>, of which I believe he is quoting from the work of Sitchin. And then Mr. Lloyd continues with, <u>And Ovid (born 43 B.C.) wrote that the legends of old stated that, "...one whole day went without the sun."</u> [4]

In the fifteenth century A.D., Jerome of Prague happened upon a peculiar tradition and artifact among the Lithuanians. These people worshiped the sun and claimed that long ago the sun ceased to shine because of a powerful king who had stolen it. The Lithuanians showed Jerome an enormous iron hammer that they believed was used to free the sun.[5]

The judgment against the Amorites by fire and meteorites, in combination with the sun and moon's extended presence, was complete in its spiritual applications because these people of Canaan were pagans who worshiped these celestial bodies as male and female divinities. For the high priest of Israel to forcibly command their own celestial gods to stand still in the sky stripped the Amorites of any hopes in escaping, for they perceived that even their own gods were unable to aid them. It is further evidenced through archaeology that Baal was worshiped (and sacrificed to) avidly in Canaan. This pagan god was the lord of storms and regarded as a fertility deity. God Almighty used the

Amorite gods against them. Be these hailstones, icy or meteoric, was a storm of great stones that slew more than half of these Canaanites.

Joshua 10:28-43. Israel refused to relent against the Canaanites and Amorites, utterly destroying the cities of Makkedah, Libnah, Lachish, Eglon, Hebron, and Debir along with all those dwelling in villages in the country. They also vanquished the army of King Horam of the city of Gezer when his troops tried to aid Lachish in her defense against Israel. The entire domains of these kings were put to the sword. Unlike Jericho, no one survived. In reference to the Israeli conquest of Canaan, Werner Keller wrote in *The Bible as History* that a trail of burned out cities marks its path and indicates an extremely shrewd strategic plan.[6]

Joshua 11:1-5. Because of the military threat of Israel, several kings in Canaan combined their forces into a massive, multi-cultural war machine with cavalry, siege engines, chariots and innumerous troops of various orders. These soldiers were from Hazor, Madon, Shimron, Achshaph, the Amorites of the northern mountains, those that dwelt in the flatlands south of Chinneroth, in the valley, the cities of the borderlands of the west, many Canaanite, Amorite, Hittite, Perizzite, Hivite and Jebusite villages and cities of the surrounding lands. The text says they were even as the sand that is upon the sea shore in multitude, with horses and chariots very many...

Concerning Jebusite and other Canaanite artifacts, over a hundred years ago were discovered ancient clay tablets written in the official Akkadian characters from Canaanite kings to their Egyptian overlord. Found in Egypt at Tell el-Amarna and dated from the 14th Cnetury B.C., they are known as the Amarna Letters. The subject of much controversy, these letters prove the historic existence of migrating Israelis into Canaan, just as the Bible details. Obviously, the requests of the Canaanite kings for archers and soldiers were never granted.

Many of the documents in the Amarna Letters of Egypt that describe the Habiri (Hebrew) invasion of Canaan were written by princes of Canaan with surprisingly Indo-Aryan names, who mention other rulers of Indo-Aryan descent. In fact, a third of these princely correspondents from Canaan have Indo-Aryan ancestry... identical with names from the Vedas and other early Sanskrit writings. Some are traced exclusively to Horite lineage.[11] Earlier in this book is found definitive links between the Horites and Amorites. The Amorites were highlanders that were worshiped in ancient India, called Aryans, the Noble Ones. Incidentally, the Sumerians of distant Mesopotamia considered the bearded, lapis-lazuli-eyed Aryans to be gods. The Sumerians themselves were the "black-headed people." It is one of establishment

Christianity's greatest secrets that the Israelites were 100% of the *Amorite* family of nations, a fact covered up by the Jewish rabbinical redactors of the older Israelite texts, later rewritten with Jewish dressing. The majority of the oldest books of the Bible were Amorite compositions "borrowed" by the Jews after the Israelites were taken into Assyrian captivity, losing their country, their culture and their *libraries* in the 7th and 6th centuries BC.

Joshua 11:6-23. The great armies of Canaan are completely slain, their cities, villages, lands, and roads searched out, kin and families killed. Hazor is defeated, all are slain, and the Hebrews become rich from the spoils of the Canaanites. All people are executed but their supplies, treasures, animals, and foodstuffs are salvaged. Joshua even succeeds in slaying more giants.

> And at that time came Joshua, and cut off the Anakims from the mountains, from Hebron, from Debir, from Anab, and from all the mountains of Judah, and from all the mountains of Israel: Joshua destroyed them utterly with their cities. (Joshua 11:21)

Obviously the Anakim were not organized in loosely fit tribal bands in scattered communities because this race of giants built and inhabited entire cities. In fact, so many giants were still alive after Joshua destroyed their cities, Hebron, Debir, Anab, their cave dwellings, and wilderness habitations, that those giants who escaped him were numerous enough to be divided into three groups that fled to Philistia.

> There was none of the Anakims left in the land of the children of Israel: only in Gaza, in Gath, and in Ashdod, there remained. (Joshua 11:22)

These same giants, the Anakims that fled from the might of Israel, were the ancestors of the infamous Goliath of Gath, the Philistine giant that the savior of Israel, King David, slew when just a shepherd boy.

Caleb was the only spy other than Joshua himself who returned to Moses with a faithful report about Canaan and the giants over forty years earlier before the slaughter of Hazor's empire. For this faith, Joshua gave Caleb the city of Hebron, the very fortress-city where they had initially encountered the three giant sons of Anak himself, Talmai, Sheshai, and Ahiman, grandsons of the mighty Arba of old.

> And the name of Hebron before was Kirjath-arba; which Arba was a great man among the Anakims. And the land had rest from war. (Joshua 14:15)

The translation of Kirjath-arba is <u>city of Arba,</u> as seen also in Joshua 15:13; <u>even the city of Arba the father of Anak, which city is Hebron</u>. The three sons of Anak are found here even after forty years. Evidently, the giants had greater life spans than ordinary men. This is further proven in that the entire nation of the Anakim were born from five giants: Arba, Anak, Talmai, Sheshai, and Ahiman, a race spread throughout Canaan. Arba and Anak were most likely dead before Moses. Although many Anakim survived the Conquest of Canaan by fleeing to Philistia, the literal three sons of Anak himself were killed in Battle at Hebron.

<u>And Judah went against the Canaanites that dwelt in Hebron: (now the name of Hebron before was Kirjath-arba:) and they slew Sheshai, and Ahiman, and Talmai.</u> (Judges 1:10)

<u>Joshua 17:14-18, 18:16.</u> The tribe of Joseph complains to the high priest that their lot in the inheritance of the Promise Land is not spacious enough to support their population. Joshua tells them that they are powerful enough to expand their territory by driving out the Perizzites and <u>giants</u> that dwell in the woodlands, even though they had chariots of iron.

For an inheritance, the tribe of Benjamin received the <u>Valley of the Giants,</u> but there is no Scripture evidence to say any giants still lived there after the Conquest.

Judges 3:5-8. The Conquest of Canaan was never completed. Israel never occupied the whole of Canaan, nor will the Promise Land ever be restored in whole to the seed of Abraham until the Messiah returns and physically destroys those who prevent Israel from living in the Promise Land. Even after conquering so much, laying waste to several <u>kingdoms,</u> there still existed five Philistine cities where the Anakim seed of Satan survived, where there still lived Canaanites, Sidonians, Hivites, Hittites, Amorites, Perizzites, and Jebusites. The Conquest was a failure, and the Hebrews have been suffering because of it for three thousand years. Their enemies were humbled, displaced, and nearly destroyed, but later multiplied against them again, as God told Moses they would.

Many Canaanite peoples are found on the monuments of Egypt. Bas-relief pictures of Egyptian soldiers battling Philistine invaders with oxen-drawn chariots show the Philistines as being one and two heads taller than the Egyptians (*Race in Ancient Egypt* by Sayce, dozens of other sources). Werner Keller in his *The Bible as History* wrote that <u>colossal figures and sculptures show us the Hittites with their big noses; the slim tall Philistines</u>.[7]

The racial characteristics of many cultures and nations were religiously engraved in Egyptian art in various temples such as Amen-Ra and Karnak.

Their precision can be seen in their depictions of the Philistines and portrayals of their dealings and confrontations with them. In this bas-relief art the Egyptians are the victors. The Philistine oxen are proportionate to the heights of the Egyptian defenders, but are dwarfed by the size of the Philistines, exhibiting that the Canaanites were truly of extraordinary stature as the Bible depicts. These artistic reliefs deal with historic events hundreds of years after the conquest for Canaan. Still, even that late in history, the Philistines were huge. C.J.S. Thompson, in his intriguing book called *Giants, Dwarfs and Other Oddities*, refers to these fascinating Egyptian monuments:

The huge images of deities, like the immense figures still to be seen at Karnak and Luxor of Egypt, and in the ruins of Memnon, show that even the early civilized races possessed a faith in Giantology and a reverence for the colossal.[8]

This art is found extensively in the temple of Amen where the Egyptian archives are in the form of carved reliefs. The walls of this ancient building serve as a vast storehouse of pictorial records. Among these archives is a detailed relief of Egyptian soldiers and Philistine warriors of greater height engaged in combat. Werner Keller states that, "They look like photographs carved in stone 3000 years ago."[9]

Also in Egypt upon the walls of the temple of Karnak are artistic and hieroglyphic records and pictures that detail the physical appearances and facial characteristics of the Hebrew prisoners abducted from southern Canaan by the Egyptian King Shishak, who attacked the Israelite King Rehoboam in the ninth century B.C.

The Hebrew towns these prisoners were brought from are named on the monuments of Karnak in praise of the might of King Shishak. The most intriguing aspect of these Egyptian portraits of the captured Hebrews is in their physical features. The pictures are not of Hebrews, but of Amorites (*Race in Ancient Egypt*). The portraits are pictures of fair-haired and blue-eyed people, characteristics found on other Egyptian monuments and picture records of the ethnic, blue-eyed Amorites and the Tammahu, or Anakim giants with their fair features. The Tammahu were the sons of Anak in the Bible, descended from Anak's giant son Talmai. Another Canaanite nation akin to the giant-kin Amorites were the Amalekites. Josephus mentions that King Saul led Israel against them and prevailed. He also took Agag, the enemies king, captive; The beauty and tallness of whose body he admired so much.[10] These Amorite-looking Hebrews were evidently descended from the pure Amorites that were never completely driven out of Canaan (then called southern Judah). The Egyptians recorded here that the Hebrews adopted the

Amorites' physical traits just as the Amorites intermarried with the Hebrews and became of normal stature and strength. This ethnic merging was exactly what the Lord commanded against, and was what probably led to Israel's fall as a national entity. Near the Amorite-Anakim city of Hebron, Ron Wyatt excavated a stone structure above a cave containing <u>three giant-sized crypts, all measuring over nine feet in length, carved into the rock walls.</u>[11]

Concerning these mysterious giant-kin people called the Amorites, an American archaeologist armed with historical evidence, relics and artifacts infiltrated an ancient cave near the 4000 year-old Amorite city of Engedi in 1979. This amateur researcher and history enthusiast took fascinating pictures of the interior of a burial crypt with tombs cut into the walls of the cave.[12] Inside the crypt were the remains of enormous men. It is rumored among treasure hunters and archaeologists alike that this area of the Middle East is full of ancient burial crypts from a time when the arid and barren wasteland had at one time been fertile and populous.

The seven Canaanite nations were weakened, but not gone.

The very pagan deities of storms, rivers, fertility, of the sun, moon, and even the stars that God Almighty destroyed before Israel, were now being worshiped by the apostate Hebrews. The groves mentioned here will be detailed at greater length in another chapter, but for now it is enough to know that there were secluded wooded areas where the stars were consulted and the celestial bodies deified. These groves were called <u>high places</u> throughout the writings of the prophets. Christian researcher James Lloyd in his *Apocalypse Chronicles* wrote that <u>the high places were locales selected for viewing the stars and planets in anticipation of the return of the "fallen ones" that had fathered the pagan gods so long ago</u> [13]

The practice of worshiping in groves derives directly from the Nephilim. In chapter 11, upcoming in this book (Albion...Isle of the Giants), is the detailed and incredible history of how the giants began this deification of trees and their relation to the night skies, and how other peoples adopted the worship and migrated northwest to the British Isles over three thousand years ago, bringing this pagan practice with them. By the time of the flourishing Celtic priesthood, the Druids erected groves all throughout the isles and continental Europe, but by this time the ritualism had shifted from the stars to the <u>spirits</u> of the giants. Earlier in this book (and still more to come) was detailed how the spirits of the giants were cursed to roam the earth as demons, evil spirits, specters, and banshees and would always be regarded as the spirits of the dead, their identity concealed because the belief in ancient giants was nigh forgotten.

The Druids worshiped the elements of Mother Earth, the spirits of fire, water, air and earth. They highly regarded the oak tree, believing that it harbored a beautiful female nymph. Called <u>dryads</u> by the early Celts, the female spirits were believed to entice men to enter into sexual covenants with them. In fact, the 18 letters of the Druid alphabet were the names of trees, <u>whose consonants stood for the months of which the trees were characteristic, and the vowels for the position of the sun, with its equinoxes and solstices.</u>[14]

Many among the ancients maintained traditions that trees contained mighty spirits that would seek vengeance if their trees were felled. These beliefs held that many tree spirits were beautiful women associated with fertility rites and practices.

These Canaanite, Druidic connections are all the more fascinating when we consider that the Bible itself refers to the Amorites as <u>Cedars,</u> and the Rephaim giants as <u>Oaks of Bashan,</u> a land once inhabited by giants.

For the sins of maintaining sexual relations with the Canaanites and following their gods that formerly suppressed them, the Lord delivered Israel to the king of Mesopotamia, who ruled them for eight years. Then the Spirit of the Lord provoked Othniel, the brother of Caleb, to make war with the Akkadians, Sumerians and Babylonians of Mesopotamia.

<u>Judges 1:1-7</u>. After the death of Joshua the high priest, God selected the tribe of Judah to again resume the conquest of Canaan by attacking the nations of the Perizzites and Canaanites. The tribe of Simeon joined them and together they invaded their domains with a great slaughter. Ten thousand men alone, not including their families, were slain in the city of Bezek where they found Adoni-Bezek, their king, who had his <u>great toes</u> chopped off. If this is a result of Nephilim deformity there is little supporting evidence. It is an extremely unusual biblical citation, however, and may be unusual because his toes were so large or he had extra ones, as often reported with giants.

<u>Judges 1:8-9, 17-19.</u> Judah destroyed Jerusalem but did not slay all of the Jebusites, which lived on in harmony with Israel. Simeon aided in the conquering of the Canaanites in Zephath and the surrounding areas and then Judah subdued and destroyed three Philistine cities, Askelon, Ekron, and Gaza.

<u>Judges 1:21-36.</u> The tribes of Benjamin, Joseph, Manasseh, Ephraim, Zebulun, Asher, Naphtali, and Dan did not vanquish the Canaanite peoples in their specific allotments of the Promise Land. In fact, the tribe of Dan was forced to live for a while in the mountains and hills while the Amorites, who

were naturally highlanders, dwelled in the more fertile valley below until the warriors of the tribe of Joseph defeated them.

Judges 3:12-30. For eighteen years then did Moab exercise dominion over Israel. A left-handed warrior named Ehud bore a concealed double-edged dagger when presenting the king of Moab with a gift in private. This king, named Eglon, was huge and extremely fat. When the king's hall was emptied for privacy, Ehud buried the dagger in the king's stomach where the shaft of the knife disappeared in the folds of fat. With the death of King Eglon, Israel attacked Moab.

> And they slew of Moab at that time about ten thousand men, all lusty, and all men of valour; and there escaped not a man.
> (Judges 3:29)

The Moabite men were called lusty, which is a description found only once in the entire Bible. Nowhere else can this Hebrew word be discovered in Scripture. The word in Hebrew means fat, large (shâmân) but does not imply that these people were out of shape physically, for these were men of valour. Evidently this revelation refers to the unique ancestral ties the Moabites had with the giants. Remember, long before the Conquest began, the Moabites migrated into the lands of the giants called Emims—whom they eventually drove out. The next chapter details more evidence of Nephilim influence in the people of Moab.

As years passed on, the Philistines of the hinterlands and coasts in Gaza, Gath, and Ashdod, fostered the giants of the Anakim clan.

Chapter Seven

The Last Bible Giants

The Philistines were a physically stronger race than Israel and after forty years of political oppression from these ruthless people, God raised up a deliverer, a man of brute strength that far exceeded any of the Philistine giants descended from the Anakim.

Samson, a Nazarite from his mother's womb, was prophesied to be born by an angel that visited his mother (Judges 13:3-4). The pure Nephilim were gone by this date, but traces of angelic lineage were evident throughout Philistia even as much as four hundred years after the death of Joshua.

The giants and Canaanite peoples were described as being <u>greater and taller</u>, <u>men of a great stature</u>, <u>mighty men</u>, and <u>men of renown</u> (Deut. 1:28, Numbers 13:32, Genesis 6:4), but none of these giants or giant-kin were equal in might to Samson, a judge of Israel for twenty years who was endowed with supernatural strength. God raised up this Hebrew to begin delivering Israel out of the oppression of the Philistines, a deliverance that King David would finish.

Samson, by his own strength, killed a lion, slew thirty Philistines for getting from his wife the answer to a riddle he'd uttered, caught three hundred foxes, tied torches to their tails and sent the flaming foxes into the corn fields of the Philistines, destroying their crops and grapevines.

Later, Samson allegedly slew one thousand Philistine soldiers with the jawbone of a donkey after breaking the ropes that bound him. But this judge, just like his people, had a problem with lust, one that ultimately cost him his life.

One day Samson entered the Philistine city of Gaza where two hundred years earlier the giants of the Anakim clan fled when escaping the warriors of Israel. He visited a prostitute's house in Gaza.

When hearing of his presence within the city, the Philistines ambushed him at the city gates. To escape their clutches he broke apart the iron barred gates on the walls and ran off into the night.

Because of his lust for a beautiful Philistine woman, Samson lost his supernatural strength after his hair was cut. He became equal in power to ordinary men because his Nazarite vow was broken. A Nazarite never cut his hair as a covenant between God and himself, and Samson was destined to be a Nazarite from his mother's womb (Judges 16:16-17).

This woman devised a way to cut his hair and the Lord departed from him, the Philistines came against him, caught him, and then gouged his eyes out once they had him securely tied.[3] But in the prison of Gaza his hair that his Philistine lover had removed began growing back.

After a while, the lords of the Philistines celebrated the capture of Samson. They held a great feast where they sacrificed unto their god Dagon, the fish god (a merman in today's fantasy literature). Samson was tied to two pillars in a colossal stone building where the feasting Philistines made sport of the blind Hebrew.

Samson prayed and the Spirit returned to him, strengthening him a final time. He pushed the pillars he was tied to and instantly the edifice collapsed, killing nearly three thousand Philistines on the roof as they fell, and many more below as the ceiling toppled on top of Samson and those underneath. All five Philistine lords were killed as well. More Philistines died at the death of this incredible Nazarite than he had slain in his entire life. And with the death of Samson began the deliverance of Israel from the Philistines. Samson's story is truly amazing when we consider that among the Philistines that he provoked were actual descendants of those giants Joshua drove out of greater Canaan. One of these descendants of Anak the giant was a giant named Goliath. The historian Flavius Josephus wrote that Goliath was <u>a man of vast bulk... and had about him weapons suitable to the largeness of his body</u>.[4]

During the reign of King Saul the Philistines made war against the tribes with the invaders encamped in the <u>Valley of Rephaim</u> as found in 1 Chronicles 11, a place called by Josephus by its Hebrew name, the <u>Valley of the Giants</u>.[5]

In a very old Jewish commentary entitled *Pseudo-Philo*, we learn that <u>Goliath the Philistine was there, and he came up to the ark.... Goliath took hold of it with his left hand and killed Hophni and Phinehas. But Saul, because he was swift on his feet, fled from him</u>.[6]

The two men killed by Goliath were priests. This account of the ark's capture is not detailed in Scripture, but the Bible does reveal that the ark of the covenant was taken by the Philistines.

Not long after the capture and subsequent return of the ark, the Philistines gathered against Israel. This was about four hundred years after Moses and Joshua led Israel into Canaan. At this time Samuel the prophet lived under Saul's reign. He foretold that a shepherd boy would be king. The prophesied king was named David, and as a young boy of fourteen or so, he ventured to see his brother at the battlefield where the Philistines and Israelites were separated by a large valley, ready for war. Beholding the might of the Philistine army, David gazed upon the enormous armored man addressing King Saul, saying, "<u>Are you not the Israel that fled before me when I took the ark from you and killed your priests?</u>"[7]

Although the Bible doesn't mention Goliath's and Saul's contentions, there are enough non-canonical old texts that reveal that Saul deeply feared this giant. It was during this military stand-off that David appeared on the scene and Goliath is first mentioned in the biblical record.

> <u>And there went out a champion out of the camp of the Philistines, named Goliath, of Gath, whose height was six cubits and a span.</u>
>
> <u>And he had an helmet of brass upon his head, and he was armed with a coat of mail; and the weight of the coat was five thousand shekels of brass.</u>
>
> <u>And he had greaves of brass upon his legs, and a target of brass between his shoulders.</u>
>
> <u>And the staff of his spear was like a weavers beam; and his spear's head weighed six hundred shekels of iron, and one bearing a shield went before him.</u> (1 Samuel 17:4-7)

Here we find that two hundred years after Samson's death, Israel is confronted with an army intermingled with giants, or at least some of the Nephilim descendants.

Remember, it was Gaza, Gath, and Ashdod where the Anakim sought refuge among the coastal Philistines.

The story of David and Goliath is profound in its prophetic applications when one realizes that David is topological for Christ at His Second Coming and the giant Goliath represents the coming antichrist of the last days. In fact, Goliath in history was a type of antichrist of the <u>seventh</u> oppression of Israel after the Conquest. In the book of Judges there is recorded seven distinct oppressions by various nations:

1. Mesopotamian
2. Moabite
3. Canaanite
4. Midianite

5. Usurpation of Abimelech
6. Philistines and Ammonite
7. Philistines (Goliath slain)

The translation of Goliath's name is <u>exile,</u> which greatly mirrors the biblical accuracy because this giant was not originally from Philistia, but was from deeper Canaan. Gath was just a Philistine city where his predecessors hid and lived until the death of the giant.

Goliath stood six cubits and a span, which is by archaic reckoning exactly <u>nine foot nine inches</u>. Og of Bashan, giant king of Argob, stood almost thirteen feet tall and Goliath almost ten, demonstrating that in four hundred years of time, the Nephilim traits were slowly being purged away genetically from the human race. Angelic ancestry was diminishing.

In between Goliath's helmet, coat of mail, breastplate, leg armor, great sword, and spear, the giant wore and carried over three hundred and fifty pounds of metal. His spear weighed thirty-five pounds, the point itself weighing twenty-five. The sword carried by the giant became legendary in traditional Hebrew literature as well. With all of this weight it is no wonder that a Philistine warrior carried the giant's shield for him.

> <u>And he stood and cried to the armies of Israel, and said unto them, Why are you come out to set your battle in array? Am not I a Philistine, and ye servants to Saul? Choose you a man for you, and let him come down to me.</u> (1 Samuel 17:8)

Goliath challenged the Israelites to send a Hebrew to fight him and let the battle be decided upon the victory of the dual. But the giant sinned against God, defying the armies of Israel, belittling the people of God by declaring he was a Philistine when this was not true. By claiming Philistine nationality, Goliath attempted to give the appearance that his challenge was equal and a fight would have been fair despite his size, which was a full four feet higher than the average Hebrew. He was actually Anakim by blood, a pure enemy of God.

And for the giant's disrespect, God Almighty met the giant's challenge with the approach of a young shepherd boy. Seeking to humble King Saul by defeating his most valiant soldier, Goliath's boast was cheapened by the presence of a boy.

> <u>And the Philistine said unto David, Am I a dog, that thou comest to me with staves? And the Philistine cursed David by his gods.</u> (1 Samuel 17:43)

By the cursing of David by Dagon, the Philistine god and other divinities, Goliath's words reveal just how spiritual this conflict was. Confirmation of this is found in a popular Pseudo-Philo text that records that Goliath boasted to Saul: "<u>I will come to you and take you captive and make your people serve our gods...</u>"[8] Only David fully realized that the battle did not belong in the realm of men, and unknown to Satan, God would move mightily in David's life to destroy the last of the Nephilim and their children from out of the confines of the Promise Land. We will learn in forthcoming chapters, however, that the giants did not meet extinction until many years later.

The Philistines were Satan's last attempt to take the Promise Land by force because he knew that by this time in history he could not stop the promised <u>seed of Eve</u>, the heavenly seed of Abraham and Star out of Jacob unless his own seed, the Nephilim, again occupied the Canaan of old. The Hebrews were now too numerous to merely pollute their bloodlines and for some unknown reason no more angels ventured forth and laid with women as they so boldly did before. Angelic sexual relations had probably ceased almost a thousand years earlier.

Satan utilized fear and numbers to instill fear into the hearts of the Israelites, but David realized that it was not their battle, the true contention being between God and Satan and the earth being the battleground. David courageously faced the giant and said exactly such.

> <u>And all this assembly shall know that the Lord saveth not with sword and spear: for the battle is the Lord's and He will give you into our hands.</u> (1 Samuel 17:47)

As he said he would, David slew Goliath as both armies watched the giant fall unconscious from the blow of a single stone to his head. David ran and stood over the giant, picked up his great sword, and chopped off his head with it. The large sword, a relic of Israel that twenty years later David again wielded and used as a weapon.[9] In Samuel 21:9, David is recorded to have looked upon Goliath's sword and commented that, "<u>There is none like that.</u>"

Seeing their hero dead, the Philistines fled.

The reason David initially picked up five stones instead of one is due to the presence of four other giants in the Philistine army. They were the direct sons of Goliath. At seeing the death of their father, David knew it was a possibility that these giants would try to immediately avenge their father's death. Before felling the giant, David told him that, "<u>For after your death your three brothers too, will fall into my hands</u>." Now why in the Pseudo-Philo text these other giants are called brothers when the biblical passages refer to them as <u>sons</u> of Goliath is not clear, but it is of interest to note that one of Goliath's sons is also called his brother in 2 Samuel 21:22.

These sons of Goliath got their revenge later. After the prophet Samuel died, King Saul consulted the witch of Endor, who prophesied that his death was imminent. At that time the Philistines found him after hunting him and his sons when they fled from battle, and killed them.

David became king and twenty years later he defended Israel against the Philistines yet again, utterly defeating them and the four giants in their ranks.

David fought with his soldiers against the Philistines on the battlefield, but he began to grow weary in battle when one of the sons of Goliath attacked him, thinking he had slain the Hebrew king. This giant was named Ishbibenob and his spearhead weighed twelve and a half pounds, exactly half of that of his father's. But David was not killed and the giant was immediately slain by Abishai, one of David's personal guardians.

The translation of <u>giant</u> in this passage is Rephaim, although it was an Anakim-related son of Goliath that dwelled among the Philistines. This greatly hints that somewhere in the misty past, the Nephilim, Anakim and Rephaim were ancestrally linked—with the Rephaim existing before the Anakim as evidenced by their earlier presence in Bible history. Josephus in his *Antiquities* wrote that this giant was a son of Araph.[10] This name confirms that Goliath was the father because Araph is nothing more than another form of Rapha (giant), from which the word Rephaim derives. Deuteronomy 3:11 records that Og of Bashan was the last of the remnant of the Rephaims; thus, it is probable that the Anakim could very well have descended from Rephaim if Arba, the father of Anak himself, was Rephaim or had some family ties with them. In-depth study of the Zuzims, Zamzummims, and Emims might unveil other links to the Rephaim as well.

Another guardian of David was Sibbechai, who slew Saph, another of the sons of Goliath. Again the Philistines were met in bloody battle where another giant was slain, a son of Goliath that was also his own brother. In 2 Samuel 21:22 we read: <u>And there was yet a battle in Gath, where was a man of great stature, that had on every hand six fingers, and on every foot six toes, four and twenty in number; and he also was born to the giant</u>. This proves that incest was practiced among the Philistine Anakim or at least done in secrecy. But the social acceptance of incestual relations in the Philistine culture is greatly alluded to in that this giant was his brother. Goliath would have had to maintain sexual contact with his own mother for this to occur, and the greatest proof lies in the fact that the unnamed third giant killed of the Philistines was likewise a son of Goliath, who had six fingers on each hand and six toes on each foot and was a <u>man of great stature</u>, a hideous giant mutant. Josephus wrote that this mutant giant <u>vaunted himself to be one of the sons of the giants</u>. And that he was <u>six cubits tall</u>.[11] This would make him nine feet in height, nine inches shorter than Goliath. The man who slew this Philistine monster was David's Hittite guardian, Sibbechai. Josephus further notes that this Hittite warrior <u>slew many of those that bragged they were the posterity of the giants</u>.[12] These four giants were killed by David and his soldiers twenty years after David picked up five stones to slay these vile people.

This 2 Samuel 21 account of these four giants records that Goliath was a Gittite. This had caused much confusion, causing many to believe there lived two Goliaths, when in fact the title Gittite is an ethnic Philistine name for <u>dweller at Gath</u>.

The fourth and last giant slain of Goliath's family was Lahmi (2 Samuel 21:19, 22). This giant's name translates to <u>warrior</u>.

The unnamed son of Goliath, the mutant with additional fingers and toes, provides light to our understanding of the dark plans of Satan. Having six fingers and toes was an unusual genetic mutation that suggests that incest was premeditated, calculated, because the dangers involved in close interbreeding have never been secret to any people, past or present. This inbreeding was probably maintained by the Philistine ancestors of the Anakim to produce larger Philistine warriors, which is supported by the fact that Goliath laid with his own mother and the translation of Lahmi is <u>warrior</u>.

With the death of this Philistine giant's son, the last giant in Scripture has fallen. In fact, there are twelve giants specifically detailed in Scripture. These are listed with the translations of their names.

1. Og, King of Bashan, Arbog (<u>crooked</u>)
2. Arba, father of Anak (<u>hero-Baal, one of four</u>)
3. Anak, fathered the Anakim (<u>collar, long-necked</u>)
4. Sheshai, son of Anak (<u>whitish, princely</u>)
5. Talmai, son of Anak (<u>furrowed, brave</u>)
6. Ahiman, son of Anak (<u>brother of the right hand</u>)
7. Goliath, Philistine giant (<u>exile</u>)
8. Ishbi-benob, son of Goliath (<u>dweller at Nob</u>)
9. Saph, son of Goliath (<u>threshold</u>)
10. Lahmi, son of Goliath (<u>warrior</u>)
11. Son and brother of Goliath, unnamed mutant
12. Rahab, woman of Jericho (<u>large, broad</u>)

A thirteenth giant is in Scripture, found in the Bible long before the twelve listed above, a mysterious figure that has two entire chapters devoted to him in this book.

All of these listed giants were either Rephaim or Anakim. Reflecting on the translation of Anak (collar), we discover that Anakim is translated as long-necked. Og was a Rephaim, which means the dead, very tall. The three Nephilim races not mentioned in this list are the Zuzims, Zamzummims, and the Emims because these giants were probably extinct long before Moses was born. Zuzim means strong people, Zamzummims means noisy people, and Emims is translated to terrible people. Though the Zuzims were likely destroyed completely by Chedorlaomer in the days of Abraham, it is possible that they escaped him and later became the Zamzummims of ancient Ammon (Deuteronomy 2:20-21).

The sixth giant listed above is most unusual. His name, Ahiman (brother of the right hand), appears to be an ethnic title. Being a son of Anak in Hebron, Ahiman must have been truly heroic. His people were feared exceedingly and present a most unusual enigma to the historian. The ancient city of Mari on the Euphrates River northwest of Babylon was built around 1800 B.C. This city is depicted in many old inscriptions from Babylonia and Assyria. Mari is described by one ancient text to be the tenth city to be founded after the flood.[13] The giant Ahiman lived in an Amorite society in southern Canaan and it is possible that the larger Amorites were considered by the early Mesopotamians as being one and the same as the Anakim giants. Old texts from this mysterious city discovered by archaeologists speak of fearsome invaders from the west called the sons of the right hand![14] This title may have been attributed to all the sons of Anak because as far southwest as Egypt the son of Anak named Talmai fathered a race of superhuman found on Egyptian monuments called the Tammahu. This Egyptian name contains the Amorite god Amurru, T[amma]h[u].

Despite the eradication of the giants during David's reign, there were still traces of Nephilim ancestral influence. One of David's trusted servants slew two lion-like men of Moab (2 Samuel 23:20).

These two Moabite warriors must have been unusually hairy and large to be mentioned at all, which is greatly supported by the translation of lion-like, which means heroic, although the root for this Hebrew word specifically implies violence and strength, traits directly related to Nephilim.

Incidentally, Moab, in ancient times after the flood, was a land belonging to giants called Emims.[15]

Since God made all nations of one blood, including Moab, then these two men who appeared as lions, hairy and large, had something other than human genes infiltrate their predecessor's bloodline.

The same soldier who slew these lion-like men was named Benaiah and also killed <u>an Egyptian, a goodly man</u> (2 Samuel 23:21). Hebrew for goodly is <u>Mar'eh</u>, meaning appearance, <u>to look up</u>, implying that this Egyptian was unusually tall. And this is exactly what we discover in the 1 Chronicles 11:23 account that reads in the Egyptian to be <u>five cubits high, a man of great stature</u>. This archaic measurement equals today's seven and one-half foot in height! This man is the last in the Bible to have his height recorded. His <u>great stature</u> is the exact terminology used when describing the Amorites, who were <u>tall as cedars.</u> In *Antiquities of the Jews,* we discover this same Egyptian warrior to be a <u>man of vast bulk</u>.[16]

Og was thirteen or so feet tall, Goliath almost ten, and this later Egyptian, over seven feet tall, was exhibiting that this decrease in height was because the Nephilim were a dying race, an angelic lineage rapidly being purged from the earth.

Since the Bible provides the cubit heights of these giant men but does not detail the heights of anyone else, then it can be assumed that the Nephilim were decreasing in stature as time progressed. Although the term <u>men of great stature</u> was frequently used concerning giants, this Egyptian is the last man in the Bible who is provided such a description. Over time, the angelic influences over the genes in the Nephilim-related peoples were weakening, each generation becoming more and more human, thus becoming less <u>enosh</u>.

Even modern scientific studies in genetics teaches us today that when different races intermarry and have children, their offspring will be a combination of hereditary characteristics from both parents, and the child will have children that will stray farther and farther from his or her parents' racial heredity if they do not continue to marry into the same racial lineage. For example, if an Oriental and a Hispanic had a child, it would take approximately three to seven generations of offspring before children would be born completely Oriental again if no other Hispanics married into the family bloodline. This same genetic phenomenon occurred to the Nephilim, who were nearly extinct by the time of David. This is proven in that after David no more giants are mentioned in Scripture, nor are any people larger than normal detailed anywhere after the reign of King David.

But concerning this large, <u>goodly Egyptian</u>, recently excavated in the Valley of the Kings in Egypt, was an ancient concealed burial chamber filled with tons of sand to prevent grave-robbing. After more than twenty feet of sand wes removed from the subterranean chamber, a large unadorned stone sarcophagus was unearthed. Archaeologists used two crank pumps and two teams of men to wedge open and topple the twenty-two ton stone lid of this sandstone crypt. Inside the crypt was discovered a perfectly preserved and ornately designed basalt sarcophagus with a painting of Isis, the winged goddess of fertility, on a coffin.

Inside the coffin was an Egyptian who lived approximately 2700 years ago, about three hundred years after David slew Goliath. This mummy was wrapped in ceremonial beads and was adorned with a large scarab beetle on his body, signifying that he was a priest of high order. Deciphering hieroglyphics of the man's life in the burial chamber, archaeologists discovered his name to be Iufaa, which means <u>one of great size</u>.[18]

Physically the Egyptians were never a tall people. Anyone over six feet would have been considered unique in antiquity, but today this is less so.

The primary reason why remains of human mummified carcasses are so rarely unearthed in tombs is linked to the ancient belief in a resurrection. Long ago tomb raiders and treasure hunters desecrated holy sites, destroying the skeletons found entombed throughout the Old World. Every archaic culture believed in a resurrection up until the time of Christ and the unbelieving Sadduccees. This conviction of a future <u>rebirth</u> is what resolved people to mummify their dead and adorn their burial sites with magnificent treasures and supplies for the journey undertaken in the afterlife of the deceased. It was believed that the dead would one day <u>awaken</u> in health and need those treasures and provisions. Marauding nomads and other tomb-pirates infiltrated these often trap-laden sites and desecrated them by looting and destroying the skeletal remains of those buried. It was a precautionary ritual practiced by such thieves to burn the carcasses to ashes of the crypts they raided, thus disabling the dead to resurrect and seek revenge for the robbery of his crypt and sepulcher. When these treasure hunters happened upon the barrows and sepulchers of enormous men, they broke their skeletons and burned their bones in fear that these giants would resurrect and deal with them brutally for disturbing their burial sites.

Josephus makes a startling claim in his incredible writings, declaring that the bones of giants two thousand years ago <u>are still shown to this very day, unlike to any creditable relations of other men</u>.[18]

Many treasure seekers found the bones of giants a valuable find, not for any scientific reasons but for extra profit. Throughout antiquity bones have harbored special powers to different peoples. James Frazier wrote in *The Golden Bough* that some of the new Caledonians drench a skeleton to make it rain, but burn it to make sunshine.[19]

Strange objects of stone and bones or other debris found embedded in rock in the fifteenth century was commonly called glossopetrae, which means "tongue-stones." These odd formations were credited with medicinal and magical powers.[20]

Neils Stensen (1638-86) examined the head of an enormous shark at the Academia del Cimento and discovered that glossopetrae were actually fossilized shark's teeth.

Many people collected these items and bones, hoping they would be charms or magical amulets. It was definitely a problem long ago to exhibit the bones of giants because thieves would steal the bodies of dead giants[21] for profit or more sinister means.

Another reason the bones of giants are so rare is that at various times in history they were valuable to those who practiced the dark arts of witchcraft.

> In the Middle Ages witches used bones to the same end, conjuring up rain and storms. They perpetuated the old belief that the bones of the dead, when handled properly, induce rain.[22]

This strange tradition finds its origins in the flood, an event that buried and fossilized bones all around the world. The larger the bones were, the more apt a ritual invocation of rain was likely to occur. How ironic that the bones of giants were used to induce rain, since it was the sins of giants and their human worshipers that caused it to rain forty days, effectually drowning them and rendering themselves to be strewn about piles of bone refuse.

If these bones were not taken for sale to pagans, then grave robbers utterly destroyed them for fear of their return in the afterlife.

> Why are the oldest libraries in the world secret libraries? What are people really afraid of? Are they worried that the truth, protected and concealed for so many thousands of years, will finally come to light?—Erich von Daniken, *Chariots of the Gods?*

Chapter Eight

Giants in Ancient Egypt

The Great Pyramid was standing when antediluvian giants stalked the earth before the flood, when Abraham visited the Nile River civilization, when Joseph ruled in Potiphar's house and then as second command of all Egypt under Pharaoh, and it was definitely standing when Moses was born and led the <u>seed</u> of Eve to Canaan. Although the pyramids are in Egypt, they are not Egyptian. The Great Pyramid of Cheops and many others found in Britain, Central and South America transcend ancient architectural knowledge in their construction and perfection in accordance with the heavenly bodies being built of stone edifices so heavy and cumbersome that not even today can be reconstructed by the machines and technologies utilized now. Many Pharaohs throughout history have tried to claim the Great Pyramid, but the fact remains that there are no idols, artifacts, or hieroglyphics within the pyramid to suggest an Egyptian origin. In the Land of Idols, could it be possible that their greatest engineering and architectural achievement could be devoid of all indications of ownership? Many Egyptian rulers have used the pyramids for various reasons through history, as storage facilities and worship centers, even putting their dead in them, but these great <u>monuments have endured from a time long before the very invention of writing, from the epoch before the Flood</u>. Cheops is dated to have lived around 3000-2500 B.C., which biblically antedates the flood. Some associate this ancient king to be Enoch himself.[1]

Richard W. Noone wrote in his book *5/5/2000, Ice: The Ultimate Disaster* that an early Arabian author named Mohammed Ebn Abd Al Hokm had written:

> <u>The pyramids were antediluvian, and they resisted the force of the great flood</u>.

In his fascinating book, Mr. Noone goes further to cite a man who lived 1600 years ago named Masoudi, an Arabic historian who translated an ancient Coptic traditional text, strangely reminiscent of Enoch the prophet.

> <u>Surid, one of the kings of Egypt before the flood, built the two great pyramids. The reason for building the Pyramids was the following dream, which happened to Surid three hundred years previous to the flood.</u>

Enoch is recorded to have interpreted the dreams of giants in the *Book of Giants,* and other Dead Sea texts indicate that Enoch's antediluvian ministry involved dream interpretation and prophesying. Biblical evidence of Enoch's ministry in prophetic visions is found in Jude 14-15 and in the translation of his son's name, Methuselah, which means my death will bring, by its most ancient reckoning of Mathusala.²

Being antediluvian, there is no way that King Surid could have been Egyptian. Egyptologists claim that their ancestors planned and constructed the Great Pyramid when in fact these ancient feats of engineering and precision belong to a high civilization long gone, antedating Egypt by at least six hundred years, but more likely to even more distant times. In Egypt, we have the suggestion that the Dynastic civilization of the third millennium may have been preceded by a far older civilization founded by survivors from a great flood, who planned the pyramids and built the Sphinx.³

Colin Wilson has produced fascinating evidence in his book *From Atlantis to the Sphinx*, showing that an ancient relic called the *Turin Papyrus* records that before any human kings ruled Egypt, the land was governed by gods and demigods.⁴ Mr. Wilson goes on to cite old Egyptian Building Texts that record that long ago Seven Sages built the Mansion of the Gods (Great Pyramid) after surviving a catastrophic flood. These Sages were identified as Builder Gods. The flood referred to here by the arcane Building Texts is not the global catastrophe of the Bible, but another flood that destroyed one third of all the cities that is detailed in the *Book of Jasher*.⁵

Interestingly, this is confirmed by early Babylonian traditions and texts that claim that the Seven Sages mentioned in the *Epic of Gilgamesh* were seven Master Craftsmen who lived before the flood and taught mankind all crafts and civilization.⁶ These builder gods are unique because of their presence in both Babylonian and Egyptian writings. Their presence may be the only explanation for why civilization suddenly developed out of nothing. Between these two classical cultures there exists no archaeological evidence of ethnological, intellectual or architectural development. Civilization just appeared. So profound was the belief in these Seven Sages that the entire human population, after the flood of Noah's day, anticipated their return. These disillusioned communities did not wait long. The Sumerian King-lists record that the pre-flood celestial kings that lived incredibly long life spans had returned again after the deluge that nearly eradicated humanity. This darkly divine kingship consisted of fifty godlike beings of which seven were powerful giants called the Seven Great Anunnaki. These giants not only brought mankind the mysticism and harmful sciences Noah suppressed at the bidding of the Creator, but these enormous god-men built the megalithic buildings, walls of Uruk (and other Mesopotamian cities), and monuments such as the Tower of Babel, all now reduced to ruins that still mystify modern archaeologists.

Just as the Egyptian Pharaohs claimed to be descendants of the early gods of Egypt, Mesopotamian rulers like King Shulgi of the third dynasty of Ur (ca. 2000 B.C.) proclaimed that he was a direct descendant of the first gods and kings of Uruk.[7]

Astonishing confirmation of this mysterious King Shulgi was unearthed in 1964 at the strangest of places—La Grange, Georgia! How this ancient lead tablet came to be in prehistoric North America will probably never be explained. This artifact is written in Sumerian cuneiform, possibly an Akkadian copy that dates itself at the forty-third year of the reign of <u>King Shulgi, a third dynasty Sumerian King</u>. This find is dated to 2040 B.C.[8]

There is no evidence in the archaeological record that any civilizations after the flood were any more advanced than those that preceded the deluge. In fact, there is ample reason to believe that intellectualism; the arts, landscaping, architecture and metallurgy, were all more highly developed than in the classical eras of post-flood civilization.

Enoch was a king who had dominion over <u>one hundred and thirty kings and princes</u> for the <u>two hundred and forty years</u> of his reign, as written in the historic *Book of Jasher*.[9] Enoch could have been the Egyptian king named Surid. The giants themselves sought Enoch's favor and desperately wanted the patriarch to intercede for them and go to the Creator, asking Him for their pardon. According to the *Book of Giants*, mentioned earlier in this book, the giants began having terrible nightmares of their impending doom and held a great assembly where they decided to approach Enoch. The Great Pyramid could have been constructed by the work of pre-flood giants in an effort of penance, directed or commanded by Enoch. An enormous altar. Frederick Haberman in his *Tracing our Ancestors*[10] wrote, <u>The Great Pyramid which was erected by the Aryan-Phoenicians   precisely one thousand years before Stonehenge circle</u>...

The Aryans are associated with sorcerer-giants, a race considered divine by the ancient Sumerians and people of India. Mr. Haberman claims that the builders were an astronomical cult that had come from the region of the Euphrates. Incidentally, this geographical area was the center of civilization both before and after the flood, and was known where giants dwelt.

Almost two thousand years ago the historian Flavius Josephus discovered ancient documents that caused him to write about the giants of Noah's time: These men did what resembled the acts of those whom the Grecians called giants. But Noah was very uneasy at what they did; and, being displeased at their conduct, persuaded them to change their dispositions and their acts for the better...[11]

Josephus goes on to describe these huge people, but what is most interesting is that Noah did not provoke the giants to merely stop committing their wicked deeds for a while, but he succeeded in causing these enormous people to perform acts for the better. Were these acts the construction of the Great Pyramid?

The measurements of the Great Pyramid and other such monuments the world over reveal themselves to be calendars based on lunar and solar modulation. There are thousands of books and articles concerning scientific and astronomical discoveries made by deciphering measurements of and within the chambers of the Great Pyramid.

Enoch the prophet, who foretold to men and giants of the coming flood, was a descendant of Seth. Josephus wrote that the descendants of Seth built the Great Pyramid before the flood as a calendar for the future and container of ancient knowledge. Concerning the Sethites and the Great Pyramid, Josephus wrote:

> They also were the inventors of that peculiar sort of wisdom which is concerned with the heavenly bodies and their order. And that their inventions might not be lost before they were sufficiently known, upon Adam's prediction that the world was to be destroyed at one time by the force of fire, at another time by the violence and quantity of water, they made two pillars; one of brick; the other of stone: They inscribed their discoveries on them both, that in case the pillar of brick should be destroyed by the flood, the pillar of stone might remain, and exhibit those discoveries to mankind; and also inform them that there was another pillar of brick erected by them. Now this remains in the land of Siriad (Egypt) to this day.[12]

From the evidence gathered, it appears that the Patriarchal Sethites assembled a force of men and quite possibly giants who constructed these monuments after a regional flood that destroyed one third of civilization. Knowing a greater flood was coming, these Sethites, probably at the guidance of Enoch or Noah, built the Great Pyramid and its eternal guardian, the Sphinx.

The peculiar wisdom cited by Josephus is <u>Astronomy</u>. An in-depth knowledge in astronomy was required to design the Giza complex. In the night sky above Egypt's desert appears the Milky Way, like a great sparkling celestial river flowing across the sky. To the right of this is the constellation Orion, which has its most renowned stars at its middle, called Orion's belt. The position of these three stars mirror perfectly the geographical positions of the three Great Pyramids on the Giza plateau, with the Nile River being mimicked by the flowing colors of the Milky Way Galaxy above.

The ancient pyramid builders believed that everything on earth is a reflection of things in heaven, so they employed their beliefs into the architecture they designed.[13]

In relation to the Great Pyramid, Colin Wilson reveals that carbon-dating tests on mortar from the structure containing organic material indicate that the pyramid had been there since the <u>middle of the third millennium B.C.</u>[14] Further confirming the pre-flood construction of the Great Pyramid, Wilson mentions the discovery of a half-inch layer of salt encrusted on the surfaces <u>within</u> the structure.[15]

The Great Pyramid is the <u>Pillar of Stone</u> mentioned by Josephus that still stands in the land of Egypt. The pillar of <u>brick</u> is the Sphinx, the cherub-looking guardian. Mr. Wilson likewise supports the pre-flood origin of the pyramid by revealing that the Sphinx was damaged not by <u>wind,</u> as Egyptologists suggest, but by water.

In Wilson's *From Atlantis to the Sphinx*, we discover that in the 1850's an archaeologist named Auguste Mariette unearthed a limestone stela from the ruins of the Temple of Isis near the Great Pyramid. This artifact is known as the Inventory Stela and is written in hieroglyphics dating back to 1000 B.C., however, as with so many other Egyptian records, the stela is only a copy of a far more ancient archive: <u>Referring to Cheops, it says, "He found the House (temple) of Isis, mistress of the pyramid, beside the house of the Sphinx, north-west of the house of Osiris."</u>[16]

Colin Wilson speculates that if Cheops <u>found</u> the temple of Isis, "mistress of the pyramid," beside the temple of the Sphinx, then we find here historical evidence that the Great Pyramid was not built by Cheops, but was built at a much earlier time. When this early pharaoh built his temple near to the side of the Sphinx, the Great Pyramid and its guardian Sphinx must have already been there. Because an ancient causeway once connected the Sphinx to the Great Pyramid, it is evident that the Great Pyramid is the <u>House of the Sphinx</u> mentioned on the Inventory Stela by Cheops.

Since there existed five Nephilim nations after the flood, it is possible that more than one giant race existed before the flood. The pre-flood world was 1656 years long. The flood occurred in 2239 BC, which indicates that the giants after the flood were somehow the descendants of Nephilim that had survived the Deluge. It is a possibility that giants built these monuments. Despite their architects' possible identity as being the giants themselves, it is a greater possibility that these gigantic edifices were a sign to the giants from God, constructed to withstand flood waters that destroyed the antediluvian cities and also deposited salt crystals inside the Pyramid that continue to baffle pyramidologists today.

Another link in the chain of evidence concerning Enoch as the pyramid builder is discovered in the *Book of Jasher*. In Chapter Two is found that one-third of humanity was destroyed by a local flood when God overflowed the Gihon River before the Great Deluge. This river is the Nile, which indicates that the antediluvian center of civilization was indeed the land of Egypt. This would make Enoch a pharaoh, and possibly the Sphinx is his one monumental portrait. The Gihon in Genesis is a river flowing through Africa so this locale cannot be mistaken. This further proves the Great Pyramid to be antediluvian. Enoch was both a prophet and mighty ruler over kings and princes, and evidently respected by the Nephilim according to the Book of Giants.

Abraham ventured into Egypt, seeking a city, whose builder and maker was God! Could it be that the Great Pyramid is an earthly prototype of the heavenly city of God designed like a pyramid in the book of Revelation? Is it a coincidence that the Ark of the Covenant exhibits a perfect pyramid beneath the wings of the Cherubim that guard it? If Egypt was truly the center of the pre-flood civilization, then the Garden of Eden that Adam was banished from could very well be the land of milk and honey promised to Abraham and his seed forever. Canaan. Even in Moses' day, one thousand years after the flood, Canaan produced gigantic grapes and other fruits and vegetables cited in the Torah. If Canaan is the Eden of old, then we can see how Cain prefigured the antiquity of Mesopotamia and its nations, especially wicked Babylonia. Cain was banished and went east, to the areas of Mesopotamia (if Eden is truly located where Canaan was after the flood). Noah and his family line had to migrate west, through Mesopotamia, to get back to the lands of his ancestors, Eden and Egypt in the west, where the Gihon flowed. If Canaan and Eden are the same land, then the four rivers in Genesis are identifiable. The Ark landed in Armenia and the Bible is the story of God's people traversing the four rivers to get back to their homelands in the west, following the Sun of Righteousness, which sets in the western heavens.

As Samson was a mockery of the physical might of the giants in Philistia, so also was the Pyramid built to mock the Nephilim and the durability of their own structures. Noah Hutchins mentions that the Great Pyramid was constructed of approximately 2.5 million stone blocks, all weighing from between 2½ tons to 70 tons, on a solid rock foundation with 144,000 granite casing blocks as a protective shield, concluding that this ancient structure, without a doubt, would have survived regardless of the catastrophe.

In *The Stones Cry Out*, by Bonnie Gaunt, we find fascinating evidence proving that only the Great Pyramid of Cheops is the original pyramid. All of the others are mere replicas, with passages that only descend to subterranean chambers later constructed by architects. They had no idea that the Great Pyramid contained a vast network of ascending passages and chambers cleverly hidden for thousands of years. Again, Mr. Hutchings' research confirms the findings of Bonnie Gaunt in that it appears that the only true and original pyramid is that of Cheops. He writes that, "The angels of Genesis 6 and their giant descendants could easily be the builders of the lesser pyramids, plus the ring of other pyramid-shaped buildings around the earth, the ancient carvings of spaceships, the huge drawings on the plains in South America, the fifty-ton stone statues on Easter Island, the monument at Stonehenge,..."

Egypt has many pyramids, but one original. This largest and true pyramid has an interior of corridors and chambers that its two contemporaries do not. The scores of other pyramids evidently built after the flood are poor replicas, many, according to Josephus, were built by the Hebrews under the bondage of Egypt.[23] Incidentally, the Book of Exodus alludes to this fact, mentioning that the Hebrews were forced to make bricks.

In *Tracing Our Ancestors* by Frederick Haberman, we read that "in another ancient papyrus do we read, 'The God of the universe is the light above the firmament; and his symbols are upon the earth.'"[24] God's symbols are in the form of architectural relics like the Great Pyramid, a colossal edifice once encased in beautiful white granite stones. The magnificence of the Great Pyramids' original structure and color created a stunning optical illusion. Because of visual distortion from distance and heat, the base of the Great Pyramid was obscured from those who looked upon the enormous building, giving it the appearance of a huge triangular structure descending from the sky itself, as one drew closer to it. This mirage was interpreted by Christians to be symbolic of the future New Jerusalem (described in the Bible) that will descend from heaven when God comes to live on earth among His people. The Sphinx dutifully guards this ancient symbol of the Creator. These architectural relics, like Stonehenge, confuse the uneducated who fail to do the necessary research, or depend upon religious dogma for their beliefs. Sometimes, however, the truth can be revealed within religious scripture when further research is done.

For example, the <u>light above the firmament</u>, mentioned in the above quote from Haberman provides the time when these ancient monuments were erected. It was in a distant age, long ago, when there was a beautiful watery <u>firmament</u> in the sky—before its collapse caused the flood, as Genesis reveals. The <u>light above the firmament</u> was of course the sun, but was diffused to some extent by this firmament. A greenhouse effect made plants and animals larger than we find today. It was a different world in these antediluvian times The creation of mysterious structures like the Great Pyramid, Stonehenge, and other marvels were not so amazing to the civilizations that created them during this time. A later chapter in this book called <u>Relics of the Gods</u> details the discoveries of many astonishing architectural wonders and the mysteries they invoke. Moderen historians are completely baffled with ancient building techniques used to construct these amazing monuments left behind by advanced civilizations, and by the giants themselves.

Stories of Goliath and the Philistine giants said to be his sons in Scripture no doubt attest to the horrid reality of the presence of giants in history. But other proofs exist beyond the memories of mythology and old histories stashed away by protective antiquaries—proofs almost as tangible as the Bible accounts recorded by pen and ink. Excavations of enormous cities with overly large portals, extremely high walls, halls, and corridors, disproportionate furnishings, unusual temples that clearly accompanied physically present deities of enormous size, megalithic dolmens that could never have been moved easily by human endeavor, forlorn altars and shrines amid desert wastes that were long ago used for the purpose of offering gods human females, and mysterious monuments throughout the entire world that remain strangely associated to the planets, sun, moon, and even many stars, especially in the Middle East. They all support the biblical evidence that ancient advanced civilizations built and inhabited by giants once thrived in a seemingly global society that enjoyed all the sciences and comforts known today such as medicinal knowledge, metallurgy, astronomy, herbalism, horticulture, agriculture, masonry, carpentry, and even an advanced form of communication.

The giants thrived from the forbidden sciences passed down to them from dark angels that transcended the mundane knowledge retained by the purely Adamic people. Instead of the Enochian astronomy the giants perverted this science into <u>astrology</u>, the art of celestial divination, and other mystical and sometimes harmful knowledge like numerology, necromancy, bestiality, divination, and various forms of witchcraft and nature worship that undoubtedly their angelic fathers, the fallen ones, had taught them, or they were born with a certain level of innate knowledge to connect them to these skills. This is why the Great Pyramid was built, to preserve for those beyond the flood what Enoch had prophesied about the true astronomy, the holy celestial knowledges that God had ordained us to know. Before the flood, God specifically said that the stars, sun, and moon were to give light and to be for signs (Genesis 1:14-16). Having a greater awareness toward the many secrets around them, the giants not only polluted the bloodlines of an entire epoch of history, but also filled the earth with alarming and dangerous information. The *Book of Jubilees* explains how the perverted doctrines and practices of the rebellious angels that were widely spread throughout antediluvian society once again surfaced to be performed after the flood. Cainan, son of Arpachshad after the flood found a writing which the ancestors engraved on stone. It contained the lost teaching of the Watchers by which they used to observe the omens of the sun and moon and stars within all the signs of heaven.[25] Cainan copied the ancient document but feared to show it to their ruler, Noah. This unique discovery must have occurred before the Babel division of tongues because Noah was still alive and Cainan could easily interpret the antediluvian writing.

Kurt Seligmann in his *History of Magic and the Occult* wrote that magic and other illicit arts were revealed to mankind by the cursed angels, betrayers of God's secrets.[26] Noah was concerned and prayed to God because of demonic activity that was increasing after the flood. He confirmed the origin of these wicked practices as coming from the angelic Watchers, as recorded in the *Jubilees* text:

> Do not let the evil spirits rule over them... and you know that which your watchers, the fathers of these spirits, did in my days... Shut them up and take them to the place of judgment.[27]

But after the flood the giants again possessed these knowledges, hinting that the origin of this demonic information was none other than the giants' fathers. This is why Joshua was told to kill all the people in Canaan, because of the godless abominations they practiced. All the nations of Canaan were guilty of practicing strange arts, rituals and magic. The ninefold charge of God against the Canaanites is found in Deuteronomy 19-20:

1. Fire sacrifices of children (20:6)
2. Consulting familiar (demonic) spirits (20:6)
3. Practicing wizardry (20:6)

4. Homosexuality (20:13)
5. Bestiality (sex with animals) (20:15-16)
6. Incest (20:17)
7. Eating blood (19:26)
8. Using enchantments (19:26)
9. Observation of times (astrology) (19:26)

The infant sacrifice to the fire god Molech was extensively performed in the valley of Hinnom at a place called Tophet. The people of Canaan believed that their god was placated by the burning of their children in smoldering fire ovens and pits. These sacrificial victims were not killed first, but cast alive into the fires of Molech. In fact, Tophet means place of burning.[28]

In *Smith's Bible Dictionary* we read:

> Human sacrifices (infants) were offered up to this idol, the victims being slowly burnt to death in the arms of the idol, which were of metal, hollow, and could be heated on the inside.

Excavations of the Tophet valley region by archaeologists have uncovered that a giant colossus was worshiped there, probably a gigantic statue of a fiery serpent with outspread arms—Molech in another form, as evidenced in a later chapter. Also unearthed in that horrific area are numerous gruesome artifacts and relics of vessels and burial urns containing dismembered and charred remains of infants and small children sacrificed in the fires. This valley is where Adonizedek (Melchizedek) met Abraham according to the *Book of Jasher*, called the Valley of Melech. Tophet was later renamed Gehenna and has, since ancient times, been regarded as a place of torment and usually associated with hell.

Consulting familiar spirits is akin to necromancy, the act of communicating with the dead, which is considered impossible by Christians. They claim that many today are deceived into thinking that they can contact the deceased by crystal balls, Ouija boards, hypnosis or channeling when in fact these people are communicating with demons, evil angels and the vagabond spirits of the Nephilim that were cursed to roam the earth until judgment.

Sacrificing children to Molech in the Hinnom Valley was also performed through exhibiting faith in idolatrous images. The power behind idols could be invoked through demonic entities that pose as gods, the dead, and even as extraterrestrial beings. Pagans, however, both ancient and modern, consider idols as a focal point for worship, being merely a conduit between worshippers and their deity, as ancient Jews would say about the golden calf or Buddhists with statues of Buddha. Concerning idols, the *Book of Jasher* says:

> And some make them in the figures of men, of gold and silver, and go to them in times known to them, and the figures receive the influence of the stars, and tell them future things...²⁹

The fact that demons exhibited what appeared to be miracles through their idols is evident in that the god Molech was sacrificed to so adamantly. People do not give up their children easily, especially to be burned slowly alive. The idol of Molech and many such others mentioned in the Bible must have seemed to perform miraculous deeds before their adherents.

Wizardry involves the elements of the earth, air, fire and water and incantations to create spells or hexes on others that are likely executed by disembodied spirits or demons rather than by "supernatural abilities" of a disillusioned sorcerer. The *Book of Enoch* claims that the Watchers themselves taught men and their giant sons hidden sciences and forbidden arts.

> ...and they taught them magical medicine, incantations, the cutting of roots, and taught them about plants, and the women became pregnant and gave birth to great giants...³⁰

After the angels that rebelled were cast into the Abyss, Tartarus, the remaining dark angels of Satan were called demons or devils from that time forward. In Greek, the word "demon" derives from the root word for knowledge. Death and rebellion resulted from eating of the tree of knowledge of good and evil. An implication in this root word for demon suggests that they have more intelligence than ordinary people, which is confirmed when, in 2 Peter, it declares that angels are greater in power and might.

> They sacrificed unto devils, not to God; to gods whom they knew not, to new gods that came newly up, whom your fathers feared not. (Deuteronomy 32:17)

The translation of "devils" in this verse is wicked demons, and is discovered only twice in the Old Testament. The other location of wicked demons is found in Psalm 106:37-38. Both references mention sacrifice; the Psalms account conveying it to be human sacrifice to Canaanite devils, or gods, as Deuteronomy claims.

Verse 38 of Psalm 106 says that Canaan was polluted with blood and verse 39 says they were defiled by their own works and went a whoring. This phrase means to have intercourse with false gods or foreigners... and mainly conveys the act of illicit sexual relations with women.

In Joshua 2:1 and 6:17 the Canaanite woman of Jericho is called a harlot. The Hebrew word used is exactly the same as went a whoring in Psalm 106:39, revealing that Rahab of Jericho was born from Canaanite sexual relations with false gods or foreigners, or as Deuteronomy 32:17 puts it above: new gods that came newly up, meaning the Nephilim and their demonic fathers. We have also seen that the translation of Rahab is large, broad, indicating a link to giant ancestry, which is further supported by Deuteronomy 32:16, which says strange gods provoked the Lord. The Hebrew word for strange can interchangeably refer to either foreign gods or adulterous gods.

Joshua was specifically commanded by God to slay these people of Canaan because of the sexual influence of these adulterous gods.

Chapter Nine

The Giant of Babylon

Many scholars today have taught and believe that giants in the Scriptures are tyrants or kings and support this claim by providing modern examples such as intellectual giant or Wall Street giant but this is deliberate misuse of the term. The archaic words for "giants" *do not convey titles*, but convey attributes of races. For example, the translation of giant is often Rephaim, which is descriptive of giants being dead and very tall. One of the greatest distortions of the terminology is found when scholars write or teach about the first king of Babylon.

Probably the shadiest character in early post-flood Bible history is Nimrod, the first king on earth, builder of Babylon. Information in Scripture concerning him is very scant, however the historic traditions of many ancient cultures recorded many interesting facts about this legendary ruler. The Bible states:

> And Cush begat Nimrod: He began to be a mighty one in the earth. (Genesis 10:8)

The Hebrew for mighty one is *gibbor*, a giant, tyrant, huge one, as read from the Masoretic text and likewise, in the Greek Septuagint, the proper rendering of mighty one is giant, huger person. The Septuagint version of the Bible is of Greek scholarship in antiquity and, as learned previously in this work, has been a valuable resource when the King James translations were somewhat obscure. The Biblical text continues with:

> He was a mighty hunter before the Lord; wherefore it is said, even as Nimrod the mighty hunter before the Lord. (Genesis 10:9)

Here, mighty is translated as gibbor again. Further proof that this indicates giant as in size is seen in that it would make little sense calling Nimrod the tyrant hunter before the Lord. A more proper translation is Nimrod the giant hunter... Even in the Paschal Chronicle, Nimrod is recorded to be Nebrod the huntsman and giant.[1] The ending of the Genesis account of Nimrod states:

> And the beginning of his kingdom was Babel, and Erech, and Accad, and Calneh, in the land of Shinar. (Genesis 10:10)

Nimrod is mentioned four times directly in the Bible. The fourth is a fascinating eschatological prophecy concerning the Antichrist of latter-day Babylon that will be explained in detail later in this book.

Babel was the site of the famous tower that archaeologists believe was a colossal ziggurat, an enormous pyramidal observatory, where the celestial bodies were studied and consulted. These strange star-temples could very well be the origin of the Babylonian zodiac so popular today. Concerning the tower, Eupolemus wrote that the structure was built by giants. Eupolemus is mentioned in *Maccabees* 8:17 of the Apocrypha, and lived during the third century B.C. He was a Greek-speaking Jew whose writings were preserved by a third century historian named Eusebius of Caesarea, six hundred years later. Eusebius wrote:

> The Assyrian city of Babylon was first founded by those who escaped the flood. They were giants, and they built the tower well known in history. When the tower was destroyed by God's power, these giants were scattered over the whole earth.[2]

Writing almost three hundred years before Eusebius in first century A.D., the historian Josephus wrote that Nimrod was a bold man and of great strength of hand... who claimed that he would build a tower too high for flood waters to be able to reach, and from this tower he would avenge himself on God for destroying their forefathers.[3]

The early historians Philo and Augustine of Hippo both wrote that Nimrod was of enormous stature, a giant and enemy of God.[4] Another interesting third century B.C. text is the book of *Judith* in the Apocrypha. Here we find in chapter 16 a song of praise by the heroine after God delivers the Hebrews from the onslaught of the mighty Assyrian general Holofernes. Remarkably, she sang that she was not attacked and killed by mighty giants... who marched down from the mountains of the north... from Assyria with their tens of thousands of soldiers.

Philo of Alexandria goes further to explain Nimrod's giant nature by commenting about his father, Cush. He wrote that Cush had a nature rather like a giant born of the earth that prefers earthly to heavenly things, and thus appears to verify the ancient fable of the giants and titans...[5]

Another indication as to the enormous physical stature of Nimrod is found in that throughout numerous ancient traditions, he was famous for his physical power. Without weapons or armor it was custom of him to battle and slay bulls, bears, lions and leopards. In warfare or hunting he wore a helmet with bull's horns affixed, one of the animals he had slain, thus spawning early legends about minotaurs and bull-headed beasts.[6]

Nimrod was also known throughout antiquity for his mastery over animals, mainly horses and leopards. His ceremonial garb included several leopard skins woven into a great cape and sash. In fact, the Chaldean (early Babylonian) translation of Nimrod is leopard-subduer.

From traditional histories of ancient Assyria and Babylonia it appears that Nimrod and his mighty huntsmen frequently set out on hunting excursions to slay wild animals.[7] After the flood (Babel was built in the fifth generation after the deluge), the animal kingdoms multiplied much more rapidly than people. Wild bears, wolves, lions and other predators wrought much misery on people, stealing away with small children, attacking travelers, and decimating flocks and herds. People began putting their faith in Nimrod and the huntsmen rather than on God who gave them authority and dominion over the animals. This is further evidenced in that ancient peoples remembered Nimrod as a deliverer.[8]

The vast majority of myths and legends of the world, past and present, find their primitive roots in the very first city built after the flood, Babylon, site of the famous tower. A casual study of myths and fables from various cultures will reveal astonishing parallels that can be traced back to Nimrod the giant and his thriving civilization on the plains of Shinar.

Nimrod is remembered by every civilized culture of antiquity and by many lesser peoples found in remote areas because the entire earth once spoke only one language, the same speech maintained before the flood to the time of Adam in Eden. Nimrod lived and fell from power during this age. The languages were divided and his memory lived on in the minds and traditions of numerous cultures.

In the Sibylline Oracles we read that after the Babel tower fell... The tongues of men were diversified by various sounds, the whole earth of humans was filled with fragmenting kingdoms.[9]

Nimrod has bene known by many shades, personified within the legends and lore the world over, deified and worshiped throughout antiquity as the deliverer and savior of the ancients, immortalized in the mythology of many peoples.

The giant king of Babylon began a system of esoteric rituals and mystical observances still carried out by the Roman Catholic Church today. When Nimrod died he was remembered as a god and later named Saturn by the Romans. So the holy Sabbath day, which God instituted, became to the pagan the satanic Saturn-day. And Nimrod today is immortalized in that he is named in one of the days of the week. It was stated by King Evander in the *Aeneid* that at least part of what became Rome (Capitoline Hill) was once known as Saturnia, which is an interesting fact if true.

Nimrod was not deified until his death. After meeting an uncertain demise he was worshiped as a divinity. One of his ancient titles was Baal-aberin, which can mean either <u>lord of the mighty ones</u> or could be translated <u>lord of the winged ones</u>. The root for Baal means <u>archer</u> and <u>horsemen</u>[10] which is significant because Nimrod was a hunter and old traditions claim he was a master of horses.

The deification of this giant is evident throughout old Assyrian art and tradition. The god Nimrod is seen with angel wings, bull's horns, cloven hooves, and the body of a lion, bull, or horse. A winged centaur. This mythical creature of Greek lore traces its origin back to the Babylonian zodiac sign called Sagittarius, the Archer, which in turn discovers its birth from Nimrod the Hunter and famed centaur. Sagittarius the Archer of the Chaldean astrological calendar is found inscribed on many ancient Babylonian coins. This stellar association to the Babel ruler Nimrod is also seen in the constellation named Orion the Hunter. Orion, in fact, specifically means <u>the hunter</u>. In Homer's epic story entitled the <u>Iliad,</u> the constellation is called <u>Huge Orion</u>, implying the stature of a giant or at least much larger than ordinary people.

In *Bulfinch's Mythology*, Orion is called a giant, described as large, but the <u>superhuman giants, who warred with the gods were of vastly larger dimensions.</u>[11]

The connections between Orion and Nimrod go further in this mythology. <u>Orion was the son of Neptune. He was a giant, with a girdle, sword, lion's skin, and club. Sirius, his dog, follows him</u>...[12] The sons of Neptune were barbarians called ogres. *Smith's Bible Dictionary* states that Orion is called <u>The Giant by the Arabs, which was Nimrod among the Chaldeans.</u>[13]

The eighteenth century researcher Alexander Hislop discovered ample evidence of Nimrod's history and published his astonishing finds in *The Two Babylons*. Referring to this most ancient king of Babylonia, Mr. Hislop wrote that he was, <u>A person of great stature and immense bodily powers</u>, a ruler over giants according to Egyptian antiquities, men of huge stature called Cyclopes that were known for being <u>the inventors of tower building</u>.[14]

This early Chaldean ruler was known widely for his hunting exploits. Recorded in the *Book of Jasher*, we find that <u>Nimrod was a mighty hunter in the field and he hunted the animals</u> in *Jasher* 7:30. Having such an acute association with animals, it is not unusual that we find that Nimrod was remembered in many anthromorphic fashions.

The Romans remembered Nimrod as a goat-legged, cloven-hoofed sylvan deity named Bacchus. This god was a satyr, half man, half goat, then as a centaur, and was friends with woodland beings and spirits called fauns, known as centaurs by the Romans of antiquity.[15] Incidentally, Bacchus derives from the Greek god Dionysus who ruled the Maenads, females who partook of his woodland revelries and orgies that were turned into oak trees for murdering Orpheus, which later inspired the beliefs in dryads by the Celtic druids who worshiped oak trees in groves and sacrificed to the spirits that swelled in them. Other followers of the god Dionysus were the satyrs.[16]

The goat-legged god with horns that the Romans also remembered Nimrod by was Fauna, a satyr deity known as Pan by the early Greeks. Pan played hunting music that instilled fear in people that wandered into his forest domains. Our English word panic derives from the name of this deity, Pan. Also, the stories of Peter Pan find their beginnings with this ancient Roman god. Dionysus, known as Pan and Bacchus, was the god of drunkenness and revelry and is historically comparative to Nimrod, the Horned One or Horned Huntsman.

In fact, one of the most famous Greek myths was inspired by the person of Nimrod himself.

The Greeks believed that long ago Zeus (Satan to the early Christians) took on the form of a flawless white bull to lure a mortal woman named Europa into following him. Once at the edge of the sea, Zeus stole away with her to the mountainous Greek island of Crete that was inhabited by the Minoans. Zeus had three sons by this mortal woman. Minos was her firstborn and later became king of Crete. In pride and arrogance this ruler claimed that he could get anything he desired from the gods since he was the son of the greatest of the gods himself. He built an altar to Poseidon, the sea god and brother of Zeus, and swore that he would sacrifice a bull to the gods if one should arise forth from the sea. Immediately, a white bull emerged from the waves.

So beautiful was this animal that King Minos added the creature to his own livestock and replaced the bull with another for sacrifice. In wrath, Aphrodite, the goddess of love, made the king's wife fall hopelessly in love with the white bull Poseidon had provided.

King Minos' wife was named Pasiphae and she told the king's master architect and craftsman about her love for the bull. So the craftsman, Daedalus, built her a wooden bull hollowed inside for her to visit her animal lover in. After having a sexual affair with the bull, Pasiphae gave birth to a half bull, half human child. The creature was called a Minotaur.[17] This is likewise reiterated in the <u>Aeneid</u>. Virgil wrote that the child of the bull and Pasiphae was <u>their hybrid offspring, child of two breeds, the Minotaur</u>.

Every nine years, seven males and seven females were abandoned within the labyrinth built by Daedalus. These hapless people were the sacrifice of the Minotaur. Tirelessly, this beast would spend his time hunting these individuals in the maze. A tireless hunter, the Minotaur was a lot like Nimrod in that he was a bull-horned giant and hunter, both being descended from giants or gods. To the Israelites of old, the Minotaur would have been Nephilim.

The Minoan civilization thrived on Crete in the Mediterranean sea between 2300-1100 B.C. Coins dating back to 400 B.C. have been excavated that depict Minotaurs, images of horned giants such as those the Norse Vikings liked to mimic when wearing their horned helms. Historically, the Minoan kingdom rapidly vanished when, about 1500 B.C., the island of Thera was destroyed by an enormous volcanic explosion from Mount Santorini.[18] From this point, the entire Minoan civilization declined, badly crippled.

The explosion caused tidal waves that continued the volcanoes' destruction throughout the Aegean Sea and Mediterranean, as far as Greece and Asia Minor. Egypt and Italy suffered from this, and 2300 years ago Plato wrote about this ancient island nation, spawning the legends from some researchers of the famous and mystical city of Atlantis.

The minotaur was the son of a demi-god, but Bacchus, the horned satyr, was widely regarded as the <u>seed of the serpent</u> because he was Jupiter's son. Jupiter appeared often in the form of a giant snake. He also had intercourse with many mortal women, one of which was the mother of Bacchus, or Nimrod. All throughout ancient antiquity before and after the flood, even previous to the recording of literature by pen and ink, on stone or metal plates, the mysterious Edenic curse was known by many cultures, having been carefully passed down by oral tradition. The Chaldean phrase "zero-ashta" means the <u>seed of the woman</u>.[19] One man named in Scripture is Zorobabel (Zerubbabel by more ancient reckoning), which means <u>seed of Babylon</u>.

In the mystery religions of Babylon, Inanna, a Sumerian goddess, replaced Eve. Inanna became Ishtar to the Chaldeans and later Mesopotamian people.[20] The <u>seed of the woman</u> then took on new meaning as it was absorbed into occult lore, being synchronized with the descendants of a <u>goddess</u> rather than a human woman named Eve. This seed was thought to someday come from the <u>stars</u>. This woman who assumed the role of Eve in the distorted version of Edenic prophecy was Nimrod's wife, Semiramus. A real person at one time, Semiramus was later deified, with her son, as a mother goddess.

Although Nimrod was a Cushite Negro with dark features, his mother-wife was fair and of angelic descent, having light complexioned features.[21] Further proof of her supernatural origin is discovered in her Grecian name. Just as the giants of old were called the Nephilim, or fallen ones, Semiramus was long ago called Nephele, or The Fallen Woman.[22]

Semiramus was remembered by the infamous antiquarian and Babylonian King Nebuchadnezzar, who is mentioned many times in the Scriptures. Two of the great archaeological excavations and restorations attributed to this wicked ruler was the rebuilding of the ancient Tower of Babel, called El-Temen-An-Ki, and the hanging gardens of Babylon, considered an ancient Wonder of the World, and once called the Gardens of Semiramus![23]

Traces of Nimrod and his mother-goddess wife can be found in the name of the very first city found in the Genesis text inhabited by giants, where the Rephaim were defeated by King Chedorlaomer in Genesis 14. The name of the city was Ashtoreth Karnaim, and is literally translated as star of the two horns.[24] Ashtoreth comes from the ancient Mesopotamian goddess I_tar (Ishtar), which means star of heaven. She is detailed in the archaic cuneiform text The Descent of Ishtar, Gilgamesh and Etana.[25] Her symbol was the eight-pointed star revered by Jews today as the star of David, a symbol allegedly harboring special powers for occultists today. The two horns (Karnaim) unveil the influence of the giant Nimrod in the city of the Rephaim.

The prophecy was a light of hope to the spiritual observer, but to the pagan mind the Edenic curse was enigmatic. Even by the time of Nimrod it had been twisted to conform to Satanic thought. Under Nimrod the giant idolatrous worship permeated through Babylonia, which largely consisted of paying homage to the Serpent of Fire erected in the plain of Shinar. Child sacrifice in incendiary ovens and flaming pits was first initiated in Babylon as a twisted rite acted out in observance to the Edenic prophecy. By offering their infants into the fires they were exhibiting faith that the true seed of the woman from the stars would come.

These rites were carried out in obedience to a twisted priesthood with warped logic, the Chaldeans who deified Nimrod and later called him king (Moloch) of fire, a savior. Before the flood, Enoch taught that one day men would be made to pass through the fire, a spiritual flame of the holy spirit that would try all men's works. But Nimrod perverted this patriarchal faith, rendering it a literal fire that burned alive the women and children of the faithful.

The Greek legend of Orpheus greatly portrays this awareness in the prophecy. Orpheus was the son of Apollo, master musician among the gods.

His wife Eurydice was very beautiful and coveted by a man named Aristaeus who chased her. While fleeing him she stepped on a serpent that bit her on the heel causing her death. Though tainted, distorted with time, this myth greatly exemplifies the Edenic prophecy... <u>it shall bruise they heel, and thou shalt crush its head</u>...

In Babylonian mythology, Ti'amat is the multi-headed Dragon of Chaos.[26] In the Bible, Satan is leviathan, the crooked serpent. In Psalm 74:14 leviathan has several <u>heads</u> and likewise, we have a good representation of Ti'amat in the book of the Revelation in the prophetic imagery of the <u>beast out of the sea,</u> with seven heads and ten horns, the Antichrist draped in Babylonian symbolism. Both leviathan of Isaiah 24:1 and the beast of Revelation are related to the <u>sea</u>, and the Antichrist beast is empowered by a <u>dragon</u> that has his capitol at Babylon. In the <u>Enuma Elish</u> account of the Babylonian creation epic, Ti'amat is characterized as the power of the <u>sea</u>, the primordial ocean in the beginning, before the world was made.[27] Later historians and writers have regarded this dragon as the original embodiment of evil.

Dark age dragons are depicted with wings and fiery breath but ancient ones were giant <u>snakes</u>. Greek dragons were basilisks, which means the <u>royal serpent</u>. Prominent Egyptians and Pharaohs had cobras affixed to their headdresses as a sign of divine royalty.

In Job 41:1-32 leviathan is a great, prehistoric-type creature that typified Satan, the Dragon. He is described in the book of Job as a great beast, a swamp-dweller, but in verses 33-34 it is revealed that he has <u>no match</u> on earth and is a <u>king over all the children of pride</u>. Lucifer also was said to be the <u>most perfect</u> in wisdom and beauty, and his initial sin was <u>pride</u> (Ezekiel 28:12-17).

Also in the Bible is a fascinating passage in Isaiah concerning the defeat of Satan as the Dragon, <u>wounded</u>, as the Edenic prophecy against the serpent foretold.

> ...<u>Oh arm of the Lord; Awake, as in the ancient days, in the generations of old. Art thou not it that hath cut Rahab, and wounded the dragon?</u>... (Isaiah 51:9)

This inspiring historical insight refers to Satan's plan to hinder the Messiah's coming by creating giants and ruining the bloodline in the <u>ancient days</u>, which refers to the pre-flood giants God destroyed with a flood, as seen in the Hebrew rendering of Rahab (large, broad). Rahab was a harlot in Jericho which was in a land of giants and giant-kin people (Numbers 13:29, 32). The <u>generations of old</u> refers to after the flood when giants, primarily the Anakim and Rephaim, populated the Promise Land. "Hath cut" means to hew down, thus the giants were cut down, which wounded the dragon both before and after the flood. Wounded here is chalal, which originally referred to sexual defilement, incest, but has a clear underlying connotation of violence. Chalal is a desecration of something holy, which synonymously means wounded. The word is special, found only twice in the Bible (the other time is detailed later and also related to the Nephilim) and associates the dragon's wound to his crime—which was the creation of large people like Rahab of Jericho, who violently went on to sexually defile the daughters of men in the days of old. Satan infiltrated the holy bloodline, desecrating it. "The arm of the Lord" from the above quote is figurative of judgment, the infliction of the wound on the dragon, for the power of a man's strength is in his arms.

Universally, through the historical epochs of all nations, evil has been personified as a serpent or mythical dragon. Where this is not held, the serpent is then glorified as deity. Many of these traditions are strangely akin to the Judaism and Christianity of today, though elements of fantasy and superstition are mixed in. Often serpents, dragons, and giants are discovered together in the tales and legends of historic people.

West African myths of the Fon people hold that the entire world is surrounded by a giant rainbow serpent (similar to the Midgard serpent of Norse belief) named Aido-hwedo. At the end of time the rainbow serpent will devour its own tail and the balance of the earth will be offset, causing the dry land to sink into the sea.[28] The rainbow serpent and sea greatly reflect the biblical account of the Edenic curse, the flood, and the rainbow of the Noahic covenant, despite their distortion.

In the West African kingdom of Benin, now called Nigeria, was worshiped a moon goddess by the natives known as Gleti. This goddess mothered a great many astral gods called the Gletivi.[29] Their activities among men are not known, however they ultimately became synchronized as the stars of heaven, a unique description of angels found repeatedly throughout the Scriptures.

The Nigerian god named Oko may have some distant relation to the Gletivi. After descending from heaven and taking up residence near the African town of Irao and residing there until he grew to an incredible age, he vanished. The natives reportedly recovered his staff, which became the only relic left behind by Oko.[30]

In southern Africa the creator is called Kalunga by the natives of Namibia. According to their belief, he was a giant who had hidden from men but frequently visited African women in secluded places regarded as sacred. The women are called <u>nelagos</u> and sometimes act as mediators between the giant god and the people.[31]

From Africa is found a startling tradition cited in *A Treasure of African Folklore* by Harold Courlander that concerns a giant named Mwooka who was a great hunter, told by the Akamba people of eastern Kenya. Like Nimrod, this giant led hunting parties while he himself only used an enormous bow.[32]

These African traditions date back to distant times before the classical eras of Egypt, Greece and Rome; to the obscure times of early Babylonia, a civilization where giants were not myth, but very real and profoundly feared by rulers and builders. Some of these giants long ago must have wandered into Africa, being remembered as the ancient Rom stone-building giants of Ethiopia and the Ad people (Adites), recalled in the Quran. It is possible that the Watusi people of Africa are descended from these giants, a strange culture of people that commonly grow to a height of seven feet or more.[33]

Depicted on the <u>Stone of the Four Suns</u> at Yale Peabody Museum is an Aztec history involving the ages of time and the god Ocelotl who represented the first age. This primordial era ended in a great destruction that eradicated the wicked <u>giants</u> that antedated their ancestors.[38]

The Sumerians too, regarded serpents as immortal in their <u>Epic of Gilgamesh</u>. Gilgamesh was the Babylonian hero who could very well have been inspired by the person of Nimrod. He received instructions from Utnapishtim (Biblical <u>Noah</u>) to find a plant that would grant him eternal youth, but while bathing in a pool of water after discovering the cherished plant, a snake stole away with the leaves. Since then, according to the tradition, snakes renew their life and vitality by shedding their skins. Gilgamesh, lord of the city of Uruk, returned home with nothing.[39]

Drawing more on the comparisons between dragons and snakes, we now turn to the Chinese. For thousands of years they have celebrated with large costume-serpents and have regarded the dragon as an imperial creature of wisdom. The traditional Chinese dragon closely resembles a large snake with a lion's head and very short forelimbs and legs, similar to the Edenic serpent before it lost its limbs and was cursed to crawl upon its belly forever.

The Egyptian arch-enemy of Re, the Egyptian creator, is Apep, the serpent of chaos. Egyptian lore of the Greek hero Hercules (Heracles by the Greeks) records that by the power of the gods, he defeated many giants. These Egyptian tales implicate Shem, the son of Noah, as being this legendary giant-slayer. Shem lived before the flood when giants terrorized antediluvian earth and even lived 502 years beyond the flood, which was ample time to witness the rise of the post-flood Nephilim. The feats of Hercules and his plights against the giants and other monsters is likewise supported by the ancient writer Apollodorus, who wrote that the gods could not rightly kill any giants unless they were aided by a mortal. Through the courage and abilities of men, gods could empower humans to slay giants.

The Greek myths of Heracles, son of Zeus, further darkly mirror Bible history. Heracles in his eleventh labour traveled to the paradise garden of Hesperides to steal the apples of eternal youth that were on a tree in the center of the garden.[40] A great serpent guarded these apples for Gaea, the goddess of the Earth, who is worshiped even today as Mother Earth.

Heracles and Gilgamesh both share many similarities such as their demigod status, encounters with giants, serpents, and plants that gave eternal youth. Is all of this myth? Or different shades of ancient truths? Gaea was the mother of titans and the spirit of the earth that is remembered and honored today. Peter Pan now flies through the minds and soaring imaginations of our children. Cartoons still immortalize the dragons and serpents worshiped long ago.

From Cuchulain the Warped One, Niflheim, the icy realm of the dead, Ragnarok prophecies of the Norse Vikings, the histories of the Tuatha de Danaan, Formorians, Firbolgs, legends of the Frost Giants, the Druids and their oaks, Dionysus and his wine, the Minotaur of Crete, the Babylonian serpent of fire, Zodiac, Orpheus, Ti'amat, the Mayan astral calendars, even the stars of Orion and many other ancient mysteries all provide hints and information concerning the powerful and shadowy figure of Nimrod the giant.

Nimrod was the son of Cush, which is evidenced also in Nimrod's Roman name, Bacchus, which derived from the Semitic bar-Cush, son of Cush. Nimrod and his mother-wife also appear together on the Zodiac, she as the Queen of heaven, adopted by the Catholics of today, and he as a representative of the seed of the woman, the child Jesus, as portrayed by the Roman Catholic Church—yet Nimrod was worshiped by the Babylonians of old. The ancient Chaldean contemporaries were the Assyrians who worshiped Nimurda, the god of war.

A careful scrutiny of the past will reveal how Nimrod came to be regarded as a god. After the flood, only Noah, his three sons, Japhath, Shem and Ham, and their four wives, were said to be left on earth. These eight people were not subject to the lifespan restrictions imposed upon humanity by God before the flood. Recorded in Genesis 6:3, God declared that man would live up to 120 years, and no more. Evidently, this stricture did not apply to those living before the flood, especially those He would spare. Antediluvian longevity had men living up to 969 years (Methuselah). Why is this? Before the flood, earth was protected from ultra violet sunrays and solar radiation from a thick atmospheric ocean, a watery canopy that magnified the heavens. The flood itself was caused by the collapsing of this protective barrier of water in the sky. Earth at that time was very fertile. Mineral-rich water and vitamins concentrated in the vegetation, this coupled with an absence of damaging UV rays and radiation had people living in perfect health for hundreds of years. Aging was extremely slow in these prime conditions. God foreknew what the cause of the flood would be, how the collapse of the firmament above (see Genesis 1:6-8) would leave men to die much earlier than their ancestors.

Two and three hundred years after the flood, Noah and the other seven survivors were witnessing the deaths of their descendants. Noah himself lived 600 years before the flood, Scripture claims he lived another 350 years after it. In the Epic of Gilgamesh, the Sumerian hero visits Noah and learns a great deal from him. Noah, named Utnapishtim in the ancient text, was apparently still alive. Interestingly, Gilgamesh has been identified with Nimrod by some, a half-giant. According to Theodor Bar Qoni from the seventh century A.D., a king named Ganmagos ruled after the flood in the days Abraham.[41]

Gangamos is Gilgamesh, an alternative rendering due to division of tongues. The *Book of Jasher* reveals that Nimrod lived and even hunted for Abraham. Just as Nimrod built the Babel ziggurat, Gilgamesh is found to have built a great wall around Uruk, the city named Erech in Genesis 10:10, that Nimrod built. This ancient inscription concerning Gilgamesh dates back to King Anam of Uruk, C.A. 1800 B.C.[42] Another comparative hint as to the identity of Gilgamesh being the person of Nimrod the giant is found in tablet II, line 47, of the Gilgamesh Epic, where the hero is said to be tall in stature, and elsewhere in the text where his head is elevated over (other) men.[43]

Being an early descendant of Noah, Nimrod could have lived for hundreds of years as well. Though not as long as the original eight flood survivors, Nimrod could have also outlived many of his descendants. Human longevity decreased rapidly as men multiplied, but not before these first generations began witnessing the deaths of their 80 and 90 year-old grandchildren.

Nimrod was either unusually large or somehow kin to those of Nephilim stock. He was the son of Cush. Nimrod's mother (Semiramus by traditional history) must have been Nephilim-kin because Cush was the son of Ham and he was, in turn, the son of Noah. Noah placed a curse on Canaan that was supported by God because of the sexual trespass involved, a sin foreshadowing the sexual unrestraint by the descendants of Ham in being involved with angels and their giant progeny. The great stature and size attributed to Nimrod by ancient scribes could be the result of his age. Like reptiles that grow as long as they live under accommodating conditions, Nimrod could have continued to grow in strength and size for two hundred years, or however long he lived.

The shadowy figure of Dagon is a mystery. Some older, unnamed historians claim it was he who taught men civilization in Babylonia. This would identify him as Nimrod himself, called a Guardian of Mankind by other sources. Nimrod, as the deity Dagon, was actually deified by the early Babylonian priests as Oannes after his death. Oannes appeared only as a <u>goat-horned fish</u>.[44]

The very first civilization after the flood was ancient Mesopotamia, which involved Sumeria, Babylon and Akkad. All three of these civilizations share pantheons of gods that all maintain striking parallels and similarities. Careful study of these three pantheons brings one to the awareness that they are descriptive not of actual gods, but ancient families, with origins in cities and regions where their descendants lived and worshiped from. This <u>one</u> ancient family, comprised of people who lived unusually long lives, were vastly knowledgeable men and women that became deified by their own descendants. Many of these <u>gods</u> have the same names as their Akkadian or Sumerian counterparts, though they are Babylonian deities. Nimrod himself is seen in many shades in these ancient pantheons. This explains why so many archaic traditions claim their ancestors were <u>giants</u>, or also how many other cultures of antiquity believed that the gods vanquished a race of giants long ago.

Chapter Ten

The Giant Wars

The first ruler mentioned on earth after the Deluge is Nimrod in the Genesis text. It is most unusual that neither Noah nor one of his three sons is revealed to be in any position of authority. Despite the fact that Nimrod was the great grandson of Noah through Ham, all of Noah's initial family still lived. Even more out of place is the fact that Nimrod is of Hamitic descent through the cursed Canaan, a bloodline foretold to sexually rebel against the Lord. And the people were under his rule.

> And King Nimrod ruled securely, and all of the earth was under his control, and all the earth was of one tongue and words of union.[1]

The earth at this time was populous, having three distinct families all speaking the Adamic language spoken before the flood, a language passed down from God to Adam. Noah lived three hundred years after the flood and he and Japhath, Shem and Ham were alive to witness the rise of Nimrod.

The ancient Hebraic *Book of Jasher*[2] states that Nimrod did not go in the ways of the Lord, so why would those of purely Adamic descent follow him? Was Nimrod the result of any mysterious sexual contacts of Cush, his father? What could have made Nimrod so intimidating that even his enemies submitted to his control? The person of Nimrod is indeed an interesting enigma. By the time Nimrod proclaimed himself king there were many hundreds of families all dwelling in Mesopotamia in small township communities and villages on the Euphrates river and on the plain of Shinar. It was during this population explosion that all of the people under Nimrod assembled.

At the beginning of the construction of the Tower of Babel the men assembled, being about six hundred thousand men, not including their families. This multitude suggests a population of over one and a half million people during the earlier part of Nimrod's reign.[3]

The first stone city to be built after the Deluge was Babel, later known as Babylon. The technical knowledge and engineering required for constructing a city and erecting a tower structure of the magnitude of Babel is colossal. Where Nimrod derived this information and ability is a mystery linked to his even more mysterious origin. Cush is only half of Nimrod's history, the other being a tainted lineage that invoked the wrath of God and destruction of Old Earth. Nimrod had a lot at stake in the construction of this strange tower. James Lloyd in his thought-provoking *Apocalypse Chronicles* wrote:

> Shortly after the devastating deluge, we find the post-flood peoples of the world all speaking one language in a unified pursuit of the star gods and goddesses. They are the offspring of Noah's three sons that built the great astronomical ziggurat known as the tower of Babel. When you realize that the first significant story that the Bible mentions immediately after the flood is the observatory at Babel, it becomes apparent that the people were looking for the return of the star gods that had disappeared during the flood.[4]

According to Jewish tradition, only the house of Noah and Shem remained loyal to the Adamic lineage and worshiped the one true Creator. The descendants of Japhath and Ham, along with many Shemites, anticipated the return of the gods from heaven who took their daughters before the flood, definitive memories passed on to the people as they were raised under the patriarchs who actually witnessed these things. Japhath, Ham and their wives told stories about the old gods and their giant sons who ruled over them.

Herodotus wrote that the very top of the Tower of Babel was a spacious temple. According to this historian, the priests would confine a female in this elevated temple in a special chamber with a richly adorned bed of incredible size. Herodotus claims that priests waited for the appearance of a god and that only the choicest of women would provoke a deity to descend.[5]

According to Kurt Seligmann in his book, *The History of Magic and the Occult*, the tower of Babel was originally a seven-stage ziggurat called El-Temen-An-Ki, which means house of the foundation stone of heaven and earth.[6] An and Ki are old Babylonian words for heaven and earth found in the name Anunnaki.

The height of El-Temen-An-Ki corresponded to its length. The square, though divided into seven, was again respected, and the old tradition of a fourfold world was reconciled with the seven heavens of later times.[7]

These architectural descriptions are based upon historic records of King Nebuchadnezzar who had El-Temen-An-Ki excavated and rebuilt, a feat that no doubt provoked God to ruin the Babylonian empire. Nebuchadnezzar also created a dark mimicry of the garden of Eden by erecting the famous Hanging Gardens of Babylon, and it's possible that his reconstruction of the Babel tower on the original site was provoked by spiritual powers more bent on subverting the works of God than what this Babylonian king was aware of. The measurements of the Babel tower indicate a cunning mind in that this colossal structure mimics the angelic city in heaven described in the Bible called the New Jerusalem, which has alignments very much like El-Temen-An-Ki. This heavenly city <u>lieth foursquare, and the length is as large as the breadth;... the length and the breadth and the height of it are equal</u>. (Rev. 21:16)

The faith in the existence of heavenly beings by the people was answered by God Almighty Himself. The people were commanded <u>to be fruitful, and multiply and replenish the earth</u>[8] but they refused to comply, instead building a city and monument for God's angels! In judgment, the Lord forced the people to obey by creating <u>division</u>, the same thing Jesus claimed that he came to perform in Matthew's gospel.[9] The people were separated into many groups according to the language they spoke. Tradition claims there were seventy languages created that day. This miraculous event occurred in the life of Peleg. Genesis 10:25 states that in the days of Peleg <u>earth was divided</u>. William Cooper in his book, *After the Flood*, recorded that the meaning of Peleg's name, as rendered in Hebrew, corresponds exactly with the Akkadian noun <u>pulukku</u>, which means <u>a dividing up of a territory by means of boundaries and borders</u>. Mr. Cooper states that the division of the peoples from Babel occurred five <u>generations</u> after the flood. The word "generations" in this context refers to a period of time, probably the traditional forty years exhibited several times in Scripture. The five generations indicated that the Babel incident transpired about two hundred years after the Deluge.

Other confirmation comes from the *Book of Jasher*, which reveals that in the early days of Peleg's life the sons of men were divided, and later in his life the <u>earth</u> itself was divided. However, this ancient Hebrew tradition adds a detail that the Bible does not. Peleg's brother was named Joktan (Yoktan) because his birth signified the time when men's lifespans were lessened.[10] From that time (around Babel) the pre-flood longevity was no longer enjoyed. Environmental and spiritual conditions known only to God provoked Him to commemorate this lessening of the lives of humanity by the birth of his brother Joktan.

The Tower was destroyed and its hundreds of thousands of builders dispersed, each taking his family to the areas where their language was understood.

<u>After the destruction of the tower Nimrod dwelt in Babel, and there renewed his reign over the rest of his subjects</u>.[11]

All who spoke Nimrod's tongue (Chaldee) followed him in the building of Babel. The Bible mentions other cities built by the Babylonian ruler: Calah, Erech and Akkad in the Euphrates regions of Shinar in ancient Mesopotamia. Akkad has been excavated.

The Englishman A.H. Layard uncovered Nimrud (Kalchu), the city which the Bible calls Calah in Genesis 10:11 [12] The Akkadians were a mighty Mesopotamian nation after Nimrod's death. For hundreds of years, Akkadian cuneiform was the universal script for trade and correspondence among nobles, sages and kings. Babel was famous for another of Nimrod's feats after God laid waste his tower-temple.

The famous hanging gardens of Babylon were erected by Nimrod and his successors above the plains of Shinar to imitate the original garden of Eden.[13]

Babel was later named Babylon, which means gate of God in Chaldee, the Fertile Crescent of ancient Mesopotamia. The reach of human civilization around 2200 B.C., during Nimrod's early reign, was shaped like a crescent, like a moon with its two ends pointing south. Incidentally, Chaldea means the moon!

The Babylonian city of Erech under Nimrod was called Uruk. It was shown by excavation to have been an important city from very early times, with great temples to the gods Anu and I_tar [Diana].[14]

After the Assyrian invasion of Babylonia, Assurbanipal had scribes search the archives of Babylon, Uruk and Nippur for old Sumerian records of Mesopotamia that he had translated into Akkadian Semitic. Among those records was found the Epic of Gilgamesh.[15]

This very old epic was translated from various relics found in the ruins in Nineveh, Assyria's old capitol. This incredible story speaks of a ruler of Uruk named Gilgamesh who was two parts god and one part man, a king of huge stature who appears after a spectacular event in Sumerian (Shinar) history when, after the flood, kingship once more descended.[16] The majority of these ancient records and annals of the earliest kings were from the city of Nippur, now called the mound of Niffar in southern Iraq.[17]

In the Epic of Gilgamesh's Introduction by British archaeologist N.K. Sandars, we find that Gilgamesh is fifth in line from the founding of the first dynasty of Uruk (after the flood) and reigned 126 years, but his son reigned a mere thirty years, and thereafter kings lived and reigned an ordinary human term.

Gilgamesh no doubt knew or served Nimrod, if he was not Nimrod himself. In *Noah's Flood* by William Ryan and Walter Pitman, we discover that the original translator of the badly fragmented Epic of Gilgamesh believed that his discoveries about the hero had uncovered the identity of the ruler that had reigned and founded the Babylonian kingdom. This is a feat attributed to Nimrod. Both ruled over 120 years, both ruled Uruk (Erech) before and after the division of tongues. According to the *Book of Jasher*, Nimrod was killed by a sword wound, so his life could have been hundreds of years.

After the flood men lived for hundreds of years, but only half the longevity enjoyed by the antediluvian people. During Peleg's life, human lifespans were considerably lessened to conform to the 120-year curse uttered by God to Noah. Nimrod lived long after the longevity lessening and his mother is the reason why. Only the biblical giants had such long lives that late after the deluge. Nimrod also ruled the city of his father Cush, called Kish by the historians.[18]

First ruled by Nimrod, the metropolis of Sumer and city of Akkad remained populated for over 1600 years until the rise of the Persian empire under Cyrus a few centuries before Christ's ministry.[19]

The Sumerians remembered Nimrod as Amar-Utu, their patron deity descended from the god Amurru, an ethnic Akkadian name for the Amorites of the Bible. Nimrod was known by several names because of the linguistic separation of peoples that gave birth to numerous cultures, all of which recalled the person and feats of Nimrod. If Gilgamesh is Nimrod then the translation of his name alludes to his semi-divinity. Gilgamesh means circle of the sun, or son of the circle of Shemesh (the sun god). The sun was worshiped long ago throughout the entire world. Anyone regarded as being a son of the sun would have to have been fathered by Nephilim.

And the subjects and princes of Nimrod called his name Amraphel... because at the tower his princes and men fell through his means.[20]

This change of name was given by his people when he established sovereignty over his subjects. From that time forward Nimrod did not rule the whole of humanity, but only those Semitic and Hamitic families in Mesopotamia. According to Stephen Jones in his *Secrets of Time*, Nimrod was 86 years old when Babel was destroyed. Nimrod is called Amraphel after the Babel incident in the Bible also.[21] This name is very revealing, describing Nimrod as a fallen giant. Amraphel has two meanings, one in Chaldee and one in Hebrew. In Chaldee it means Keeper (Guardian) of the gods and in Hebrew this name contains the words rapha and nephel, conjoined to spell Amraphel, the fallen giant. "Rapha" means giant and "nephel" is a description of something that has fallen violently like Nephilim, the fallen ones.

The reason no giants (like Rephaims from rapha) are found in biblical genealogies is because the angels that appeared as huge gods and their giant offspring took women they wanted to secluded areas outside the contemporary civilization of that time to foster a race of giants and enormous people like Nimrod and Gilgamesh. Nimrod's mother was one of these isolated giants, perhaps a Nephilim-kin priestess born from an early half breed race deified by early humans in Mesopotamia. The sexual curse proclaimed by Noah is exemplified in the person and biblical revelation of Nimrod, the fallen giant. In the second tablet of the Gilgamesh epic is an allusion found in lines 46-49 that those who are born and grow up to be tall in stature are only born in the mountains.[22]

Another reason why this mysterious race of giants appeared in early Babylonia is cited by Maureen Gallery Kovacs in her translation of the Epic of Gilgamesh. She writes that for unknown reasons, Mesopotamian kings may have practiced an unusual custom of having sexual intercourse with brides before their husbands did, and that these practices were ordered by the counsel of Anu.[23] Considering the fact that Mesopotamian kings are one in the same with the ancient Sumerian kingship that descended from heaven both before and after the flood, this order by the "supreme god" appears now to have been a sinister design premeditated to foster a race of giants.

Many of the tyrants of old were born under similar circumstances. Gilgamesh, as mentioned earlier, was two parts god and one part man. His mother was an obscure goddess who was worshiped in Uruk in her palace-temple and his father in the king list is rather mysteriously described as 'lillû' which may mean a fool, or a demon of the vampire kind.[24] Since the discovery of the Gilgamesh Epic, scholars and historians have discovered that a King Gilgamesh truly did live and rule Uruk in the third millennium B.C. So why don't they believe in his self-proclaimed ancestry? Before Gilgamesh ruled in Uruk, a King Lugulbanda lived who was considered to be a god, married to a Sumerian goddess named Ninsun, and who just so happened to be the mother-goddess of King Gilgamesh. Mesopotamian myth or something more?

In Jeremiah 36:4, the Bible mentions a book written by Baruch. Today we have an accurate translation of this informative book called the *Apocalypse of Baruch*. In these writings are found, in chapter 10, the Greek form of the vampire demon mentioned in the Epic of Gilgamesh. In Sumerian, Gilgamesh's father was described as lillû, what later became Lilin in Greek and then Lilith. In the Apocalypse writings these Lilin are mentioned in the same context as the Sirens and dragons. The Sirens are said, in the Ethiopic text of Enoch, to be the wives of the wicked angels that appeared on earth.

The Baruch commentary states that male and female demons named Lil and Lilit belong to Assyrian and Babylonian demonology. They were thought to attack men and women in their sleep. In Isaiah 34:14 these types of mysterious and sexual demons are mentioned. The translators, however, have called them the "satyr" and the "screech owl," when in fact these are blatant mistranslations. "Satyr" means he-devil in Hebrew and "screech owl," which is only mentioned one time in the Bible, does not mean owl at all, but night monster (night demon, according to *Baruch*).

These Lilit demons are evil angels in a female human form that seduce men and give birth to their children. The Sumerian hero Gilgamesh was a son to one of these Succubi, a demoniac mentioned in the Sumerian King-Lists as an unnamed figure described as a lillû. Even so early after the flood the angels were very busy. And then there is Sargon I in Werner Keller's book, *The Bible as History*, where we find:

> Cuneiform texts have this to say of King Sargon, the founder of the Semitic Dynasty of Akkad in 2360 B.C.: "I am Sargon, the powerful king, the king of Akkad. My mother was an Enitu priestess, I did not know any father..."

Priestesses were confined in lavish bedchambers at the top of the tower of Babel and no doubt atop many lesser ziggurats and temples in later cities. Maureen Gallery Kovacs, in her very literal translation of the Epic of Gilgamesh, adds in her introduction that she believes Gilgamesh was taking some sexual advantage of the women in Uruk.[25] Were Nimrod, Gilgamesh and Sargon of angelic ancestry? Even Alexander the Great of Greece claimed to be a son of God by divine conception, which was untrue. He merely sought the prestige enjoyed by the kings of old, echoed in Greek mythology. The Epic of Gilgamesh poems antedate the Homeric epic by at least one and a half thousand years.[26] Yet still, their memory remained up until the time when the true Son of God appeared, according to Christians, and up to now.

Through archaeology we have determined that Nimrod's people truly believed that he was of heavenly origin. In Frederick Haberman's book, *Tracing Our Ancestors*, we find that the earliest sculptures of Nimrod, the king is the figure with the wings and tail of a bird.[27] Sir Henry Layard in his excavations of Nimrud and Nineveh discovered many of the winged stone images, and in his book called *Nineveh and its Remains*, states that the images look remarkably like the cherubim of Scripture.[28] Even after Nimrod's death he was remembered as being angelic. Concerning excavations of ancient Assyrian relics, William Ryan and Walter Pitman in *Noah's Flood*, state that larger-than-life human figures were unearthed at Nimrud.

The merging of words to form titles was not an uncommon practice, like Amraphel. A prime example of this tradition is discovered in the name of the god Uranus. This deity finds its most primitive origin in the Chaldean civilization of Ur, a city-state established under Nimrod. Ur was the most important pre-Akkadian city where the Sumerian creator god Anu was worshiped. The city and god later became synchronized into Uranus: [Ur][Anu]s. Ur-Nammu is another ancient god that ruled in Mesopotamia of Amorite origin, their god <u>Amurru</u> being the base word in <u>Ur-Nammu</u>.

Another example is found in the Semitic name Ashurbanipal. This king of Assyria was a collector of books who had, at one time, the most diverse and largest library in antiquity. He ransacked foreign archives and temples for lost and secret documents dating back to Sargon I (2350 B.C.).[29]

"Ashur" in Ashurbanipal means <u>star of Ur</u>. The ancient library at Nineveh antedates the reign of King Ashurbanipal by a thousand years, to the time of <u>Hammurabi</u>. It was in this archaic collection of tablets and stellae that the Akkadian text <u>Epic of Gilgamesh</u> was found by the Assyrians.[30]

Hammurabi is nothing but an ethnic derivation of <u>Amraphel</u>. Hammurabi was a <u>keeper of the gods</u> and great Babylonian lawgiver. Nimrod was remembered by the later Hebrews as Tammuz, a personage called Dumuzi by the older Sumerians. Dumuzi means <u>the true son</u>, a name that reveals that the ancients all believed in the Edenic prophecy of the <u>seed of the woman</u> that was to come. Further proof that Hammurabi and Nimrod are one and the same is found in that Tammuz and Hammurabi both have the Amorite god Amurru's name embedded within their own! H[ammur]abi and T[ammu]z.

I_tar (Ishtar) was Dumuzi's wife and mother goddess, a woman long ago named Semiramis in Babylonia. Tammuz was killed and annually mourned,[31] which was considered an abomination in the book of Ezekiel 8:14; <u>there sat women weeping for Tammuz...</u> Dumuzi was considered a <u>son of the gods</u> so his death was commemorated yearly.

The most ancient name of Nimrod's wife is <u>Semiramis</u>, a queen of Babylonia whose name betrays her unusual origins. Semiramis appears to be a merging of two ethnic groups, the Semites and Amorites [Semi][Ramis=Amurru]. If this is correct, then we know that it is through her and her Amorite-angelic family that Nimrod came to be a giant. Nimrod was the son of Cush and Semiramis. Cush was already very old when his son was being raised. By the time Nimrod came to power his father was dead and Semiramis, Queen of Babylonia still lived youthfully, blessed by her dark, angelic longevity. Enamored with his own mother, Nimrod took her as his wife and she remained queen.[32]

The Edenic prophecy was well preserved in those early centuries after the flood and interestingly, Nimrod, being the son and husband of a woman regarded as being a goddess, was himself regarded as a deliverer and savior of the people, blasphemously called Zoroaster by the early Chaldeans, which means literally seed of the woman (zero-ashta).[33] After her son's death, Queen Semiramis had Nimrod deified as being the fulfillment of that promised seed that was foretold to come and die for the salvation of humanity.

In *After the Flood* by William Cooper,[34] it is discovered that the Amorites invaded Babylonia, which means land of the gate of God. The Amorites ruled and were remembered by the Akkadians of Mesopotamia as the Amurru, a name found distinctively in the name of the Babylonian law-giver H[ammur]abi, an Amorite name. Hammurabi literally means Amurru the Ham[ite god] or [the god] Amurru of Ham. Nimrod was Ham's grandson. This clarifies why Amraphel, a Chaldean name, indicates in Hebrew that its bearer was related to giants (rapha). Am[raph]el conveys a link to the Rephaim family of giants that lived among the Amorites in Canaan in the days of Moses and before. In fact, even the Amorite god Amurru is found in the Chaldean name [Am]raphel! Nimrod was an Amorite giant. Even as late as 1400 B.C., Amorite giants lived. King Og of Bashan ruled over the Amorites in southern Canaan. This giant's bed was 13½ feet long and almost half as wide (Deut. 3:11).

The Amorites were called the race of Martu by the Sumerians, an ethnic name synonymous with Marduk, the Babylonian name for Nimrod.[35]

Hammurabi is directly associated with the ruins of the Tower of Babel.[36] Stephen Jones in his work *Secrets of Time* also links Nimrod and Hammurabi as being one and the same king. Nimrod, under his Amorite name Hammurabi, desired to again rule the earth. Temples in his cities were erected to various angelic gods that were receiving their women as gift offerings for fertility, often in the form of virile priestesses. Once powerful enough to wage war against those other cities built by the Babel refugees, Hammurabi spread his kingdom.

> The empire of the kings of Sumer and Akkad collapsed in 1960 B.C. under their [Amorite] irresistible attack. The Amorites founded a number of states and dynasties. One of them was eventually to become supreme: The first dynasty of Babylon, which was the great center of power from 1830 to 1530 B.C. Its sixth king was the famous Hammurabi.[37]

And thus began the conquests of Nimrod. Under his Amorite dynastic name, he waged war against the whole of the Euphrates city-states that were populated from the families he once ruled over.

For Ham's sexual unrestraint, his seed through Canaan was cursed. Ham's descendants through his <u>other</u> children were <u>not</u> cursed, only his lineage through Canaan. Nimrod was in this cursed bloodline, son of Cush, who was the son of Canaan himself. Instead of submitting to the prophecy of Noah that Ham provoked, Nimrod attempted to thwart it.

> And he said, Cursed be Canaan; a servant of servants shall he be unto his brethren,
> <u>And he said, Blessed be the Lord God of Shem; and Canaan shall be his servant.</u>
> <u>God shall enlarge Japhath and he shall dwell in the tents of Shem; and Canaan shall be his servant</u>. (Gen. 9:25-27)

Before the construction of the Tower complex at Babel, the son of Cush was named Nimrod. After the Tower he was called Amraphel. Then, when he arose to power once again, he was named Hammurabi by the Amorites who also fell under the curse of Noah because of their sexual relations with Nephilim or fallen angels masquerading as gods. Many rulers of antiquity had birth names, personal names, and family, ethnic, dynastic and throne names, and some even had deified names and titles attributed to them once they where dead. Nimrod was one of the kings. He was by far the most influential and feared man during his lifetime and for many centuries later. His life gave birth to hundreds of legends and myths. Amraphel and Hammurabi are merely two different titles for a king that lived over 200 years. He may have had other names, but they are still hidden in the past. Perhaps they will soon be discovered and the life of yet another ancient and popular personality will unveil itself to be just another facade of the infamous Babylonian ruler which the Bible names as Nimrod. The fact that Hammurabi was believed to be the sixth king of Babylonia does not contradict the biblical record. Gilgamesh was the <u>fifth</u> ruler of Uruk, of Babylonia. Amraphel was second, Nimrod first, all are the same.

The date 1960 B.C. appears to be too late, according to many Bible chroniclers, for Nimrod's reign. But in all actuality if the flood did occur around 2400 B.C., as most believe, then the fall of Sumer and Akkad at 1960 B.C. is strikingly compatible. Human population growth would have been accelerated because of polygamy, <u>all</u> women considered it honorable to produce as many children with their husbands as possible. Some men had dozens of wives and as many concubines. According to the *Book of Jasher,* Noah's grandson Cush was already very old when he fathered Nimrod.[38]

Another reason why Nimrod was known by Hammurabi is because he was not defeated at the coming of the Amorites into Babylonia. Nimrod was empowered. If Nimrod was truly of giant ancestry then the Amorites were his ancestral cousins. This relation to the Amorites has fascinating implications concerning the future Antichrist and his campaign in the last days. Everything about Nimrod and his life serves us as a prophetic outline of the career of the Antichrist. These incredibly buried revelations are expounded upon in detail in coming chapters.

Like Ninsun, mother and goddess of Gilgamesh, Nimrod's mother must have been an Amorite priestess or of direct Nephilim descent. Forged by Lucifer himself in his war against the prophets of God, it is very possible that Nimrod's mother was a disguised fallen angel (succubus) who seduced his father Cush and married him. Further proof that Nimrod was empowered is found in Genesis 10:10-11. After the Babel fall, Nimrod built (or rebuilt) Babel, adding the cities of Erech (Uruk), Accad and Calneh in the beginning of his kingdom. Verse II goes on to say that, and out of the land went forth Asshur, and builded Nineveh. Alexander Hislop in *The Two Babylons* reveals that the translators rendered Assur as a proper name when it is not, being in reality the passive participle of a verb that in Chaldee (Ashurah) means to make strong, or means to make prosperous in Hebrew.[39] Properly rendered, Genesis 10:11 still refers to the exploits of Nimrod, reading, Out of that land he went forth being made strong, and builded Nineveh.

Nimrod in the Assyrian dialect is named Ninus, who was the first king of Assyria, according to Justin Martyr, Trogus Pompeius, Diodorus Siculus, and Apollodorus, all cited by Mr. Hislop.[40] Nimrod founded Assyria and built Nineveh, which literally means the habitation of Ninus.[41]

Although the Bible does not specify what kind of empowerment Nimrod gained, it is evident that his kingdom was strengthened by the people of Sumer in southern Babylonia, Queen Semiramis' direct kin. Earlier in this book we've identified these mysterious descendants of Amori. They were Amorites, or Sumerians. The city of Sumer can be seen in [Semir]amis' name. Named Amar-utu by the Sumerians, Nimrod is further associated to these Amorites because elements of their population in Sumer were called the race of Martu, a name embedded in a[mar]u[tu].[42]

The Semites (Amorites) when they invaded Mesopotamia inherited most of the Sumerian gods, but they altered their names, their mutual relations, and many of their attributes.[43]

It is a very real possibility that the Amorites infiltrated Babylonia before Nimrod's fall at Babel and loss of totalitarian control. The Amorites are mysterious and the Sumerians are equally perplexing to both historians and ethnologists. Both cultures abruptly appeared, grew and effortlessly conquered early Babylonia. Situated in southern Mesopotamia, the city-state of Sumer was inhabited not by dark-skinned Akkadians or swarthy Chaldeans, but by a fair-featured and highly advanced race of seemingly superhuman people. These people of Sumer were no doubt Amorites, tall and maintaining sexual relations with the angels, their <u>kingship from heaven</u>. Incidentally, they were descended through Canaan, the cursed lineage.

Another piece of evidence possibly linking the hero Gilgamesh with Nimrod is the startling fact that the oldest copies of the <u>Epic of Gilgamesh</u> were written in the Sumerian language, a language unparalleled by any other form of writing in antiquity. Interestingly, Maureen Gallery Kovacs in the introduction of her translation of the <u>Epic of Gilgamesh</u> states:

<u>There is no doubt that Gilgamesh was a real historical figure who ruled the city of Uruk at the end of the early dynastic period</u> (circa 2700-2500 B.C.).

If the Babylonians of Uruk (Erech) were akin to those of Accad and Sumer then it becomes apparent that Amoris progeny lived among them–the Amorites. In the whole of Scripture the Amorites are evil, unrepentant and directly associated with <u>giants</u>. Sometimes they are described as huge people. Few times there is anything good to say about them. The Amorites were from Canaan but they invaded Babylonia and ruled over the Shemites there for a while. However, they returned to their native lands, where the Nephilim were extremely active in sexual programs bringing up populations of giants that would fight against the Israelites when they came to claim their inherited land. The historic connections between the Amorites and Nimrod are shady and very ancient, but this history begins in one of the most unique stories of the Bible.

Probably the most overlooked and misunderstood story in the Bible involves Nimrod and the Amorites. It is the <u>first</u> war mentioned in Scripture and occurred in the early part of Abraham's life. Now under the name of Amraphel, King Nimrod of Babylonia sought to rule Elam in the east. Before the great dispersion of Babel, a ruler named Chedorlaomer had been under Nimrod's dominion but now that the languages divided the people, this ruler was King Chedorlaomer of Elam.

Several decades later, after the world was a much more populous community, Nimrod assembled <u>seven hundred thousand men</u> and met the hosts of Chedorlaomer, to bring him back under his dominion. The armies clashed and Nimrod's campaign was put to a stop. With six hundred thousand dead soldiers before him, Nimrod returned to Babel with a hundred thousand men. Chedorlaomer was not only victorious, but enslaved Nimrod (Amraphel) so that he would pay a tribute every year. The servant had become master. In the *Jasher* account, even the wickedly renowned son of Amraphel, named Mardon, was slain in battle.[44] Many of the deeds and attributes of Nimrod were confused with his son Mardon. Mar in Chaldee means rebel[45] and interestingly, Nimrod was remembered as Mars, god of war, Marduk and Amar-utu. By the Amorite-Su[mar]ians! Amazingly, ancient Assyrian historical archives reveal that long ago Elam conquered and overran Babylonia.[46] Chedorlaomer became emperor over the vassal kings of Amraphel of northern Shinar. These tablets also convey that Tidal assembled many tribes and peoples under Chedorlaomer.

> And it came to pass in the days of Amraphel king of Shinar, Arioch king of Ellasar, Chedorlaomer king of Elam, and Tidal king of Nations; that these made war with Bera king of Sodom, and with Birsha king of Gomorrah, Shinab king of Admah, and Shemeber king of Zeboiim, and the king of Bela, which is Zoar. (Genesis 14:1-2)

The *Book of Jasher* text concerning Genesis 14 lists Chedorlaomer, Tidal, Arioch and Nimrod, king of Shinar, further proving that the biblical person Amraphel is indeed the famed Nimrod. In Genesis 14, Chedorlaomer of Elam imposes his rulership over the cities of Babylonia, Canaan and Assyria for twelve years. In the thirteenth year of his rule, five of the Canaanite cities rebelled.

Amraphel was king of Shinar. The word king here is an ancient Semitic title, melekh, from which the fire god Molech derives. Melekh implies that Amraphel was regarded as having his power and authority sent from heaven. The name Shinar is found seven times in the Bible. All seven references are directly linked to Nimrod, Amraphel or the future Antichrist! Shinar means land of the two rivers, and refers to the regions of Babylonia and Chaldea, the lands where the Sumerians inhabited.

Arioch, King of Ellaser, means lion-like and is likewise discovered seven times in scripture. All seven are also related directly to Babylon. In another language, Arioch means servant of the moon god,[47] which further confirms Arioch's rule in early Babylonia and Chaldea, for the latter is translated the moon. In the Assyrian Tablets, Arioch's name is Eri-aku and is identified as being the nephew of King Chedorlaomer.[48] Arioch's kingdom of Ellisar is mentioned only twice in the Bible, both times allied to Amraphel and in both of the verses that Amraphel is located (Gen. 14:1, 9). Ellasar is ancient Thelasar, the realm under Nimrod that later became Assyria. In fact, in Micah 4:5-6

Nimrod is specifically called the <u>Assyrian</u> in a prophetic context amid historic symbolism. The prophet Ezekiel was also aware of the person of Nimrod as a giant and a possible historic foreshadowing of a greater antichrist to come:

> <u>Behold, the Assyrian was a cedar in Lebanon with fair branches, and with a shadowing shroud, and of an high stature.</u> (Ezekiel 31:3)

In ancient times <u>Assyria</u> had very broad dimensions, encompassing Babylonia and nearby Assyria. Nimrod's connection to archaic Assyria was unveiled earlier in this book, showing he built Nineveh and that both Nimrod and Arioch were descendants of Queen Semiramus, Nimrod being her son made husband and Arioch her grandson.[49] Arioch was also Nimrod's grandson, later worshiped by the Greeks as a war god.[50]

Like Amraphel and Arioch, King Chedorlaomer is only discovered in the fourteenth chapter of Genesis. His name means <u>servant of the god Lagamar</u>. He was an ancient Persian king of Elam, which means <u>high land,</u> and encompassed what later became Persia.

The fourth king is Tidal (<u>terrible</u>, or <u>fearfulness</u>) and like the previous three kings, is found only twice in the Bible, those being in Genesis 14. Tidal was king over the tribes and nations between the Caspian and Dead Seas and is also discovered on the Assyrian Tablets.

Fourteen years after Chedorlaomer began his rule over Canaan, Assyria and Babylonia, he marched an army of Elamites, Babylonians, Assyrians and Canaanites into Canaan to put down a rebellion led by the kings of Sodom and Gomorrah. This army was 800,000 soldiers strong.[51]

The hosts of Chedorlaomer destroyed Ashteroth Karnaim (<u>star of the two horns</u>), where many Rephaims dwelt. Rephaims here is directly translated as <u>giants</u>. The name of their city implies that they observed the stars and celestial bodies. The Rephaims are also mentioned <u>seven</u> times in the Bible, five times in the phrase "Valley of the Giants" (Rephaims). Ashteroth Karnaim was a giant city in Bashan where the enormous sons of Anak and the Amorite giant, King Og, lived in the days of Moses much later.

Nearly 1800 years later, Karnaim is still a fortified city <u>which was almost impossible to besiege or even reach because of the narrow passes that led up to it,</u> according to the writer of the Apocryphal 2 Maccabees text. Initially, this most ancient city carved out by Rephaim giants, mostly killed in Chedorlaomer's campaign, was called <u>Ashtaroth</u> Karnaim, in honor of a goddess of Canaan who was later named Atargatis by the Greeks. This goddess was worshiped in a pagan temple as far as the third century B.C. and also cited in 2 Maccabees 12:26.

After defeating the giants in Bashan, the Elamite armies advanced through ancient Ammon and drove out the Zuzims. These people were giants related to the Zamzummims.[52] They appear only once in Scripture. Zuzims derives from <u>ziyz</u>, which means <u>wild beast</u>, but in its present and plural tense it means <u>terrible ones</u>.

The third Nephilim race defeated by Chedorlaomer were the Emims in Shaveh Kiriathaim. The Emims appear once in the Bible in present tense; the other two times much later after they were gone. Concerning the region of Moab, we find

> <u>The Emims dwelt there in times past, a people great, and many, and tall, as the Anakims. Which also were accounted giants, as the Anakims, but the Moabites called them Emims.</u> (Deut. 2:10-11)

The home of these strange and very large people, Shaveh Kiriathaim, means <u>plain of the twin cities</u>. It is intriguing that Chedorlaomer invaded Canaan from the north and advanced southward to Sodom and Gomorrah. Furthermore, it is peculiar that only giant nations are destroyed. *Smith's Bible Dictionary* says <u>it was on the plain Kiriathaim that the Emims were smitten by the eastern kings who plundered Sodom</u>.[53] The Elamite federation from the east must have been specifically led by God through Chedorlaomer to eradicate the giants so that the descendants of Lot, hundreds of years later, could inherit Ammon and Moab as seen in Deuteronomy 2. If the kings of Sodom and Gomorrah were relying on military support from these Canaanite giants then King Chedorlaomer extinguished that possibility with a southbound advance through the heart of Canaan. Another reason why this Elamite ruler chose to attack from the north is because Tidal ruled many of the northern Canaanite countries bordering Sodom and Gomorrah and was probably adding to Chedorlaomer's forces as the federation traversed the lands of Canaan on their southern trek.

In *The Bible as History* by Werner Keller, we read that the <u>giants are possible survivals of ancient pre-Semitic elements in the population</u>.[54] These <u>elements</u> are angelic. Once the division of languages separated the peoples, the fallen angels called <u>kingship</u> by the early Sumerian King-Lists gave birth to giant and heroic sons through ordinary women, taken from their homes and families.

Chedorlaomer also invaded the mountains of Edom, mount Seir specifically, and killed the <u>Horites</u>. This mountainous land was prepared by God for the descendants of Esau.[55] These Horites were also mysterious, being giant-kin peoples called the Horims, cave dwellers. Werner Keller also wrote that the biblical Horites were not a Semitic people... the names on many Hurrian documents indicate that at least the princely caste must be reckoned as Indo-Aryan. This is interesting because the Aryans, according to the Indians who wrote about them so extensively in their *Vedas*, describe them as being fair-skinned and blue-eyed, a tall people described exactly the same way by the Egyptians who knew them as the Amorites.

The armies of Chedorlaomer then turned into Kadesh and destroyed the lands of the Amalekites, and then turned to their Amorite neighbors in Hazezon-tamer. The federation of four armies then made war against the combined forces of the five Sodomite armies. The onslaught resulted in Sodom's defeat and flight.

This rebellion and war is very unique in Scripture. It is the first recorded confederation of nations, the first time giant nations and their cities were mentioned. It is the only place where Chedorlaomer, Amraphel, Arioch and Ellasar are found by these names, and the only place in the Bible where the five kings of Sodom are named. Their names indicate that they were extraordinary rulers of unusual strength and ability.

Bera, king of Sodom, means son of evil. Gomorrah's king Birsha was regarded as the offspring of a god. His name means son of divinity or son of godliness, yet the name has an underlying implication of wickedness. Interestingly, Gomorrah itself means people of fear.[56] Amazingly, Birsha is found on the Ebla Tablets excavated in Syria, archaic records confirming his rule in Gomorrah.[57] Shinab was the king of Admah, his name having a dual meaning, being hostile and change of father.[58] What unnatural situation does this unique name refer to? King Shemeber too has a name with a twofold meaning, one being he who soars on high and the other was splendor of heriosm,[59] a direct descendant of the might men which were of old, men of renown (heroism) in Genesis 6:4—the Giants. He ruled the city of Zeboiim. Bela is enigmatic in origin, believed by some to be the prophet-king named Balaam in the Bible[60] and the *Book of Jasher*. Balaam's name means a stranger. It was he who caused the Midiantish women to seduce the Israelites in the days of Moses. He was a sorcerer-diviner of unusual power, definitely of Nephilim ancestry (hence stranger). In fact, all these kings were giant-kin, descended from angels. Their names support this. Son of evil, son of divinity, wickedness, hostile and he who soars on high. The latter is reflected best in the biblical prophecy against the demons found in Isaiah 10:33 that foretells that the high ones of stature shall be hewn down...

It seems evident that God Almighty used King Chedorlaomer to humble Nimrod and his Amorite allies influencing him to wage war against the angel-worshiping nations of the giant Rephaims, Emims, Zuzims and the giant-kin peoples called the Horites which were merely Amorites of a different locale. The inhabitants of these five Sodomite cities were Amorites of the lineage through Canaan. They were Nephilim-kin and much larger than the purely Adamic nations. Gomorrah is from Amôrâh, an ethnic Canaanitish word from which Amorite comes from, the descendants of Emer, fourth son of Canaan. Emer was Nimrod's uncle, born many years before and was already the chieftain of his family of dozens, long before Cush had Nimrod at a very old age. Further proof that Chedorlaomer specifically targeted the giants is found in the writings of Josephus, who wrote that, <u>these kings had laid waste all Syria, and overthrown the offspring of the giants</u>.[61]

The *Book of Jasher* reveals that these cities had four judges that ruled over each one, called Anunnaki by the Sumerians, rulers and Wise Ones. In *Jasher* 4:18 the fallen angels are called <u>judges</u>. The giant Anak who fathered the biblical giants called the Anakim was one of these mysterious judges, or guardians, as the ancient Mesopotamians remembered. In fact, Sûmeria means <u>land of the Guardians</u>.

Arba in the Bible was the father of Anak.[62] He lived in a city called Kirjath-arba (city of Arba), which was called Hebron during Moses' life when the sons of Anak terrified the Israelites because of their enormous size. Like the four judges of Sodom and Gomorrah, Arba was a giant, a Guardian of Hebron, whose name actually means <u>one of four</u>! Concerning the number of judges being four, we also see in the *Book of Jasher* that before the destruction of the Amorite capitol named Hazor (Chazar) <u>four mighty men, experienced in battle,</u> stood before the city's gates with swords and spears and would not allow the Israelites to approach the city walls. Mighty men here are <u>gibborim</u> (giants, tyrants, huge men) and they must have been truly large and intimidating to keep an army back for a while. Four ordinary soldiers could not keep back an entire invading force. However, these gate guardians were killed and the city destroyed.[63] Amazingly, over three thousand years later this custom of having four giant protectors per city was remembered and artificially adhered to in the British Isles!

> <u>Several cities in the provinces also had their giants, and we learn from an ordinance of the Corporation of Chester in 1564, "The pageant for the setting of the watch on St. John's eve was directed to consist of, among other things, four giants according to ancient custom."</u>[64]

In *Jasher* the four judges of Sodom and Gomorrah had beds <u>erected in the streets</u> to measure the heights of all newcomers by the lengths of the bed. This was done by force. The foreigner was abducted by six men who laid him on the bed and measured his height, against his will. Often, the ordeal resulted with the death of the stranger.

Further evidence that these cities were Amorite dwellings is found in Genesis. After rescuing Lot from the Sodomites who fled from Chedorlaomer, Abram had a dream from God about his descendants being captive in a strange land (Egypt)... <u>but in the fourth generation they shall come hither again: for the iniquity of the Amorites is not yet full</u>.[65] This dream was a prophetic allusion to the defeat of the Amorites by the <u>seed of Abraham</u>, descendant of Noah, of Enoch, of Adam, son of God. This dream was a confirmation of the Edenic prophecy of the contention between Satan's seed and the <u>seed of the woman</u>. Abraham's seed would grow in Egypt to become a mighty people able to overcome the Amorite giants, beginning with Nimrod.

The Bible clearly states that Abraham was from <u>Ur of the Chaldees</u>, a city in northern Babylonia in what ultimately became Assyria. This city called Ur is not to be confused with the Sumerian city of Ur in southern Mesopotamia. Ur or Urfa in the north is near Haran, a place mentioned in the Bible where Abraham's father Terah died, about six hundred miles from the southern Sumerian Ur.

Urfa is very near the Euphrates River and still maintains early traditions concerning King Nimrod and Abraham. Other indications identifying this region as the patriarchal homeland is the fact that nearby towns are all named after Serug, Nahor, and Terah, Abraham's forebears. The Ebla Tablets also locate <u>Ur in the territory of Haran</u>.[66] Interestingly, the first occupants of Haran were called H[ur]rians, and later Ururians. According to the Hurrian (Nuzi) tablets, Ariphurra was the founder of the Chaldeans, named Arphaxad in the Genesis text.[67] The Assyrians knew his descendants as being the <u>Kaldu, who were adept astrologers, magicians, and mathematicians</u>.[68]

Like the Babylonian Anunnaki, Sumerian Igigi, and biblical Nephilim, the Chaldeans were originally a race called the <u>Khaldises</u>, an order of divinities, themselves descended from a god or giant specifically named <u>Khaldis the Mighty</u> on an inscription of Argistis near Van.[69] The Chaldeans of Nebuchadnezzar's time were Chaldee by name and practices only, normal people being nothing in stature and prestige compared to their Khaldi forebears.

Before Abram's journey to Egypt from Mesopotamia, Nimrod was determined to kill him because of an earlier dream that Abram had when he was back in Chaldea. God told Abram to go to the land of Canaan, out of the reach of injury from Nimrod.⁷⁰ A unique parallel arises in the biblical and *Jasher* texts concerning Nimrod and Abram. The Bible states that Nimrod was a mighty hunter before the Lord (Genesis 10:9) and in the informative and ancient *Book of Jasher*, mentioned in the Bible,⁷¹ we discover, And Nimrod King of Babel, the same was Amraphel, also frequently went with his mighty men to hunt.⁷² Mighty men is here *gibborim*, also. Nimrod may have hunted more than just animals.

The traditional story is that God knew Nimrod would seek Abram and He raised a powerful grandson to Abram through Isaac... Esau, a mighty hunter. The *Jasher* story of Nimrod's death reminds us of the old adage, "Live by the sword, die by the sword." Nimrod heard of the exploits of Esau the great hunter and went to Canaan all the way from Babylonia to kill this rival. Nimrod lived to 215. He was born before Abram and outlived him. Esau slew Nimrod with a sword to the head in a one-on-one duel. This unnatural death indicates that Nimrod would have lived much longer, perhaps another two hundred years because he was of angelic ancestry on his mother's side. Semiramus was her traditional name.⁶⁹ ⁷³ She was regarded as a goddess.

The history of Nimrod is a prophetic mirror of the future rise, fall, and resurrection of the Antichrist's campaign in the last days. Nimrod's name after the Babel fall was changed to Amraphel (the fallen giant), but he reestablished his reign in Mesopotamia for a while and was then named Hammurabi by his angelically descended allies, the Amorites. This all foreshadows the Antichrist's fall from a sword wound to the head (Rev. 13:3, 12, 14) and his apparent and miraculous recovery. In mimicry of the resurrection displayed by Jesus before hundreds of witnesses, the Antichrist will perform this dark parallel, becoming the Hammurabi of the future, if the prophecy is right. This false messiah is the ultimate personification of the seed of Satan.

This kinship with Satan is confirmed in the name of Gilgamesh (gilgal-shamash), which is a combination of two words meaning circle and day sun, forming the descriptive name that means circle of the day sun. The ancient Babylonians called the sun the day star, a title mirrored in the biblical text of Isaiah 14:12 where Lucifer is found, which means light-bringer, and is called in the verse son of the morning which is actually translated daystar. Shamash was the sun god known to the early Mesopotamians, a deity personified from the day star, worshiped as a male divinity unified with their Ishtar and Innana, goddesses of the moon. Gilgamesh is therefore biblically referred to as a son of the daystar, Lucifer. Nimrod was of the Nephilim.

Chapter Eleven

Albion... Isle of the Giants

The most ancient historical evidences of Britain and Ireland's history derive from the oral traditions and myths of these and other European people. It is within these legends that pieces of actual history are found and where we also find information solidly in support of the biblical history of giants. Long before any humans attempted to colonize the isles of the present day United Kingdom of Western Europe, the Nephilim were already there.

> The Greeks of the early ages knew little of any real people except those to the east and south of their country, or near the coast of the Mediterranean. Their imagination meantime peopled the western portion of this sea with giants, monsters, and enchantresses.[1]

But was this imagination? The whole of Greek society thrived hundreds of years after Israel conquered and drove out the Anakim and Rephaim of Canaan and Philisia. The Bible reveals that the giants fled west from Canaan, to Gaza, Gath and Ashdod (Joshua 11:21-22), to coastal cities and regions in Philistia. This maritime nation was already in ruins by the time of the Greeks. The Philistines were worshipers of Dagon, a fish god, and Ashtoreth, a mother goddess from the stars. There exist many clues that these Nephilim-kin people had fled Philistia by sea and migrated to the ancient island of Albion, Briton of old.

> According to the earliest accounts, Albion, a giant and son of Neptune, a contemporary with Hercules, ruled over this island, to which he gave his name.[2]

This giant established his kingdom long before the Philistines reached the Briton shores. But Albion the giant, if factual, must have dwelled in the isles after the greatly remembered flood that initiated the Ice Age, an age that the Norse believed the Frost Giants ruled. In the Bible the five giant nations were the Emims, Zuzims, Anakim, Rephaim and the Zamzummins, but in the *Encyclopedia of Fairies* by Katharine Briggs,[3] we discover that the first unnamed inhabitants had perished in the great flood, but after this the fierce giants called the Firbolgs and the Fomorians were the first inhabitants of the British Isles. Where did these two giant nations come from? In the *Encyclopedia*, the Highland Fomorians were a race of giants.

Evidently, the Fomorians were a different clan of giants than the Firbolgs, the former inhabiting Briton (Albion) and the latter residing in Ireland. The giant Albion himself, according to the evidence, was a Fomorian. A third giant clan was present on the Isles called the Foawr. This name closely resembles the Old English word for giant, gawr. In the *Encyclopedia of Fairies* they are described as stone-throwing giants and could be an ancient lineage of the Fomorians. The origin of these three nations of giants must have been in Canaan, Babylonia or the older Mesopotamian city-states that Nimrod ruled over after the flood. These are where the Bible indicates that the Nephilim occupied until driven out by other nations who descended from Noah.

It is possible that Albion and Anak the giant are one in the same, or related. These Fomorians and Firbolgs might have migrated from war-torn Canaan in the days of Joshua and the Israeli conquest. They possibly arrived to the Isles around 1400-1200 B.C., or, and more probably, these giants are Emims that were driven out of ancient Moab sometime between 2000-1700 B.C. It is possible that King Chedorlaomer in Genesis 14 did not eradicate them all, but some fled.

> The first inhabitants of Ireland, according to ancient traditions, were the Firbolgs, who were conquered and driven into the western islands by the Tuatha de Danaan. The Firbolgs became the first fairies of Ireland, giant-like grotesque creatures.[4]

The Tuatha de Danaan invaded by ship. They were a warlike nation of people of inhuman stature. Dagda was their High King, the battle-lord of this great race of Danu, the Tuatha de Danaan. Danu is described as a mother goddess, which further links these mysterious maritime people to the ancient Philistines and Anakim exiles. The Canaanites and Philistines worshiped Anat, Antit, I_tar (Ishtar), Ashtoreth and the most ancient Mesopotamian goddess Inanna, all known as mother goddesses, called Queen of Heaven or Mother of the Gods. After killing King Saul and his sons years after David killed the giant Goliath, the Philistines worshiped Ashtaroth (1 Samuel 31:10).

Anu and Danu are one and the same mother goddess. Like many other deities, they come from different origins and are the result of a cultural merging of people who combined their gods. Her previous personages worshiped in Canaan and traced back to Sumer and Mesopotamia descend through cultures of old back to the Anunna:

<u>The ancient Sumerian records confirm the astral lineage of the descendants of Anak, for ancient tablets repeatedly speak of "The Anunna, Gods of heaven and earth."</u>[5]

Danu was recorded to be the ancestress of the Tuatha de Danaan. The majority of cultures past traced their descent from a great male historical figure, an archaic yet well-remembered patriarch like Albion or Anak of the giants. On the surface it appears to be that the Danaanites find their origin with a female, Danu,[6] and being Philistines with a history found in the Bible, this would be an oddity. However, when traced back to Canaan, the male counterpart to the Danaanite's ancestry emerges. While the Philistines trace their descent from Ham and then Noah, so did the Fomorian giants![7]

In the ancient Sumerian belief, the Anunna were also called the Anunnaki. <u>Ki</u> is the Sumerian word for <u>earth</u> and <u>Anu</u> was to them, long ago, a male divinity who had once lived among them but was originally from heaven. The Anunnaki of Mesopotamia back then (biblical Anakim) were considered to have resulted from a union of heaven (anu) and earth (ki). The Anunnaki were giant offspring of the gods.[8] A perfect example from the *Book of Jasher* of these mysterious beings is found in the name of a sage in Nimrod's court in Babylonia named <u>Anuki</u>.[9] Even in the archaic epic of <u>Gilgamesh,</u> the god Anu lived at one time on earth. This giant boasted that "<u>Gilgamesh is my name, I am from Uruk</u> (biblical Erech) <u>from the house of Anu.</u>"[10]

It is true that after the conquest of Canaan by the Israelites, the Philistines remained in Philistia even until today, being called the Palestinians[11] or the biblical <u>Pelishtim</u>[12], however, once David and his men killed Goliath and four of the giant's sons, the Philistine families that were larger from intermarriage with the Anakim exiles fled, knowing that they were being specifically targeted for extinction.

The male divinity worshiped by the Philistines was Dagon, a merman, half fish and half man. Living so much of their lives at sea and on coastal cities, it was important to them to pay homage to an aquatic deity. Evidence of the ancient Philistine presence in Briton and Ireland exists strongly in that merman and mermaids were believed to exist by the early inhabitants of the Isles. Though tainted by tradition, we can see how these fantasy creatures originated, being the children of Dagon. Dagon was worshiped in Philistia and Canaan as early as 1900 B.C. In chapter ten entitled <u>The Giant Wars</u> is cited historical texts proving that even the early Assyrian tyrant Sargon I worshiped Dagon. In these lands a goddess named Anu was also worshiped.

As time progressed through the centuries, Dagon and Anu became synchronized into Danaan. Tuatha de Danaan literally means <u>peoples of the</u>

goddess Danu, but the relationships between the deities are more complex. Anu, in a feminine tense is Ana, the base word found in the roman goddess Diana Di[ana]. She was a moon goddess called Ashtoreth in Palestine. She was Canaan's supreme female divinity.[13] Illustrations of Diana in *Smith's Bible Dictionary*[14] depict her with conjoined legs and fish fins over her feet. Other images of her have her wearing fins instead of feet. A mermaid. Dagon was also worshiped in a female form named Derceto.[15] Fascinating historical information about this fish god can be found in *The Rephaim*, by Miss Fanny Corbeaux. The center of Diana's cult was in Ephesus in Asia Minor, the ruins of her temple being one of the Seven Wonders of the Ancient World called Aysaluk, the city of the moon.[16]

Powerful evidence that the Philistines migrated to early Ireland and Briton is discovered in the name of the Tuatha de Danaan's High King, Dagda. This king's name derived from Dagon, their national fish god. In fact, the Hebrew word for fish is dagah, or simply dag.

The Philistines and many other Canaanite peoples were astutely pagan. They worshiped nature and sacrificed to Ashtoreth to ensure human and agricultural fertility. These places of worship were wooded areas on hills and mountains, high places forbidden by God where the powers of nature, in a feminine sense, were deified and the stars, in a masculine sense, were consulted and followed after the pattern of zodiacal ritualism. The name of the primary fertility goddess was Asherah, the Hebrew word that likewise means a grove.

The paganism of Canaan extends far into human history into the realms of the ancient Euphrates civilization under Nimrod and then later, Sargon I took these regions by force and adopted their beliefs, especially in Dagon.[17] Further evidence is found in the early Britons in the Celtic priesthood that have traced to ancient Chaldea[18] the system of their beliefs. From Chaldea (Old Babylonia) spread the occultic observation of worshiping Baalim and the groves in Judges 3:5-7.

Initially practiced by the pagan Canaanites and then adopted by many Israelites as recorded in the Bible, these tree-altars and groves were imported to ancient Briton by the Philistines and were discovered throughout the Isles by the early Trojan settlers. Later this pagan practice was incorporated into the nature worship of the early Druids and Celts who religiously regarded oak trees as sacred, thus making oak groves holy ground. This remnant tradition finds its origins not with the Philistines, but with the Anakim and Rephaim giants who worshiped the oaks of Bashan, gigantic trees in southern Canaan. In the Bible the giants later became symbolized by these enormous trees, the oaks of Bashan.[19] An old British proverb cited by Katherine Briggs is, "Fairy folks are in old oaks."[20] An interesting link between oak trees, fairies, and giants in Canaan that lived in Ashtaroth (The Star) is the fact that fairies in all the old tales among the Isles were starworshipers![21] The mythical Dryad, a female spirit called a nymph or fairy, was believed by the Druids to live only in oak trees. The appearance of deified oak trees and pagan groves permeated through continental Europe as the Celtic and Druid influence spread abroad. It was Moses who led the Israelites through Bashan, killing the giants and then Joshua destroyed the high places throughout Canaan. Og of Bashan was slain in the Conquest, a giant king who was descended from the Rephaims and Amorites that fought against Chedorlaomer in Genesis 14 and lost. The Anakim giants fled to Philistia, seeking refuge in Gaza, Gath and Ashdod on the Mediterranean Sea, but it was the Philistine worshipers of Dagon that carried the pagan oak beliefs to early Briton.

Incredibly, discovered on a rock in southern Ireland is this inscription: "We are Canaanites who fled from Joshua the son of Nun, the Robber."[22] But aside from all this proof there are yet other pieces of evidence linking the seafaring cultures.

Another clue as to the Anakim-Philistine presence in historic Ireland lies in the intriguing facts that both nations were sea-faring, both were giant or giant-kin peoples, and both spoke the same language![23] The answer to how the Philistines spoke the same language as the island Firbolgs and Fomorians can only be discovered in the Old Testament. The Philistines were mariners long before they colonized the southern coasts of Canaan and northeast Egypt. In fact, Philistia is translated land of sojourners. The origin of the Philistines has been traced back to old Crete, called Caphtor, long ago. Caphtor was an island nation in the Mediterranean Sea. In Genesis 10:14 the Philistines are said to come from the Caphtorim. In Amos 9:7 it reads, the Philistines of Caphtor. These people were already of great stature long before they migrated to Canaan. Nephilim influence in their ancestry derived not from the giants of Canaan, but from the giants of much older times called the Avims. In Deuteronomy 2 is an extensive history of the geographical regions inhabited by the giants and giant-kin peoples of old. Explained therein is the Emims, Zuzims and Zamzummims' defeat by the descendants of Noah, the Ammonites, Edomites and the Moabites. This eradication was actually begun hundreds of years earlier in the days of King Chedorlaomer of Elam in Genesis 14. Also mentioned are lesser Nephilim nations of giants, but ones smaller than the pure Nephilim-stock giants like the Anakim and Rephaim. These are the Horims, who lived in the ancient caverns that the city of Petra was hewn from by the early descendants of Esau. The other race was called the Avims. The Avims were a mysterious race of giant-kin people that lived on the coast of Canaan until the Philistines sailed from Caphtor and invaded their land, destroyed them, and dwelt in their stead (Deut. 2:23). The land of the Avims was then called Hazerim until their defeat by the early Philistines.

The Philistines then established Philistia in the land of the giants called Avims. These Avims then lived among the Philistines, submissively, as the Anakim and the Rephaim exiles of Canaan who fled from the hosts of Israel in the fourteenth and thirteenth centuries B.C. Other Avims may have fled by ship to Albion, becoming the Firbolgs. Whatever the case, the language of the giants was the same, a language known by the Philistines because of their complex history of coinhabiting cities and regions with giants. The Firbolgs must have originated from Canaan somewhere, be they former Avims, Anakim, Emims, Horims or Rephaim, in order to have spoken the same language as the Tuatha de Danaan (Philistines). Even Homer in his Odyssey uses the names Danaanites and Phaistos interchangeably as allies of the Greek invasion of Ionia and the Trojan enemies.

Centuries after expelling the Avims, it appears that the Philistines then followed them to the western frontiers, away from human civilization. To Albion, a safe haven and land of refuge. Just as the Philistines conquered them in the past, the Tuatha de Danaan then again conquered the Avims, who were known to the ancient Irish and Britons as the Firbolgs. Twice destroyed, the Avims disappeared or were merged into the Danaanite culture since both spoke the same language and it was customary for the Philistines to absorb their enemies rather than eradicate them.

In reference to the Isle of Albion, Frederick Haberman cited evidence in his book *Tracing Our Ancestors*, that mining and smelting operations were carried on by an eastern superior race. This writer further provides ample proof that such a race came from the east, which is proved by the ancient stone circles and alignments, which are identical to those of Syria, Persia, and the highlands of Tibet.[24] Also, megalithic dolmens called giant's beds are found in India, east Asia, Canaan, South Sea islands, in Europe and on into Britain, indicating a great mass migration in early times.[25]

This mysterious race abruptly appears as a southbound trek of ancient Philistines that appeared on the northernmost edges of civilization as a massive migration by land and ships along the coasts of the Mediterranean. The Hittites fell, along with every other Canaanite nation that opposed their presence. There is considerable evidence in Homer's Odyssey that the Greek-allied Phaistos warriors under Agamemnon were Philistines who aided in the fall of Troy and Ionia.

<u>Terrifying reports heralded the approach of these alien people... a trail of burning houses, ruined cities and devastated crops.</u>[26]

These Philistines marched and settled into the Hinterlands between Canaan and Egypt, provoking the Pharaohs to build their border defenses. The Egyptian historian Manetho wrote that Egypt fell dramatically when <u>unexpectedly from the regions of the east, came men of unknown race</u>.[2]

Once a vassal-state of Egypt, the city of Ezion-geber was later occupied by Philistine-Phoenicians. This port city is just a few days walk from the Anakim and Amorite cities of southern Canaan and the borders of the land of Philistia on the Mediterranean. Among the ruins of Ezion-geber are earthenware smelting-pots that have <u>the remarkable capacity of 14 cubit feet</u>.[28] Having an enormous furnace for refining metals, this industrious place once produced copper. <u>Nowhere else in the Fertile Crescent, neither in Babylonia nor in Egypt, was such a great furnace to be found</u>.[29]

In *The Bible as History*, Werner Keller reveals that similar furnaces, smaller replicas, were excavated in the Philistine city of Gaza. But still, Mr. Keller asks the obvious question: <u>How was copper refined in this ancient apparatus? Smelting experts of today cannot solve the mystery</u>.

Ezion-geber was on the coast between Egypt, Midian, Philitia and Canaan on the northern Sinia waters of the Red Sea called the Gulf of Aqaba. Its metals were exported by land and sea. <u>From Ezion-geber the ships set sail on their mysterious voyages to distant and unfamiliar shores</u>.[30]

Early Albion could have been visited and surveyed by early Philistine-Phoenicians, and even colonized. The fact that prehistoric mines and quarries have been discovered support this. Being a sea-faring nation, these people knew Albion was an ideal land to settle. Perhaps there is truth that the metallurgical practices of creating alloys, mixed metals, began with the giants, men of <u>mixed</u> lineages. The ages-old *Book of Enoch* has dozens of references to this. The Nephilim infiltrated Philistine culture because they chose to settle off the coast of Canaan in giant-infested lands. They learned the techniques of mining and the making of alloys from the giants they conquered and lived among them. This is greatly supported by the intriguing fact that Ezion-geber literally translates to <u>backbone of a giant</u>! What fossilized relic was found there by the Israelites to cause them to name this city in such an unusual way?

True to their Canaanite nature, the Philistines, or Danaanites, began building their warriors through selective breeding, attempting to produce larger and more powerful offspring like Goliath. In an *Encyclopedia of Fairies*[31] we find that after defeating the Firbolg giants, the Tuatha de Danaan began a widespread program of interbreeding with the Fomorians. The Danaanites were initially inferior to the Fomorian race, a people described as monsters and giants that were frequently sacrificed to.[32] Just as these Philistines had done with the Anakim giants, they grew larger and more powerful warriors by sexually uniting themselves.

Beat into submission and heavily outnumbered, the Firbolgs allied themselves to their Danaanite masters when war broke out in Albion. With remnants of Firbolgs in their army, the Tuatha de Danaan waged war against the indigenous Fomorians for full dominion of the Isles. After years of contention, the war was ended in the famous and often thought legendary battles of Moytura.[33] Dispersed but not extinct, the Fomorians became roving bands of nomadic giants, hermits, and were scarcely seen.

Many years later the Isle of Albion was a quieter place. Only in the faraway hills and mountains did small gangs of giants, Firbolgs, Fomorians and Foawr roam, and in the dark fens and marshes lurked solitary giants that were seen hardly at all by those who lived to tell about them. The descendants of the powerful Philistines, these Tuatha de Danaan ruled Albion but they themselves were a weaker strain than before. Without enemies, the Danaanites softened, their communities no longer advanced, but became tribal. It was then that the first purely human invaders arrived to the Isles.

The Tuatha de Danaan were defeated and driven underground by the invading Milesians. They retreated to an underground realm.[34]

This fantasy underworld realm inhabited by the defeated Danaanite giants was long ago called Tir Nan Og, the Land of Og. Here is startling proof in the Canaanite origin of the Danaanites, for Og was king of Bashan and a once renowned giant in Canaan. The Celts remembered him as Ogmius, a type of Hercules who put down many giants. Other traces of Canaanite history and memory are found in the names of Dagda's (Dagon of the Philistines) sons. Angus Mac Og is one, a giant and god of ancient Ireland of the Tuatha de Danaan,[35] and Ogme the Champion, who is detailed in one of the most ancient books of Ireland entitled, *Lebor Gebar*.[36] Interestingly, Goliath the giant is called a champion in the Bible, and *gebar* derives from the Hebrew word *gibbar*, which means giants. This dateless time of Ireland's history is literally translated as the Book (Lebor) of Giants!

Tir Nan Og was called the Land of the Young[37] because of the incredible longevity of the Danaanite people. This magical land was also reckoned as a Land of the Giants,[38] their long lives bolstered by magic, for by their enchantments they could resist the power of death.[39]

These invading Milesians, mentioned above, are mysterious in that little is known of their attack on the Tuatha de Danaan. However, Miletus was an ancient seaport in Ionia, an area occupied by the Trojans. It is most likely that these Milesian invaders were refugees of Troy after the city was burned by the Greeks. Frederick Haberman in his book *Tracing Our Ancestors* cites proof that an expedition of adventurers from the Trojan Ionic state of Miletus set out on a voyage <u>at an early date in the annals of Miletus</u>.[40]

As cited earlier, the first fairies of Ireland, often regarded as evil fiends and spirits, were the Firbolgs when the Danaanites defeated them. Now, suffering defeat themselves, these people were then driven underground, allegedly becoming fairies. This old belief in the origin of fairies is fully supportive of the ancient Enochian account that the spirits of the giants were cursed by God to roam the earth as demons and foul spirits until the day of Judgment.

<u>Danu was the ancestress of the Tuatha de Danaan, who later dwindled to the Daoine Sidhe, the fairies of Ireland.</u>[41]

The giants were the offspring of sexually disobedient angels and mortal women, taken by force or given in sacrifice to these angelic beings who were then regarded as <u>gods</u>. The Daoine Sidhe were the demons, ghosts, wraiths, spectres, goblins, trolls and other fiends that the giants had become when their physical bodies were destroyed. Katharine Briggs states, <u>Various theories of the origin of fairies are presented; fairies as the dead, or alternatively as "of a middle nature betwixt man and angel, as the daemons thought to be of old."</u>[42]

This middle nature is what this entire book is about. The Nephilim were <u>fallen ones</u> from heaven who thought to wrest the throne of God. They were a hybrid race of heavenly and earthly origins, resulting from the union of <u>Anu</u> and <u>Ki</u>, creatures or beings that now continue their war against the Creator through men. When contemplating the origin of fairies it is often suggested by the early Britons and Celts that fairies were the <u>souls of those drowned in Noah's flood</u>.[43] This comment and belief could well be accurate, since giants lived before the flood and were killed in the waters. Without the guidance of biblical texts in the first millennium B.C., these early Britons and islanders knew that the giants were fathered by angels and associated their presence with the flood. The <u>Daoine Sidhe,</u> according to Lady Wilde in *Ancient Legends of Ireland,*[44] were the remnants of fallen angels: <u>Some fell to earth, and dwelt there, long before man was created, as the first gods of the earth, others fell into the sea.</u>[45]

The history of the peoples now living in the United Kingdom once called Albion goes back over three thousand years and is directly related to the Milesians. Just like the giants, these people find their origin in the Bible. In this excursion into the fascinating past of the British people we will find how the Milesians came about.

The eighteenth descendant of Japheth, son of Noah in <u>Alanus</u>, is recorded in ancient genealogies to be the great grandfather of Dardanus. This man built a city and named it Troy after his son <u>Trous</u>. With Trous begins the Welsh genealogies and Geoffrey of Monmouth's <u>Historia Regum Brittanae</u>.[46] The Dardanians initially settled <u>around the area of Troy, whose coastal regions are known today as the Dardanelles</u>.

It was with Trous that the Trojans came about in their famous and now excavated city of Troy. This city's history is old and complex. In fact, Werner Keller in his book, *The Bible as History*, states that <u>a second Troy had long been standing upon the ruins of the first</u>.[47] These ruins were discovered by Prof. Heinrich Schliemann at Hisarlik in Asia Minor (ancient Ionia). He successfully shocked the world by breaking through the facades of Greek myth by digging up the Trojan city. These most renowned people were written about over 2500 years ago in Homer's <u>Odyssey</u> and <u>Iliad</u> and then hundreds of years later by Virgil in the <u>Aeneid</u>. The founding of the city of Troy <u>must have occurred in 1520 B.C. at the latest</u>.[48] The actual fall of Troy was told by Eratosthenes of Alexandria, Egypt, to have taken place in 1183 B.C.[49] More recent research from diverse sources agrees that Troy fell in the year 1229 B.C.

The Trojan war is a story of immense passion and sorrow, of a great people driven out by the Greeks, of Achilles and Agamemnon and their involvements with the Olympian gods who overcame the gigantic Titans. Many of these gods were actually men of historic prestige like Dardanus. This ancestral founder of the Dodanim (the ancestors of the Trojans) <u>was deified by his descendants and worshiped under the name of Jupiter Dodanaeus (here we have a mingling of the names of Japheth and Dodan)</u>.[50] The Roman name Jupiter derives from the name Iupater, which in turn finds its beginning in Iapetos, the Greek name for Japheth of the Bible.[51]

The Trojans trace their lineage through Tiras back to Japheth, son of Noah. They worshiped the deified version of their forefather Tiras, calling his name <u>Thurus (i.e. Thor), the god of war</u>.[52] Thor is the prime deity of the Norse, recognized by the old Celts and highly regarded throughout the entire ancient and modern European pantheons. Thor fought against the Frost Giants, protecting Asgard, the realm of the Norse gods and Yggsdrasil, the tree of life. William Cooper in his thought-provoking research, *After the Flood*, finds evidence that Thor is uniquely connected to the ancient Trojan city of Troy.[53]

After the destruction of Troy in Ionia, the Trojan survivors fled to a predetermined location:

> On arriving at the place of rendezvous, numerous fugitives of both sexes were found, who put themselves under the guidance of Aeneas.⁵⁴

Troy was burned to the ground, the capitol of the Trojan state. Aeneas was a valiant warrior and descendant of Trous, listed as one of the principal leaders of the Trojans. He led the Trojans to Italy where they remained for several decades. Aeneas' great grandson was named Brutus. He was considered to be a Trojan noble, but born in Italy.

From Italy, Brutus led an armada of 320 sails to a certain island, which they found destitute of inhabitants, though there were appearances of former habitation.⁵⁵ Other accounts have Brutus' fleet at 324 ships.⁵⁶ Knowing that this was not a place to colonize, he sailed further west, happening upon another colony of Trojans ruled by a man named Corineus. Corineus is listed in the early British genealogy as a possible cousin of Brutus around 1100 B.C., which remarkably coincides with the traditional date of the fall of Troy, being 1193 B.C. So just over ninety years after the fall of Troy, the two colonies merged to become one body of exiles, a small nation.

The Milesians mentioned earlier were also from Ionia, from the city of Miletus, a Trojan city-state. Miletus was a port city and it's more likely that Corineus was raised among the Trojan exiles of Miletus after the Greeks burned Troy. Corineus is famous in history for destroying a race of giants, so it is he that probably led the Milesians to Albion where they defeated the Tuatha de Danaan. The name of their commander was Duke Corineus... who could overthrow even gigantic opponents.⁵⁷ Unfortunately, because the giants were not completely gone from the Isles, Corineus retreated to a lesser island where Brutus found his colony. Corineus fathered Gwendolen (1081 B.C.), who became the wife of Locrinus, son of Brutus.⁵⁸ This was after Briton was established and Albion was no more. After joining forces with Corineus, Brutus led the ships to the shores of France where they were violently attacked by settlers on the shore. Sailing on, Brutus followed the instructions of a mysterious prophecy. In *Milton's History* is cited a quote from a Trojan goddess, recorded by Geoffrey of Monmouth:

> Brutus! Far to the west, in the ocean wide,
> Beyond the realm of Gaul, a land there lies,
> Seagirt it lies, where giants dwelt of old.⁵⁹

In the research of Frederick Haberman we are given an alternative translation of this prophecy, which reads, in the last line, ...giants once possessed, now few remain, instead of "where giants dwelt of old."⁶⁰

Brutus searched for a seagirt land, an expansive island good enough to build a kingdom. Gaul was mainly Germanic so Brutus knew his destination was further north along the coast of Europe. But before arriving to this ancient giant realm, they passed another island, not dissimilar to their destination.

> The Cyclopes were giants, who inhabited an island of which they were the only possessors.... They dwelt in caves and fed on the wild productions of the island.[61]

The Cyclopes were giant sons of the sea god Poseidon, named Neptune by the Romans. These are the giants that the Greeks claimed inhabited the western islands. The primeval giant Albion may have been a Cyclops. Homer described the Cyclops as being a brute so huge, he seemed no man at all.[62] Albion was also a son of Neptune.[63] Herodotus described a community of people where far north of the regions of the Scythians, dwelt men among them who had but one eye.[64] Pliny also cites a most archaic tradition about a race of one-eyed people called the Arimaspi, who lived beyond Palus Moeotis.[65]

In the *Odyssey* and the *Iliad* we discover Cyclopean islands, but they are not the island home sought by Brutus. Albion is also pictured as a Cyclops because these giants were also called ogres in Virgil's *Aeneid*. In traditional Irish lore, the ogres are giants called Formorians.[66] The *Odyssey* refers to one of the giant sons of Poseidon as Eurymedon, commander of the Gigante in the olden days, who led those wild things to their doom and his.[67] Detailing his travels at sea among the western islands, Odysseus says, "In the next land we found were Kyklopês (Cyclopes) giants, louts, without a law to bless them... Kyklopês have no muster and no meeting, no consultation or old tribal way, but each one dwells in his own mountain cave..."[68]

The Titans are the Gigantês who warred with the gods long ago. Homer wrote his epics with haunting accuracy in chronology and geography. A number of antiquated sources told of islands that harbored giants. So prevalent was this belief that even to this day, walls and edifices constructed of enormous boulders of various shapes, form-fitted together, are still called Cyclops walls.

After sailing many days north of the Cyclopean islands, Brutus anchored his fleet on the enormous island of Albion. Albion was, in a manner, desert and inhospitable, occupied only by a remnant of the giant race whose excessive force and tyranny had destroyed the others.... And there the hugest giants dwelt, lurking in rocks and caves, till Corineus rid the land of them.[69]

Upon arriving to the island, Brutus became king and named it Briton. According to William Cooper in *After the Flood*, the Britons (former Trojans) did not establish themselves until 1104 B.C., approximately 300 years after the end of the Ice Age, caused by the Flood in 2348 B.C. (Ussher's Chronology). Other than the Frost Giants, no one lived on these isles before the Fomorians, Foawr and Firbolgs because of the inhospitable conditions and glacial terrain of prehistoric Briton. The polar ice caps extended dramatically closer to the equator during the Ice Age, a freezing epoch that endured for almost a thousand years. This frozen land is what preserved so many of the giant megalithic relics still standing today in Ireland and Briton.

Knowledge of these large western islands was not new. Throughout the first millennium B.C., Phoenician sailors told stories of the giants that darkly mirrored the mythology that told of these cyclopean savages on the isles of the Great Sea. Aristotle wrote, <u>In this ocean, however, there are two islands, and those are very huge, and are called Brittanic, Albion, and Ierne...</u>[70] Brutus knew that an enormous island existed somewhere out there, beyond the edge of the know world. Even in the ancient Hebrew Torah commentary called the *Book of Jasher*,[71] the isle of Brittania was known and inhabited as far back as the fourteenth century B.C.

In a most incredible work of research containing evidences of both ancient and modern giant remains called *Giants, Dwarfs and Other Oddities,* by C. J. S. Thompson, M.B.E., is a confirming statement concerning Corineus: "<u>There are many other stories of giants in Cornwall, a county which abounds in legendary lore, and is still the home of fairies and the "Spriggins," who are believed to be the ghosts of giants who guard hidden wealth.</u>"[72]

Brutus built Trojanova (New Troy) while Corineus organized hunting parties that fed the people and occasionally fought off <u>remnants of the giant race</u>. Corineus had already been to this island and defeated the Tuatha de Danaan a decade or so earlier, but now, reinforced with more and younger Trojans from the ranks of Brutus, he renewed his campaign against the giants and Danaanites, and almost drove them to extinction. This intensity was most likely motivated because the Danaanites themselves were a part of the forces that aided the Greeks in destroying the Trojan states on the Mediterranean in Ionia. Also called the Phaistos in Homer's *Odyssey*, these epic Danaans were the Philistines of Canaan.

Those who followed Corineus became known as the Cornish people. They settled part of the isles known today as Corinea. The giants <u>were in greater numbers there than in all the other provinces</u>.[73] He did not put an end to the giants on Briton though, or giant-kin people, but he did succeed in decimating their populations and drove them deeper into the wilderness so they no longer posed a threat to Trojanova's sovereignty. <u>They forced the giants to fly into the caves of the mountains</u>.[74] Trojanova was known by several names over the millennia as the Britons lost some remnants of their past and history over the expanse of time. However, the historians of old did not forget and have made us aware that Trojanova is none other than London, England today.[75]

As centuries passed, the Britons, Celts, Norse and other European peoples began warring against each other, and the threat of marauding giants were forgotten. But they still were lurking out there. Reports filtered into the cities from distant stretches of the country of large beasts, monsters and even giants even as late as the sixth and seventh centuries A.D. Occasionally encountered by hunting parties was the dreaded Athach, which means monster or giant. This large humanoid beast haunted lonely lochans or gorges in the Highlands. Like Grendel's mother in the epic poem *Beowulf*, some of the athach beasts were female.

Akin to the Athach was the hideous Direach, a giant descendant of the Fomorian Cyclopes. It had one eye in the middle of its forehead and was known by locals long ago as the desert creature of Glen Eiti in J.F. Campbell's *Popular Tales of the West Highlands*.[76] As we will find shortly, the Direach was not the only one-eyed giant residing in the hills.

A subterranean monster thought to surface occasionally was the Ciuthach, a cave-dwelling giant of long forgotten antiquity. In the *Celtic Review* (vol. IX) we find that the legends of the Ciuthach may have an ultimate historical basis.[77] This Ciuthach was evidently more primitive than the Gruagach, which is described as a supernatural wizard, often a giant. The word Gruagach means the hairy one.[78] Like the spell-casting Tuatha de Danaan, these giants were regarded as wizards.

The common denominator between the names of all these giants is the -ach suffix, which evidently is indicative of larger than normal size. Ath[ach], Dire[ach], Ciuth[ach] and Gruag[ach] all describe male beasts; however, there existed other creatures that were noticeably female. In fact, the earliest appearance of a female giantess is the Tuatha de Danaan queen named Fuam[ach] in *Gods and Fighting Men* by Lady Gregory.[79]

The Caille[ach] bheur of the highlands was a blue-faced hag who seems to be one of the clearest cases of a supernatural creature who was once a primitive goddess, possibly among the ancient Britons and Celts.[80] She is related to the Caille[ach] bera, which is a class of gigantic hags in the mountain wilderness of Ireland. Later, she became reckoned as an evil spirit or fairy, much like the Danaanites.

To further link these monstrous hags to the giants of the Tuatha de Danaan and Firbolgs are the tales of the Black Annis. This female giantess was reclusive, a nocturnal hag ever so tall with long stringy hair, large teeth, and feared by mothers with newborn children. The Black Annis was a witch giantess that ate people, with an appetite for infants. The name of this dark fairy, Annis, derives from the Celtic mother goddess Anu, which is a form of Danu of the Tuatha de Danaan, Danaan being a composite of Dagon-Anu (Ana-feminine form).⁸¹

Said to be a descendant of an ancient bloodthirsty goddess, Black Annis was one-eyed, livid-faced and long clawed.⁸² It appears that this Annis hag was similar to the Direach, a giant descendant of the Fomorian Cyclopes. Long after the lore and legends of giants passed on to the realm of mere fable, the British and Irish of the Dark Age and Middle Age eras still told of gaunt, wandering hags with bluish skin and unusual height. Like the female Grendel in Beowulf, called an accursed outcast (line 1267), the Annis and Cailleach lived among ruins, caves and secluded woods, rarely daring to encroach upon human territories.

Another forlorn demonic like Grendel is an archaic being from the underworld named Aillen, a restless remnant of an elder race, long ago forced by mortals into the other world beneath the Irish hills.⁸³ Aillen was a musician of the Tuatha de Danaan of former times, until Corineus destroyed his race. Aillen was reduced to a hideous form that stalked the surface world only during All-Hallow's Eve (Halloween). This evil fairy is also described in *The Enchanted World...Night Creatures*, as a full two heads taller than any human.⁸⁴ This physical description is significant because of its Egyptian parallel cited earlier in this book, where the Philistines are depicted in Egyptian artistic reliefs as exactly two heads taller than their Egyptian adversaries. This elder race was none other than the Anakim-related Philistines from Canaan. In fact, Annis appears to relate directly to Anak, which finds its origin from the Sumerian Anunna, a supernatural being that fathered the giants. *Smith's Bible Dictionary* also confirms this unique size difference, stating that the Anakim were a race of tall people, who lived in Hebron.... They appear on monuments of Egypt as tall and light colored, and are called the Tammahu, from the Hebrew Talmai. Talmai was one of the great giants that the ten spies feared when they searched out Canaan, a son of Anak himself.

Another direct link the Tuatha de Danaan maintained with Canaan and their Philistine ancestors was their affinity for music and the playing of instruments. Like Aillen of the Danaan fairies, no people were more devoted to music than the inhabitants of Canaan... an inexhaustible treasure house of musicians.⁸⁵

The fairies became increasingly popular as the fear of giants subsided and became distorted with time and through inconsistent oral traditions. The more renowned fairy folk were elves and goblins, both enchanting and sometimes ghastly remnants of the legendary Tuatha de Danaan that lived below Ireland. Mermaids and mermen were feared greatly as harbingers of destruction to the

British and Irish, who had no bridges to Europe or North America, save by sea.

But be they land or sea, the common link between the physical traits of the various kinds of fairies on the British Isles and continental Europeans are the random deformities discovered when fairies are more closely examined. These include cleverly hidden mutations, aberrations, webbed fingers or toes, cloven hooves for feet concealed with long dresses, and even cloven hands, bone deformations, missing limbs, etc. People associated these defects with evil, with fairies being considered demonic servants of the devil. It is quite probably that these mutations were caused by normal people engaging in incestuous affairs, genetic mutations caused by inbreeding. This was a very common practice among the biblical giants, forbidden by God, but passed down into human society. These unfortunate children were regarded by the ignorant commonfolk as "children of the devil," and fairies. But it is true that not all of these cases were natural. The historic defects in fairies can be found more extensively in *An Encyclopedia of Fairies* by Katharine Briggs.[86]

These same deformities are what gave the son of the Philistine Anakim giant Goliath twelve fingers and toes. Inbreeding among the Nephilim nations and its mutating effects became so pervasive in ancient Canaan, that giant-kin peoples were raised to expand the gene-pool, found in nations such as the Avims, Horims, Sabeans and the Philistines. Because of genetic disfunctions unforeseen by the Nephilim, these giants forced lesser and weaker pure human nations to pay homage to them by sacrificing their daughters over to them, as concubines for the giants.

The Canaanite nations were expelled from the Promise Land because they feared the Rephaim and Anakim that ruled over them. They were guilty of giving over their daughters to false gods. The Almighty told Abraham that in four hundred years his descendants would become a great nation, as the stars of heaven. This could not occur immediately because, as God stated, the sins of the Amorites was not yet full.[87]

The Amorites were inbreeding with the giants, becoming a giant-kin nation of extraordinary stature, also found in the art of the Egyptians, as cited earlier in this book. God was patiently giving the rebellious Amorites a reason for Him to destroy them utterly. Like the other Canaanite nations, the Amorites were defeated and lost all trace of their ethnicity. But some of the Philistines made it to Albion. And these Danaanites, after being greatly diminished and subdued in war, maintained constant intercourse[88] with the early Trojan settlers. This contact gave birth to more people of incredible size that will be examined later in chapter 14, The Bones of Giants.

Chapter Twelve

Epics of the Giants

Giants are the most common and thoroughly ignored presence in the vast majority of ancient literature. From the four thousand year-old *Epic of Gilgamesh* to the late one thousand year-old poem *Beowulf*, giants are discovered in fascinating accuracy when compared to the biblical accounts of the Nephilim. Between these two historic epics are the famous Homeric epics called the *Odyssey* and the *Iliad*, both lengthy stories about gods and giants that archaeologists and historians marvel over even today. The Roman poet and writer Virgil continued this art form of epic preservation in his articulate collection called the *Aeneid*. His contemporary in the first century B.C., Ovid, also wrote about the giants and their conflicts with the gods and mortals.

So far, in this book, we've discovered historic information about giants as recorded by Homer, Virgil, Ovid and many other epic writers, even in the Gilgamesh text. However, it is this latest epic poem entitled *Beowulf* that we learn the most stunning and intricate insights into giant history and beliefs. "This ancient poem was truly preserved by God, for only one burnt copy of the thousand year old epic remains and it is located today in the British Museum."[1] Under Catholic persecution long ago, all known copies of *Beowulf* were burnt and their owners punished severely.

> Beowulf is the sole survivor of what may have been a thriving epic tradition, but it is great poetry. Approached as an archaeological relic, it is fascinating. Taken as a linguistic document, it is a marvel, a mine of revelations and controversies. It gives us vital information about many things that scholars would like to have much more information on.[2]

Long ago, as far back as a few decades after the flood, bards and sages would tell stories, weaving their history into a poetic cadence, often using harps or other instruments for effect and entertainment. Entire stories line by line were memorized and told with great effect. Later these traditions passed from being solely oral to written epics that preserved the oral stories and beliefs in new artistic forms that earned their tellers high esteem and a good living.

Even today, these poems are hauntingly vivid despite their translations no longer having the effect of rhythm. Like the power experienced within the pages of our Bibles, these ancient epics echo of times magically familiar to us, deep within our being.

> These are stories of folklore and romance, which run back from the medieval courts through Celtic legend and minstrelsy to archaic Sumer, and perhaps further, to the very beginning of story telling. [3]

William Cooper has put together a very scholarly and convincing argument for the historicity of the ancient Old English epic *Beowulf*, identifying names in the poem in archaic Danish and Anglo-Saxon genealogies, including the Geatish warrior, Beowulf himself. This research is found in William Cooper's book *After the Flood*, a fascinating and new look at ancient and modern Anglo-Saxon history.

The Anglo-Saxon race, along with the Geats, Swedes, Gauls, Norse, Celts, and Scythians, among others of European ancestry, are all more recent descendants of people who trace their bloodlines directly back to Mesopotamia, to the patriarchs Japheth and Noah. The Norse remembered the giants as enemies of the gods, evil Frost Giants that terrorized their ancestors during an ice age long ago. The Celts recorded their battles with the last Firbolgs and Fomorian giants and then later, with the Tuatha de Danaan, all huge and violent peoples. And now, in *Beowulf*, is discovered a knowledge of evil giants by the ancient Danish and Geatish people. The author of this famous poem is no longer known, lost in the mists of history and Catholic oppression, but his belief in the existence of giants and their biblical history is unquestionable. In Burton Raffel's creative translation of *Beowulf* we read:

> He was spawned in that slime, conceived by a pair of those monsters born of Cain, murderous creatures banished by God, punished forever for the crime of Abel's death. The Almighty drove those demons out, and their exile was better, shut away from men; they split into a thousand forms of evil-spirits, and friends, goblins, monsters, giants, a brood forever opposing the Lord's will, and again and again defeated.[4]

It is interesting to us today that the author of this poem believed that monsters and giants were born of Cain and were banished by God, a parallel found in Genesis when Cain himself killed Abel and was banished by God to depart from Eden. Before the flood, when the sons of God rebelled sexually against God and impregnated women, this hybrid union gave birth to the giants. The Nephilim. It was probably Cainite women who fathered the giants after being abducted by these fallen angels. Also of interest is the connection made by the author between giants of the Bible to times *before* the flood, identifying the fathers of these giants, indirectly, as being fallen angels or demons.

The belief of old that giants and demons were one and the same has incredibly ancient origins. The writings of Enoch, another epic-like collection of stories, revelations, and prophecies concerning angels and giants confirmed this connection long ago. The book of Enoch explains that when giants die, evil spirits shall proceed from their flesh, because they were created from above, from the holy Watchers was their beginning... evil spirits shall they be upon the earth, and the spirits of the wicked shall they be called.[5]

John Milton reflects this archaic belief in his modern epic of the seventeenth century entitled, *Paradise Lost,* in which we read that the original fallen angels became fairies, having sons of enormous stature long ago that in more contemporary times have become diminutive:

> ...in bigness Earth's Giant Sons
> now less then smallest Dwarfs...[6]

William Cooper's genealogy of the Royal Geatish House has Beowulf living from A.D. 495-583. The members of Beowulf's family and ancestors as listed in the poem are also discovered in the genealogy and traced directly back to Noah by ancient chroniclers such as Geoffrey of Monmouth in his *History of the Kings of Britain*. Having a definitive place in northern European history, the writings in *Beowulf* thus strengthen the writings of Enoch concerning the giants and their demonic relations. In Burton Raffel's translation of *Beowulf*, in the back of the book, is an Afterword by Robert Creed. In this Afterword we find more proofs that this epic contains many verifiable events, a work of true history. Concerning *Beowulf*, Dr. Paul Carus wrote in his book, *The History of the Devil and the Idea of Evil:*

> There are innumerable legends which preserve the old conception and simply replace the names of giants by devils...[7]

The entire plot of the *Beowulf* epic concerns these giants. Already by the time of this saga, the giants were no longer existing as a civilization. Beowulf traveled to help the Danes kill Grendel, a fierce beast that haunted the fens and swampy moors. Before his famous stand against the creature he boasted, "I drove five great giants into chains, chased all of that race from the earth."[8]

Here is evidence that the early Anglo-Saxon people regarded the giants as a race and not regarded as random mutations caused by inbreeding. This is not unusual and nor would it have been contended by the first millennium B.C. and A.D. Britons, Celts, and Norse, all who incidentally trace their ancestry to post-diluvian patriarchs who had lived long ago, when giants were a much more common threat.

Beowulf kills a monster called Grendel, a beast that lived among reptilian creatures with sharp claws and teeth. William Cooper cites evidence and provides photographs of archaeological relics of stone and clay figurines of prehistoric-like creatures. Dinosaurs. In his book, *After the Flood*, he reveals astonishing historical proofs and records of these and other creatures, now extinct, that evidently lived in the swamps and lakes of Europe over a thousand years ago. A complete list of 71 zoologically applied terms in *Beowulf* is in Cooper's fascinating book.

After the defeat of Grendel in a wrestling match where Beowulf tore off the monster's arm, bards immediately compose songs and poems of Beowulf's bravery, weaving their lyrics into older songs about heroes long ago. The unknown narrator states:

> ...There were tales of giants wiped from the earth by Siegmund's might.[9]

The writer of the poem describes these verses of Siegmund as being from old songs, revealing that the giants were a part of their distant history. Just as the people alive during the epic's story have been identified in early genealogies, so also has Siegmund been discovered in the genealogy of the East Saxon kings as Siegmund, fifth descendant of Sledd.[10]

This archaic race was believed to have been born of Cain before the flood. Speaking of Cain, the writer states, And he bore a race of fiends accursed like their father.[11]

To the author, all demons became monsters, fiends and giants. After Beowulf killed Grendel, the monster's mother ate a Danish warrior in King Hrothgar's renovated hall, beginning her revenge. One of Beowulf's soldiers was eaten the next night as well. Beowulf meets the fog-giant Grendel and defeats him.

> ...he then encounters Grendel's mother, the giantess of the marsh whence the fog rises...[12]

Traced back to early Briton, we find many parallels concerning the giants in Beowulf and the giant remnants detailed in the previous chapter, Albion... Isle of the Giants. There were hill giants, mountain giants, storm and fog giants, all related to the Firbolgs or Fomorians. In *Bulfinch's Mythology* are found huge mountain giants allied to the Frost Giants that warred against the Norse gods. Grendel is also described as being very large in the Time-Life Books collection called *The Enchanted World...Night Creatures*:

> Although manlike, that being was no man. Huge and hairy, it shambled through the night mists of fell and fen...[13]

Beowulf hunted the mother of Grendel (a female giant) in a swamp and found her among the ruins of an ancient hall that the creature was using for a lair. His own sword useless against the she-beast, Beowulf wrestled her as he had done her son. Unlike any woman today, this monster had incredible strength and pinned Beowulf to the stone floor of the dilapidated building.

> Squatting with her weight on his stomach, she drew a dagger, brown with dried blood, and prepared to avenge her only son...[14]

Beowulf had entered the swamp with the mindset of defeating the giant without a weapon, as he had done her son. Or so he boasted. But during the unique conflict, Beowulf frees himself from her grasp and sees:

> Hanging on the wall, a heavy sword, hammered by giants, strong and blessed with their magic, the best of all weapons, but so massive that no ordinary man could lift its carved and decorated length.[15]

This passage calls to mind the many citations in this book concerning the metallurgical practices of the giants, of the Anakim of the Bible and Anunnaki of Babylonian antiquity, both of which have their name derived from ancient words for metals, as expounded upon in earlier chapters. These giants mined rare and precious metals and were smiths that incorporated vast intelligence, alchemy and adept metallurgical skills into their weaponry. Today, people regard giants as being clumsy, unintelligent and mythical, but not long ago they were perceived as agile, malicious and highly skilled, with their workmanship considered of magic.

Another unique connection we see in the person of this giantess in relation to the old Celtic and British beliefs in giant hags and witch-giants, is the fact that in the epic *Beowulf* this female giantess is also called a monstrous hag.[16] She is also called a horrible hag, fierce and wild.[17]

After slaying Grendel's mother in the ruins, the hero returned.

> ...but all that Beowulf took was Grendel's head and the hilt of the giant's jeweled sword...[18]

Grendel was not a single creature but the name of the mysterious giants known to hide in the swamplands, away from human civilization. The *Beowulf* epic makes careful mention of other monsters, great beasts that fit perfectly into today's versions of prehistoric creatures. In *After the Flood*, we discover that many prehistoric animals became extinct because climatic conditions after the deluge were more frigid compared to the global tropical weather before the flood. This atmosphere and weather promoted the growth of such great beasts as the dinosaurs. The flood caused global cooling with an ice age, where Frost Giants became the greatest threat because the enormous reptiles were dying.

The *Book of Enoch* indicates that the rebellious angels known as the Watchers were imprisoned during the flood as a foreshadowing of the eternal imprisonment these sexual angels will suffer. After the flood, these angels were again released. And when the angels shall ascend, the waters of the springs shall again undergo a change, and be frozen.[19]

The global cooling effected by the flood and the collapse of the aquatic atmosphere that entrapped earth's geothermal heat and magnified the sun's light, initiated an ice age in which the northern and southern poles and regions for thousands of miles became desolate, frozen, glacial wastes. Only the equatorial lands were habitable for nearly five hundred years after the flood, which is why most archaeologists concede that the cradle of civilization was in Mesopotamia, which was merely the land where the descendants of Noah multiplied. They became nations that eventually began wandering away as the ice melted and the earth became a warmer place.

Because of these colder climates, the reptiles and creatures no longer grew to their former sizes, nor lived as long. But remnants of these creatures survived and dispersed to areas around the world more suitable to their nature. And the warm lakes, fens, swamps and marshes of Finland and Denmark were one of these havens. It is a possibility that the Loch Ness Monster is more fact than fiction because of this historic occurrence.

Grendel was personified as a demon by the author of *Beowulf*. Being an early Christian writer this is not unusual, however the word grendel was used in the English transliterations to describe such phrases as terrifying ugly one,[20] solitary walker,[21] terrible,[22] evil doer,[23] devil,[24] accursed outcast,[25] fierce in battle,[26] and giant.[27] The word for giant is found in line 426 of the epic, *Thyrs*, which refers to the male Grendel Beowulf killed first.

Earlier we learned that the Fomorians (Irish giants of old) were hideous in appearance and could easily be described as terrifying ugly one(s). Since no good giants are found in Scripture, it is not surprising that giants have been universally associated with the devil and evil-doing by scores of historical texts and traditions. The description of Grendel being <u>terrible</u> fits perfectly with the biblical giants called Emims, for <u>terrible</u> is the translation of their name. All the giant nations, the Anakim, Rephaim, Emims, Zamzummims and Zuzims were warlike, <u>fierce in battle</u>. No Nephilim people ever knew peace.

There is little description of Grendel except for these and other literal translations of the creatures called <u>Grendel</u>. In fact, in the *Beowulf* text we discover that Grendel is said to walk <u>like a man</u>, an attribute very rare, save for humans. This proves Grendel was no ordinary monster. Speaking to Beowulf, King Hrothgar said,

> <u>"I've heard that my people, peasants working in the fields, have seen a pair of such fiends wandering in the moors and marshes, giant monsters living in those desert lands. And they said to my wise men that, as well as they could see, one of the devils was a female creature. The other, they say, walked through the wilderness like a man, but mightier than any man..."</u>[28]

This description of the beasts gives forth the image of a giant humanoid creature. Although other fierce reptilian animals are described in *Beowulf*, it appears that the Grendel beasts slain by the hero were giants that lived in some ancient ruins in a swamp. The peasants mentioned by the king could discern that one of the creatures was female from a distance. If truly reptilian, this would never have been so easily noticed. Also, reptiles or amphibian creatures have no <u>hair</u>.

After slaying the first Grendel's mother, Beowulf then decapitated her and <u>carried that terrible trophy by the hair</u>.[29] Admittedly, Beowulf had killed giants before, but this Grendel was the first giantess he's slain.

If these Grendel beasts were descended from ancient Nephilim giants, then they would have been intelligent. The giants were forgers and metallurgical masters that definitely retained the intelligence to have a written language. Here in this archaic Old English poem is found astonishing historical accuracy in what is regarded today by the intellectual elite as mere myth. Beowulf used a <u>mighty old sword</u>[30] to kill the giantess in the ruined hall where Grendel dwelt.

> <u>He gave the golden sword hilt to Hrothgar, who held it in his wrinkled hands and stared at what giants had made, and</u>

> monsters owned; it was his, an ancient weapon shaped by wonderful smiths...³¹

This inspiring rendition by Burton Raffel calls to mind the biblical stories of trophies kept in remembrance of the giants so popular in Bible history.

Earlier in this book is cited the Scriptures where the giant named Og was killed and his 13½ foot bed was kept as a trophy by the Ammonites. And then David killed Goliath with his own giant sword after knocking the Philistine giant unconscious with a stone. The sword of Goliath was kept in a temple and many years later was wielded by David again.

> The old king bent close to the handle of the ancient relic, and saw written there the story of ancient wars between good and evil, the opening of the waters, the flood sweeping giants away, how they suffered and died, that race who hated the Ruler of us all and received judgement from his hands. Surging waves that found them wherever they fled. And Hrothgar saw runic letters clearly carved in that shining hilt, spelling its original owner's name...³²

This enormous sword given to King Hrothgar of the Danes was called an ancient relic almost fifteen hundred years ago! The Sumerians and Akkadians of Babylonia remembered the smith-giants of old, calling them Anunnaki and Anakim. Goliath was a descendant of the Anakims that fled Canaan and found refuge in Philistia, away from the conquests and bloody campaigns of Joshua and the invading Israelites.

When David killed Goliath he took the giant's sword as a trophy of his feat—as Beowulf had also done. Both heroes gave these relics away. The amazing aspect of this giant sword hilt is the runic letters. The runes were used only by initiates in mysterious Celtic and Druidic worship and practices. As cited earlier, the Celtic and Druid beliefs migrated from greater Canaan and ultimately from the regions of Chaldea in Mesopotamia. The runes were called moon letters long ago, specially imprinted with light wax, invisible unless held up to the moon or candle to be read through the paper, thin vellum, or parchment. Runes developed from the ancient Akkadian cuneiform letters, crescent-shaped letters resembling little moons. Remarkably, Chaldea is translated as the moon. This runic inscription upon the hilt of the sword was probably inscribed by Tuatha de Danaan people, enormous in stature and from Canaan and Philistia, as cited throughout this book.

The details in *Beowulf* concerning the flood are uncanny in their biblical accuracy. The flood was issued by God because of the utter chaos wrought by the giants. If the rebellious angels had not sexually integrated with humans and the giants were not a hostile presence among God's people during the days of Jared, Enoch and Noah, then the Creator might have judged the earth in a very different way. But He did not. Nor is there any biblical evidence that Noah was told to warn anyone of the coming flood. Earth was corrupt and God washed her clean.

Also, the *Beowulf* text reads that the flood was caused by <u>the opening of the waters</u>. This unique phrase is descriptive of the collapse of the firmament above, as detailed in the Genesis creation account. This marine atmosphere rained upon earth, sending <u>surging waves</u> over the planet. This abundance of water caused global cooling. A drop in temperature around the world caused the north and south poles to accumulate ice rapidly because they are the farthest distances from the equator. To relieve the immense stress and weight at the poles, the arctic regions fragmented and still continue to do so, sending glaciers and icebergs toward the equator.

A Roman epic writer and historian named Ovid also wrote about the giants, metallurgy, and a flood that destroyed them with their wicked practices.

> Then comes <u>the Age of Iron, and the day of evil dawns... man tore open the earth and rummaged in her bowels. Precious ores the Creator had concealed... were dug up.... So now iron comes with its cruel ideas. And gold with crueller... But not even heaven was safe. Now came the turn of the giants... They coveted the very throne of Jove</u>.[33]

Ovid lived over forty years before Jesus and may have still been alive at the age of eighty or so during Christ's ministry. Being a Roman citizen and being a scribe, Ovid had access to many ancient archives and traditions recorded by former scribes. His information is eerily aligned to the biblical records concerning the giants and their rebellious nature. According to Roman and earlier Greek beliefs, God destroyed these giants with thunderbolts, and then later, the Creator flooded the earth to kill men. Ovid wrote that Jove addressed the other gods, saying, "<u>When the giants, whose arms came in hundreds... reached for heaven, I was less angered. Those creatures were dreadful but they were few-a single family. But no...I have to root out, family by family, mankind's teeming millions.</u>"[34]

At the end of Burton Raffel's translation of *Beowulf* are two sections of interest, an Afterword, and Glossary of Names. The Afterword is a detailed study of the historical applications of *Beowulf* by Robert P. Creed. This research provides many insights into the people of ancient Denmark, Sweden and other relative European people mentioned in the poem. Like William

Cooper in *After the Flood,* he puts forth very persuasive evidence in the historical accuracy of *Beowulf.*

In the Glossary of Names at the very end of the Raffel translation is a list of the characters in *Beowulf* and their relationships to each other, as well as information that historians have gathered about these ancient people.

In the Glossary we find Grendel. The text states that the etymology of this title is perhaps related to the Old Norse word grindill (storm). This comparison is interesting because of the Norse belief in Frost Giants. The icy realm of the dead to these archaic Icelandic people was called Niflheim, a word directly derived from Nephilim, the fallen ones. The giants of Bible antiquity were known as the Dead Ones, being the Rephaim, which is plural of rapha (dead; very tall), a unique Hebrew word having a dual meaning. So Niflheim of Norse memory could very well be the icy realm of Rephaim, the dead. Remembered as Frost Giants, the Norse also associated these giants as storm-bringers, akin to grindills. Storm giants. Even the word giant in Old English, gawr, is comparable to the Hebrew word for huger man, which is *gibbar*, found in Genesis 7:4; mighty men which were of old, men of renown.

The Anglo-Saxons and Norse were racial cousins, their ancestry sharing distinctive parallels, along with many other European peoples such as the Gauls, Celts and Danes.

In modern occult lore, found extensively in adult fantasy role-playing games and other fantasy books, is discovered the Frost Giants, Fomorians, Firbolgs and ogres, all giants driven out of ancient Canaan and Europe by the early Britons, Celts and Norse invaders. This same occult lore, which explicitly details the appearance and traits of these Nephilim-kin nations, also features the enormously feared Storm giants—the Grendels.

Their ancient civilizations lost to the judgements of God, the giants migrated further west, to Gaza, Gath and Ashdod in the thirteenth century B.C.[35] These giants and giant-kin peoples are identified in Homer's *Odyssey* and revealed earlier in this book as the Phaistos (Philistine-Phoenicians), and the Danaans, who allied with the Greeks under Agamemnon at the destruction of the Trojan states and their capital city, Troy. The Danaans migrated to ancient Albion, where they battled Nephilim refugees from Canaan and possibly remnants of giant Rephaims, Emims and Zuzims, who fled from Chedorlaomer, who had tried to eradicate their race in the days of Abraham. These giants were called Firbolgs by the early Trojan colonizers under Brutus and Corineus, who'd fled from the Greek invasion of Ionia. For a complete historical account of the Tuatha de Danaan's arrival to Ireland and battles with the Firbolgs, read *Gods and Fighting Men*, by Lady Gregory.[36]

By the first millennium A.D., the giants as a civilization anywhere on earth were no more, reduced to solitary walkers like the Grendels, vagabonds and swamp recluses so degenerated, they were incapable of reading the runic inscriptions on the old relic hilt given to Hrothgar, a weapon made by their own ancestors. Like the Yeti of Tibet's mountains and desolate reaches and the Sasquatch of northwestern America and British Columbia, the Grendels were a forlorn, bestial remnant of an ancient and powerful race cursed by God, best described in *Beowulf* as an accursed outcast.[37]

Like Beowulf of the Anglo-Saxons, a hero lived long ago among the Sumerians, Babylonians, and Akkadians named Gilgamesh. And not unlike Beowulf, this royal figure has been identified as being a real personage of distant antiquity, the king of biblical Erech ruled by Nimrod, called Uruk in the *Epic of Gilgamesh*. Also, just as the Geatish hero slew a giant at the edges of human civilization, Gilgamesh killed a giant much larger than himself, even though he himself was of partial giant ancestry. The giant slain by the Sumerian hero was named Humbaba, the Guardian of the Cedar Forest.[38] This Cedar Forest has been located by archaeologists as being in Lebanon, but interestingly, the *Epic of Gilgamesh* has been discovered in fragments as far as Canaan near Megiddo, a land once inhabited by enormous people.

What makes the *Epic of Gilgamesh* so much more unique than *Beowulf* is the archaic symbolism discovered throughout the ancient text that corresponds beautifully with biblical passages. Unlike *Beowulf*, which does not contain many parallels with biblical history, the *Gilgamesh* tablets not only reflect Bible history but reveal astonishing revelations through symbols found only in our Bibles. It unveils a lost language, a form of communication preserved by the Bible's writers, but lost to contemporary civilization.

> My son, in Uruk lives Gilgamesh; no one has ever prevailed against him, he is strong as a star from heaven.

The term star of heaven is representative of more than one idea. In line 107 of the first tablet of *Gilgamesh*, the hero is said to have strength as mighty as the meteorite of Anu. This word kisru was translated meteorite in the text, but this Akkadian noun could also be accurately rendered–lump of metal.[39]

This phrase hints again at the heavenly metallurgical practices taught by the Watchers and their giant offspring. To be compared with a star of heaven was an honor akin to being called god-like. On old Sumerian and Akkadian texts and monuments, every symbol of a god was also connected with a star.[40]

In previous chapters we discovered intriguing passages in the Bible located in both testaments that describe and associate stars of heaven with angels, which are revealed to be greater in power and might than ordinary humans. Gilgamesh is herein compared with a supernatural being, which is further seen in the *Gilgamesh* epic.

> He will come in his strength like one of the host of heaven.

The art of conveying vital information through unobtrusive symbols permeates throughout Scripture. In the epic is found that Humbaba was also called watcher of the forest. The title Watchers is found in the very old books of Enoch, Jubilees and even the Bible, in the book of the prophet Daniel. The Watchers were guardians and Humbaba was doing just that. This rebellious order of angels fathered the giants, which is reflected in the *Gilgamesh* text.

> In the forest lives Humbaba whose name is hugeness, a ferocious giant.

Symbols were used by ancient writers to reveal things often misunderstood or not believed, and protected the writers from criticism when others openly defied them. Having written in symbols, the authors could easily apply another meaning to thus appease any dissidents. Dr. Paul Carus most articulately explains the usage of symbols and encrypted writing:

> Symbols are not lies; symbols contain truth. Allegories and parables are not falsehoods; they convey information. Moreover, they can be understood by those who are not as yet prepared to receive the plain truth.[41]

Humbaba is killed by Gilgamesh, the giant being identified as a north Syrian, Anatolian or Elamite god.[42] The parallels found in this ancient Sumerian epic that correspond with the Bible go deeper. The biblical giants called the Anakim are the same Nephilim race as the Babylonian Anunnaki. Like the Philistine-Anakim giant Goliath in the Old Testament, we discover that Humbaba the giant had a sword of eight talents. As David kept Goliath's sword and Beowulf the giant sword hilt of Grendel, Gilgamesh took this enormous sword. The fact that Humbaba was a giant guardian conveys that he was keeping post for others or for something of value, and this is what is discovered by Gilgamesh. After slaying the giant, the Sumerian hero came across the sacred dwellings of the Anunnaki.[43] Anakim giants of the Bible were renowned for their height and metallurgical skills. Gilgamesh later traveled to visit Noah, who was named Utnapishtim in the Babylonia-Akkadian version, and heard a story about antediluvian life and the flood. The *Epic of Gilgamesh* is fascinating and should be studied by all serious Bible students.

> He was wise, he saw mysteries and knew secret things, he brought us a tale of the days before the flood....

Chapter Thirteen

Relics of the Gods

Four thousand years ago thrived advanced civilizations whose vast and complex engineering feats still remain with us today in thousands of archaic sites, structures, and artifacts.

These stargazers of old possessed knowledge that our modern fathers of astronomy have merely <u>rediscovered,</u> their ancient wisdom and arcane ingenuity being adopted into our textbooks as recent discoveries.

Like the great pyramid in Giza, their knowledge was immortalized within the architectural confines of their structures. Many of the archaeological relics still stand intact as they did for millennia ago, inspiring fantastic stories and legends passed down by hundreds of generations in cultures spanning over every continent on earth.

South America boasts ruins containing blocks weighing as much as 40 tons (80,000 lbs.). How these gigantic stones were elevated still remains a mystery, a feat we cannot match today. These forlorn monuments are still being discovered beneath the foliage of South American jungles and continue to reveal, by architectural design, the times and seasons when certain planets and constellation were visible, including the equinoxes, the positions of the sun, moon, and other stellar bodies in relation to the earth, and many more astronomical revelations that prove that incredibly strong and intelligent men long ago retained scientifically accurate calendars that were as reliable as those we have today.

The South American city of Tiahuanaco is a pre-Incan city complex of enormous edifices and stone works. Two huge monoliths, the gates of the sun and moon, were each constructed from single stones weighing as much as 100 tons, 200,000 lbs.[1] Constructed by engineers utilizing building and planning techniques far too advanced for the two thousand year-old ruins, this city was complete with an amazing sewage system and water works. Local traditions claim that a race of giants build these monuments and incredible structures, but this notion is dismissed with the same intellectual prejudice evoked by locals who try to explain the origins of other ancient prehistoric sites around the world. Often the oral traditions of primitive natives are more accurate than the assertions of archaeologists. Old Yucatec beliefs convey that a previous race left behind great temples and heavy monoliths, and the Seri Indians to the north told stories of an ancient race of giants now extinct.[2] The impressive ruins still standing, left behind by the Toltec Empire, antedate the Aztecs by a thousand years.[3] The Aztecs believed that these archaic people were taller, swifter, and wiser than normal humans.[4] The fall of these mysterious Toltecs is ascribed to the deity that had descended from the sky named Titlacahuan, which means, We are his slaves. The Toltecs subsequently fell into ruin.[5]

Many of the abandoned stone buildings regarded as sacred by the Tarahumara Indians were left behind by their ancestors long ago, who were called the Raramuri, an evil race in former times until God was said to have destroyed them. These Indians hold that the skeletons of the Raramuri are still found in many caves where they died while attempting to hide from God.[6] Interestingly, the name Raramuri identifies these ancient people as Amorites, sun worshipers of the ancient second millennium B.C., from Mesopotamia and Canaan. The Amorite-Sumerian deity Amurru is embedded within Rar[amuri], with the prefix "Ra" being the Egyptian word for Sun God.

Evidently, many North and South America cultures believed that they were visited by deities from the heavens. The Jicaque traditions truly stand out because they claim the ancients were banished from the Earth's surface and thus rose into the sky, becoming stars![7] The fascination of ancient men being in or from the stars is traced back to the first civilization after the flood. The flood was not so much a supernatural event, but rather the result of a major astronomical phenomenon. The melting of glacial landmasses could have effected the climate change and eventual flooding of the continents, but more probable proof is cited and explained by Immanual Velikosky in his book, *Worlds in Collision*. He scientifically explains how Venus was initially a comet that closely orbited earth long ago, before being caught in the sun's orbit, with its gases solidifying into a planet. This ancient, erratic fly-by caused intense stress on the aquatic atmosphere earth once enjoyed (a firmament above, which we've on a few, separate occasions), destroying it. This oceanic atmosphere collapsed and flooded the earth.

Still standing in Chichen Itza, Mexico, is a giant architectural relic left behind by the Mayan civilization. The building is an apparent celestial observatory, one of a group of star-temples thet were constructed strategically in accordance with other observatories that were aligned with solar bodies, so that the Mayans could predict the exact times of lunar and solar eclipses with scientific accuracy, thought possible only in recent times.[8]

The rotation of earth as observed by the Mayans may reflect why the Mayan calendar was cyclic, involving a series of endless catastrophes and renewals of the earth. Their calendar began after the flood, an event they remembered and claim was the end of the previous age, and beginning of the present one.[9]

Where could these people have acquired such sophisticated information? These Incan, Aztec, and Mayan civilizations were isolated for thousands of years away from the rest of the world. Or were they?

Maps dating a thousand years old have been discovered that are but mere replicas of even more archaic maps and charts of long-forgotten authorship that illustrate perfectly the seven continents, including islands and rivers. These ancient cartographers navigated the seven seas long before Magellan or Columbus set out on their landmark voyages. Explorers from forgotten civilizations and distant antiquity, long before Cortez or Lewis and Clark, charted the rivers, mountain ranges, and regions throughout ancient America. This includes the accurate coastline of Antarctica, completely buried today in a polar ice cap, but seen today in early surviving maps like the Piri Reis and Finaeus maps. Who, so long ago, could have charted the arctic seas and coasts of the Antarctic before the ice cap appeared? It was evidently not there until the last ice age.[10]

Another mystery in North America is the gigantic earthworks of stone and soil found on the Mississippi River in Illinois that resemble truncated pyramids so ancient that the untrained eye can easily mistake them for natural hills. Among many beliefs concerning these and other earthen mounds throughout the United States, is the idea that a civilized race of giants constructed these colossal monuments.

One of the most carefully designed cities of distant antiquity is the Indus Valley civilization of Mohenjo-Daro. Dated to the third millennium B.C., this ancient city was already in ruin by 1800 B.C. for reasons unknown to historians. Many modern cities of the twentieth and twenty-first centuries were not planned and built as carefully and meticulously as Mohenjo-Daro. The remains of the homes, courts, alleys, gutters, sidewalks, streets, hostels and public and governmental buildings and temples were constructed of masonry not unlike many of today's edifices.

Thousands of pictographic relics and inscriptions have been excavated since the city's discovery in 1922, but their strange language has yet to be translated.[11] It is very possible that this most ancient site was excavated and rebuilt after the flood by people who wandered there from Mesopotamia. If this were an antediluvian city (the third millennium partially antedates the flood), then this would explain the uniqueness of the pictographic language unknown to historians, and found only at this archaic locale. Although there is no indication of the presence of giants among these mysterious people, there is the presence of advanced engineering knowledge and city-planning. But further, the city is too ruinous to determine the size of its occupants. Its remote location has placed it outside the traditional biblical areas for its time, which provokes the suspicion that Mohenjo-Daro could have once been an Amorite (Aryan) dwelling-place, where giants were raised outside of the contemporary civilizations of old.

> The civilization of the Indus Valley also has some very early beginnings. Prof. Waddell, who has done diggings and research in this location, shows by ancient Indian official king-lists and chronicles, that this civilization's recorded history extends back to 3100 B.C.[12]

This remote date biblically antedates the flood and may be slightly anachronistic, however, traces of Aryan presence have been found all throughout ancient India, even in Mohenjo-daro.[13] Earlier in this book is cited considerable evidence from biblical records, Egyptian reliefs, and the old Sanskrit Vedas of India, that the fair-featured Aryans were regarded as terrestrial gods with celestial parentage, great people called the Anakim in the Bible, Tammahu on Egyptian monuments, and Amorites by the early Mesopotamians.

Though the long forgotten king lists of India do reach far into the past, even to the precipice of the third millennium B.C., they have no pre-flood history to substantiate a dynastic beginning at 3100 B.C. In the old Indian Sanskrit writing called the Rig-Veda, the supernatural Aryans survived the flood, but an antediluvian past is still nonexistent.[14]

Concerning these seemingly indigenous Aryan-Amorites of India, there was found unearthed in the Chinese desert of Takla Makan in 1985, a naturally mummified woman, her flesh in an incredible state of preservation ... estimated to be 58 years old, and was fully adorned in an unusual diagonal, twill-weave blouse, boots, and jewelry. This unique woman's skull was strangely pointed; she had a long, narrow nose and thin lips, blond hair and deep-set eyes. What most surprised her discoverers was her almost six-foot height. This humanoid fossil was dated at 1000 years before Christ.

Her amazing descriptions are very similar to the Indo-Aryans and Canaanite Amorites, and even the Anakim giants of much greater size.

This intriguing woman naturally mummified due to the arid climate, with atrophic dehydration of the corpse causing severe contraction of her tendons and ligaments, which drew her bones closer together. In life, this most ancient woman stood over six-foot tall and the males of her racial culture were no doubt typically taller. This 3000-year-old mummy openly defies the evolutionary concept that modern man is further developing in size from primordial hominids. Very few women today stand to a height of six feet.

Her ancestry is further proven by excavations of lost Indo-European texts discovered at her gravesite and their decipherment using Sanskrit writings.[15]

Henry Mouhot of France heard of an ancient, ruined city complex hidden deep in the jungles of Cambodia. In 1860, he ventured into the mysterious depths of the tropical forest and into a vast stone city called "the ruins of Angkor" (also called Angkor Wat today). This deserted metropolis in the jungle is almost 38 square miles of bare and cracked foundations, causeways, temples, water canals, shrines and habitations of various sizes. Its irrigation network is complex in design and exhibits the fact that the builders had architectural methods and planning unparalleled until recently.

Archaeologists have determined throughout the meticulous excavations that Angkor was a city destroyed and rebuilt several times. It was the largest city in the world in A.D. 1000, housing about 500,000 people. But this thousand year-old Hindu city was only a rebuilt remodeling of an even more ancient metropolis dated two thousand years *earlier*, to 1000 B.C. When the mystified Henry Mouhot asked the Cambodian natives over a hundred years ago about the city's origins, he was told that the jungle civilization was built long ago by giants.[16]

Although this book has extensively detailed giant activity in the traditions of eastern peoples, and especially in the traditional Bible lands, it is evident that larger than normal people have lived elsewhere and left behind their influence upon many people. Even in America. Although America is the most ignored region of the planet by archaeologists, there have been some startling discoveries in the past two centuries. Discovered in Eureka, Nevada, in 1877 were the fossilized remains of a human leg partially embedded in quartzite. The remains measured 39 inches from the toes to just above the knee cap.[17] This person, if still alive today, would stand over nine feet in height!

A nine-foot tall man is difficult to conceive of. Most would rather confine the presence of such huge mysterious people to the stories in our Bible, but the truth is, there are a few giants still alive today, among us. The *World Book Encyclopedia* exhibits a photograph of a man in the Middle East who stands seven feet ten inches! A modern giant. He is located under the giant entry. The *Guinness Book of World Records* also exhibits men of incredible height. Remnants of giant ancestry can be found throughout society today.

There is no end to the possibilities of what archaeologists might unearth if only the New World was regarded more seriously as the domain of lost civilizations that were evidently here. But even without modern scienctific approaches to native American history, there is still a tremendous amount of evidence already uncovered about these forgotten civilizations.

In the blistering Mojave Desert lies an enormous picture on the ground that can be seen clearly only from a high altitude. Such pictures are regularly seen around the world and are referred to as geoglyphs, earth pictures often found in North and South America and in Britain. This Mojave geoglyph is called the Blythe Giant, named after a nearby California town[18] The Mojave Indians claim that a wicked giant terrorized their ancestors.

Native American neighbors of the Mojave Indians were the Navajo that dwelt in the New Mexico/Arizona regions. These Indians worshiped a god of war named Nayenezgani, who they believed once lived in the San Juan Valley area. According to the Navajo people, long ago during an age now almost unremembered, lived a wicked race of powerful giants all over the earth. These fierce and large people assembled and made war against humanity in an attempt to destroy all humans, but before they could succeed, the god Nayenezgani descended and killed them off with a great calamity. The most fascinating aspect of this Navajo tradition is the unique translation of this god's name. Nayenezgani literally means slayer of alien gods.[19]

In South America, there are huge pictures of giants and humanoid figures all over the expansive Nazca plateau in Peru. Geoglyphs of animals, intricate designs, and simple patterns can be seen from high altitudes, their origins unrecorded and just as mysterious as the giants themselves. Giants in Central and South American Indian lore are usually relegated to the ancient time and said by some to have been the first race.[20] In Popoluca lore, the giants not only lived as a powerful historic race long ago, but according to them, both male and female giants are still extant as forest-dwelling cannibals.[21]

In Chile lies the mysterious Atacama Giant, a bulbous-headed figure over 300 feet from head to feet that strikingly resembles a tall version of today's E.T.[22] Thousands of miles away, far north of these ancient earthworks and designs are discovered great geoglyphs of giants in East Sussex. Called the Long Man of Wilmington, this old chalk design is a giant that stretches upon the ground at a height of 231 feet. This artistic relic has been dated to be twenty-five centuries old and could be an inscribed memory of the dreadful Firbolg and Fomorian giants that had once roamed freely through the Isles.

Even North America boasts of dozens of earth patterns and ancient circle sites of various sizes, wheels of stone circles upon earthen mounds or amidst open areas where they could better be viewed from the sky. Bighorn Medicine Wheel in Wyoming is one example of the more popular circle-stone sites. Like the pre-Incan Nazca earth art, these shapes are not easily recognizable from the ground. In fact, the vast majority of geoglyphic designs and patterns were not discovered until the advent of flying in this last century.

The presence of geoglyphic art and earth pictures that can only be viewed from the sky proposes a great mystery to those unaware of the true history of our most distant ancestors. These ancient people of Mesopotamia built huge step pyramids with astronomical implements of stone to record the events in the heavens. Solar and lunar calendars were scrutinized, and the skies searched nightly for strange developments that could be signs of the gods returning.

These enormous star temples have been excavated by the hundreds and can be found in many varieties, and were discovered in the Americas as well. Called ziggurats in the Middle East by archaeologists, these stone observatories had no function other than for celestial purposes. In the Bible, the very first building mentioned is the tower of Babel, an edifice destroyed by God and believed by many to have been a ziggurat. In Britain today are geoglyphs of men and horses. The most famous is the Cerne Giant, a 180-foot figure holding a knotted club aggressively, and exhibiting an erection that earned him the name of the Obscene Giant by locals. English lore claims a giant Danish man was beheaded there, but the presence of an erection on the naked giant, however, appears to contradict the English claim that a Danish soldier died and instead hints to more distant times. The details in the geoglyph appear to relate giants as having violent sexual tendencies. This geoglyphic relic could very well be from a pre-Celtic era when the Formorians or Firbolgs, the ancient Irish giants, inhabited these isles or from later, when the mysterious Tuatha de Danaan occupied early Ireland and Britain.

Stonehenge and other neolithic monuments could be related to giants. Stonehenge was originally a circle of about 75 megaliths, some weighting as much as 100,000 lbs. These colossal stones were transported from a blue dolerite quarry 130 miles away. How were these incredibly heavy and cumbersome boulder-sized rock slabs carried? Perhaps there are historic ties between the ancient Tuatha de Danaan and Formorians and the hundreds of other stone monuments throughout Britain and northern Europe.

In the old text called *History of the Kings of Britain* by Geoffrey of Monmouth, Stonehenge was called Chorea Gigantum long ago, which means Dance of the Giants.[23] Local traditions differ, some claiming that Irish giants built them and others telling of angry gods who petrified a group of giants around a bonfire. One of these traditions, supported almost a thousand years ago by Geoffrey, is that Merlin the Magician, a man of great learning long ago, said that Stonehenge was erected by an ancient race of Irish giants who carried the stones from Africa![24]

Stonehenge is known the world over, but is not the only mystery left behind by giant architects. Silbury Hill in England is also a prehistoric site, a mountain of earthwork 130 feet high and covering an area of almost six acres. It could very well be an antediluvian pyramid that was reduced to rubble by the rushing flood waters.

Europe boasts of the largest known megalith in the world, which today lies broken in four huge pieces at the edge of an ancient burial site. The monument is called the Fairy Stone and originally stood 65 feet tall before an earthquake felled the colossal rock in 1722.[25] How could ancient men have carried and erected this 350-ton (700,000 lbs.) monument?

Frederick Haberman in his book, *Tracing our Ancestors*, cites an interesting connection:

> The giants which Brutus encountered in large numbers, as told in the Chroniclers, were no doubt the early Aryans, who reached the western isles almost a thousand years previous [circa. 2100 B.C.]—the people who piled up ancient mounds and erected the circles and other megalithic monuments.[26]

The Aryans, as we've revealed earlier in this book, were of much greater size, called Anakim, Amorites, Indo-Aryans, and many more names. Exactly who constructed these incredible buildings is hidden far in history, but like the tall, mummified remains of the Aryan woman excavated in the Chinese desert of Takla Makan cited earlier, the skeletal remains of these large people are unearthed in the European Isles as well, providing us further insights into Britain's misty past. In A.D. 1184, King Henry II learned that the remains of the legendary King Arthur were buried at the Abbey of Glastonbury. But if this body belonged to the mythical king, it would be difficult to prove. At the site indicated by King Henry, monks excavated an 8 foot tall skeleton with a crushed skull, which evidently caused the person's demise. Lying in the grave beside this unusually tall man was a small female skeleton.[27] In the nineteenth century, a man named Robert Hunt studied many artifacts and megalithic sites in Old Cornwall and discovered near Dartmoor that the people in those parts believed that their land was long ago inhabited by giants.[28]

Other examples of enormous edifices are the huge stone-hewn faces on Easter Island that the Polynesians have no true memory of erecting (although they claim they did), nor do they have the technical capability of such a feat. The Sacsahuaman stone temple, with overly large steps that ascend up to an enlarged chair-like recess, is another unexplained megalithic monument. Erich von Daniken theorized in his highly controversial book, *Chariots of the Gods?*, that these steps led up to a throne for giants. Though his perceptions as to the origins of extraterrestrials is contrary to the findings in this book, Mr. von Daniken's theory may be more accurate than he believed.

The enigmatic stone structures and unexplained monuments not only appear in the British and Pacific Isles, North and South America, continental Europe and the Far East, but in the often overlooked desert wastes of Saudi Arabia and the Middle East—ancient areas that were once flourishing, subtropical regions now buried in the sunburnt sands of growing deserts. Even the old Muslim beliefs held in the writings of Quran reveal that long ago, in the south of Canaan in Arabia, giant-kin people existed. The Ad people were tall in stature and were great builders in the Arabian peninsula, ancestors of the fourth generations from Noah.[29] This lineage is probably Amorite, from Emer. The fourth in the lineage was Nimrod, being Noah's great grandson, who was empowered by the presence of Amorites in his early kingdom. The Ad people described by the Islamic traditions resemble the Amorites. They are detailed in the Arabic text as having a stature tall among the nations.[30] These Ad people were later known as the Thamud, people who cut out huge rocks in the valley.[31] These rocks are described as dolmens, called giant's beds all throughout Arabia and Canaan (Palestine and Iraq today), and are located as far north as Ireland and Britain and at hundreds of sites in between the Isles and Saudi Arabia. In reference to the Thamud, the *Presidency of Islamic Researches, IFTA* commentary reads that the remains of their buildings show that they were gifted with great intelligence and skill.[32]

But the evidence of giants today is not restricted to things such as ancient buildings and skeletal remains. Historical and modern evidence continually surfaces from Tibet and North America concerning eyewitness accounts and physical evidence of giants today. Deep in the Himalayas of Tibet is believed to be a Bigfoot-type creature referred to as the Abominable Snowman. Known as the Yeti, this reclusive giant wanders the snowy regions of Tibet's mountains and thick forests foraging for food. Though passed off as a comical farce and mere myth by Americans and others outside of Asia, the Yeti is both feared and respected in Tibet.

The legendary cousin of the Yeti is Bigfoot, also called Sasquatch by the Salish Indians of British Columbia and the northwestern states of America.[33]

Vast compilations of eyewitness accounts and research of footprints far too large to be human, has been conducted for many years. Evidence from animal carcasses and footprints have led most Bigfoot researchers and hunters to estimate that the Sasquatch stands between nine and ten feet in height and weighs approximately seven hundred pounds. It is possible that these creatures may not be of the same stock or genus as the various biblical giants, but they are giants nonetheless.

Sasquatch is described by the Indians as a lonely giant, hairy and bipedal, closely resembling a humanoid ape. Footprints in soil and snow have been photographed to a great degree and studied. It is doubtful that the two isolated creatures, Bigfoots and Yetis, are hoaxes. Both the Yeti and Sasquatch were encountered long before American or other non-native explorers and scientists began documenting information about these creatures. Both of these creatures must, in some distant connection, have something akin to the ancient Nephilim. Bigfoots are described as intelligent and keenly aware when they are being observed. It is an odd occurrence for a Bigfoot to exhibit violent outbursts and the creatures have an extremely developed ability at vanishing into thickets and woods. Unlike the evolutionary scientists and their propaganda, the Yeti and Sasquatch are not primitive forms of hominids, but highly intelligent vagabonds left behind by a race of giant men that died out a very long time ago. The northwestern areas of America, with its expansive forests, along with the valleys, caves, and slopes of the Himalayas, provide perfect refuges for these remnants of giants.

Footprints found of these creatures are not often photographed due to the fragile condition of the evidence. Ice melts and dirt washes away with water. Erosion destroys much of the most perfectly preserved footprints. But petrified mud cannot be lightly regarded. The most fascinating footprints of giants ever discovered is located, petrified, in the Paluxy river basin in Texas. The location is called Dinosaur Park in Glenrose. These ancient human barefoot prints are 22 inches long and found amid dinosaur tracks. The existence of the giant footprints in Texas is solid evidence of the Biblical veracity concerning the Nephilim and early post-flood history.

Evolutionary scientists have misinterpreted the assorted layers of strata caused by flood sediments deposited according to their weight and density by attributing them to geologic ages of millions of years. According to these scientists, the dinosaurs lived up until 65 million years ago on the supercontinent they have named Pangaea, but many dinosaurs were alive later, sometime before the flood, to coincide with man and the human tracks, found together in Texas.

The deceptive intentions of evolutionists is concealed within the name of this alleged supercontinent. Pangaea is an occultic title blatantly honoring two Greek divinities; Pan and Gaea. Both, we have learned earlier, derive from more ancient non-Greek deities that find their origin with none other than Nimrod the giant, and his mother-wife named Semiramus. Pan was the satyr (devil) and Gaea the spirit of Mother Earth and mother of the giants, the Titans. Nimrod was the first legendary King of Babylon, according to Masudi, and married to his mother and first queen, Semiramus. Their incestuous offspring was the Akkadian deity, Tammaz. Nimrod, one may recall, is credited for building the Tower of Babel.

The collapse of the vapor canopy and resulting flood caused global cooling that resulted in thick ice caps at the north and south poles. This explains how ancient maps chart the coastlines of Antarctica when today they are hundreds of feet below the ice, and how prehistoric creatures and tropical vegetation have appeared petrified in the frozen rock of Siberia, Greenland, and other polar regions.

Christian minister, researcher and writer, Noah Hutchings, cited in his work *The Great Pyramid... Prophecy in Stone*, tangible evidence of this devastating polar shift:

> On August 30, 1996, a news report given over Canadian television reported the discovery of a frozen forest only eight hundred miles from the north pole. This was not petrified wood, but preserved trees with the roots of the stumps still embedded in the soil.[34]

During the vapor canopy years the entire earth, even at the poles, had a warm climate due to a greenhouse effect. After the canopy collapsed and the flood was over, the atmosphere changed. It became cooler, especially near the poles where ice formed and it snowed, freezing the forest mentioned above in this newly-created wasteland. This sudden cold snap caused a rapid Ice Age, which took about 1000 years to melt (more on this can be found in the Epilogue).

All this shows that our geologic history is different from what we've been taught. The giant that left his footprints in Glenrose, Texas, is powerful proof that the evolutionary time frame of Pangaea and geologic ages is far exaggerated. It also proves without dispute that the Biblical version of flood sedimentation and later continental division is real.

American archaeologist, Ron Wyatt, excavated a peculiar amphitheater-like complex with an enormous stone that was evidently placed there like an altar, near Dogubeyazit, Turkey. Mr. Wyatt states that, "It was obvious that whoever stood upon this altar was quite a bit taller than we are, for the step is about three feet high." Extremely large stones were used in the surrounding edifices, even a very large boulder balanced upon several upright stones. Mr. Wyatt declared that whoever erected these rocks must have been, "...very strong, because today many of the large rocks could not possibly be moved by humans without mechanical assistance."[35]

The presence of enormous artifacts has baffled man from the very earliest of times. Even Josephus claimed that in his time (first century A.D.), the bones of giants were displayed and studied.[36] The ancients associated mystical places such as Stonehenge and other rock monuments or bones discovered in caves or barrows, with bizarre and often demonic activity. Evil spirits haunted these forlorn ruins. Gods descended and performed strange rituals. Devils danced among these giant rocks during full moons. Fantastic creatures such as trolls, imps, and dwarves were often believed to have accepted or left behind gifts, a tradition mimicked today by those who leave Santa Claus milk and cookies.

Unknowingly, many parents are guilty of continuing this pagan tradition by planting money under their children's pillows, while giving the teeth of children to tooth fairies.

The origins of much folklore and myths actually derive from the mysteries proposed by ancient men who wondered where these strange monuments came from. It was the prevailing opinion in antiquity to assume these Nephilim relics were associated with the gods of lost and forgotten worlds detached from our own. In fact, one of the greatest examples of the Scriptural precept of cyclic history and reoccurring occultic beliefs (as the Mayans believed in their cyclic calendar), is the ancient and recent emergence of the belief in extraterrestrial life.

Chapter Fourteen

The Bones of Giants

Viking navigators sailed the oceans of the northern hemisphere from continental Europe through the scores of islands in the United Kingdom to Iceland, Greenland, and the untouched coasts of North America. These often-misunderstood people are labeled as savage and barbaric by historians and writers because of their apparent size and battle prowess when, in fact, the Vikings were astronomers of the highest caliber. Unlike the Chaldean astronomer-priests and Egyptian adepts who gazed up at the heavens for omens and celestial consistency, the Vikings lived by the stars and constellations, navigating to remote corners of our world on dragon ships once thought to be inadequate for long sea voyages.

The Vikings were racially a very large people. The men of Viking clans were known to have stood almost eight feet tall, though their average heights were measured between six and a half and seven feet.

The earliest known text that unveils the enigmatic lives of the ancient Vikings is called the Ibn Fadlan Manuscript, an eye-witness account over one thousand years old written between 921-926 A.D. by an Arabic ambassador named Ahmed Ibn Fadlan. This man went on a journey into the far north on an errand for the Caliph of Bagdad, into the snowy regions far beyond the domains of the Arabian empire. Fadlan encountered a company of Norse Vikings, calling them "Northmen," and wrote, "Never did I see a people so gigantic: They are as tall as palm trees, and florid and ruddy in complexion... all carrying an axe, a dagger, and a sword, and without these weapons they are never seen..."[1]

Like the Phoenicians, the Vikings charted many formerly unknown lands and islands, but unlike the eastern sailors, these men discovered hundred of sites and megalithic monuments scattered throughout the seas, remnants of a race of mysterious sailors of far greater stature than themselves. Naturally, the Vikings assumed these enormous forlorn ruins were all that was left of the Frost Giants, deeply embedded in their traditional memories since the Ice Age after the flood. The giants remained, but the Ice Age did not.

Almost a thousand years after the flood, the Ice Age was reduced from its former expanse and the poles became much like we know them today. By this time the Frost Giants had become the Formorians of Albion in prehistoric Briton, and the Firbolgs colonized Ireland and many isles after migrating from the east. Phoenician merchants told of one-eyed giants on many islands and thus gave birth to the Greek legends of the Cyclopes.

Later, Tuatha de Danaan fleets arrived and the Formorians and Firbolgs were driven into the wilderness by these Philistine giant-kin people. The remains of these people are scarce because of their ancient Canaanite-Philistine practices of burning their deceased. Large Philistine burial pots have been discovered full of ashes by archaeologist Ron Wyatt.[2] Even these pots are a rare find because the Philistines were a sea-faring race who worshiped Dagon, a fish god, and believed that their dead must be returned to him. This fascination with cremating the bodies and bones of the dead may have something to do with the copper-smelting city of the Philistines called Ezion-Geber (backbone of a giant). Erik Wahlgren in *The Vikings and America* wrote that, many a Viking, too, left his bones on a foreign beach or perished in the waves...[3] Like the Philistines, the Vikings were a mariner race who believed in disposing of the bodies of their deceased. Unlike the Philistines, however, these Nordic people burned their dead on funeral pyres or within ceremonial burial ships.

Another reason why giant human bones are a rarity is because of the destruction of giants' remains by tomb-raiders, fearful of these enormous men resurrecting and seeking revenge. And then there were arcane and ritualistic practices of burning giant bones to induce rain, a tradition no doubt inspired by the flood that drowned the wicked giants of those distant times.

As mentiioned earlier, the skeletal remains of huge Amorites were discovered in ancient burial crypts at Engedi by Ron Wyatt, who also unearthed the jaw bones and fossilized remains of giant men at Dogubeyazit, Turkey. Wyatt also exhibits a picture of a human thumb bone next to a ruler that measures 3¾ inches, a length over twice as long as any average man today. He claims it is the petrified bone of a pre-flood man.[4] Two thousand years ago, Flavius Josephus wrote in his greatest work, *Antiquities of the Jews* that, The bones of these men [giants] are still shown to this very day."[5]

Concerning the Amorites, the Chinese Takla Makan desert has yielded the remains of their Aryan cousins. The six-foot tall mummy of a female with a pointed skull, similar to the ancient Sumerians, is detailed earlier in this work. Like the thousands of accounts of Himalayan giants and the reclusive Yeti, this mummy's skull hints to ancestral links between the Amorites, Aryans, and the often-thought mythological Bigfoots. These documented accounts of the enormous man-like creatures called the Yeti in the mountains of Tibet are made more powerful by the fact that traditions exist of a race of giant men that once lived in the Himalayas.[6]

Also, mentioned earlier in this book, is the bizarre discovery in 1877 of a human leg fossilized in quartzite found in Eureka, Nevada that measured an astonishing 39 inches from the foot to the knee.[7] This leg must have belonged to a giant before the flood who stood at least 8½ or 9 feet tall. The presence of quartzite hints to an antediluvian origin.

Many more skeletons and artifacts of giants will be unearthed when archaeologists cease to study the thousands of dateless stone circles, megalithic ruins, earthen mounds, barrows and tumuli, and begin digging under them. The countless multi-ton stone monuments called giant's beds, or dolmens, found strewn about the wastes of every region that giants were believed to have lived, from India, Arabia, Iraq, Northern Africa, Canaan, France and the British Isles, need to be excavated under to find the buried remains of these mysterious people. Seldom is this done, but when it is the finds are rewarding. During the reign of King Henry II, an eight-foot tall human skeleton with a damaged skull was found in 1184 A.D.[8]

Unearthed in the early part of the nineteenth century at an old Roman Catholic chapel was a huge lead coffin, which was found to contain a skeleton of heroic dimensions, measuring 8 feet 3 inches.[9]

On December 17, 1615, a man named Jacob Lemaire was investigating a site at Port Desire in England when, to his astonishment, he unearthed the skeletons of men which measured between 10 and 11 feet from beneath several rock-buried graves.[10]

The geoglyphic chalk outlines of the Long Man of Wilmington and the 180-foot Cerne Giant could very well have been made by those who feared or remembered the giants. Ten and eleven-foot tall men are truly shocking, even greater in stature than the nine-foot, nine inch Philistine giant, Goliath. Could these enormous skeletons once have belonged to Tuatha de Danaan men or the monstrous Firbolgs and Formorians?

Stonehenge and several other dolmen circles (referred to as dance of the giants by Geoffrey of Monmouth) might be ancient graveyards having very little astronomical significance. Also in England are dozens of rock and earthen mounds perhaps containing the remains of unknown men. The largest is Silbury Hill, a 130-foot artificial hill of rock debris and earth that could have once been an antediluvian pyramid. What colossal remains lie beneath this ageless ruin?

With the abundance of physical and architectural evidence attributed to the giants of old and the diverse and antiquated traditions and legends of their presence long ago, it seems only fit that their remains be found and studied. Every nationality, culture and race has left us their remains in architecture, art, traditions, or other tangible evidences of past presence, even as long ago as the mystifying Sumerians, so it is ridiculous to think that races as productive and destructive as the giants would not have left us reminders of their once terrifying occupations.

Giants keep on cropping up on all parts of the globe: in the mythology of east and west, in the sagas of Tiahuanaco, and the epics of the Eskimos. Giants haunt the pages of almost all ancient books. So they must have existed.[11]

Already in this book we have cited these texts, some thousands of years old, written by Homer, Virgil, Ovid, Josephus, Pliny, Philo of Alexandria, Herodotus, Eusebius, and many others no so long ago, but still hundreds of years before our time.

Although most of these accounts seem to be authentic, there may have been some intellectual dishonesty due to the abundance of traditions and lack of physical proofs. For example, Pliny tells us that a certain giant named Gabbaras was brought to Rome by the Emperor Claudius Caesar from Arabia.[12] How true this is might be questionable to those who consider that the Hebrew word gibbar means "giant," and that Pliny states that Gabbaras' height was nine feet nine inches, the exact measurements of Goliath in II Samuel, an ancient biblical text no doubt studied by Pliny.

Human oddity researcher Frederick Drimmer in his book *Born Different* wrote:

> For hundreds of years physicians and anatomical museums have collected the remains of giants and human oddities and exhibited them.[13]

In 1833, road workers dug up an ancient grave containing some bones of large size, a skull of abnormal proportions, and a gold vest. Ancient documents reveal that these remains belonged to a giant named Benlli who lived around 500 A.D., and was long ago called the Giant of the Golden Vest.[14] This gold-encased leather vest is now held in the British Museum. 500 A.D. aligns perfectly with the *Beowulf* epic and its story of a giant called Grendel that vexed King Hrothgar of the Danes.

In the churchyard of a village named Hale, in England, is a twelve-foot slab with an inscription that reads:

> Here lyeth the bodie of John Middleton the Childe. Nine feet three Born 1578. Dyede 1623.

A portrait of his hand was made and placed in Brasenose College Library, which shows it to be seventeen inches long. Not long ago, John Middleton's grave was opened where, allegedly, some bones of great size were found.[15]

Cajanus of Finland (1714-49) stood 9 feet 3.4 inches tall according to his contemporaries, however, the measurements of his right femur in a Dutch museum shows that he probably stood 7 feet 3.4 inches tall.[16] His upper torso and neck may have been abnormally extended like the ancient biblical Anakim (long-necked) giants, which would given him additional height that the femur calculations fail to convey.

Born in 1736, Cornelius McGrath of Tipperary, Ireland, stood 7 feet 8 inches tall. Today his skeleton stands in the Trinity College at Dublin.[17]

The skeleton of Charles Byrne stands 7 feet 8¾ inches, in the Museum of the Royal College of Surgeons of England. In C.J.S. Thompson's, *Giants, Dwarves and Other Oddities*, we find that

> The skeleton measures 7 feet 8¾ inches, and the bones, generally, are well proportioned to the extraordinary height of the individual. The cranium is long and narrow and much depressed, with a low retreating forehead.[18]

Again we discover one of the most common physical traits shared among all the skeletal remains of giants from Sumer, India, Tibet, and the United Kingdom—abnormally long and narrow craniums.

The bones and skeletons of ten and eleven-foot tall men are completely inhuman. These remains are the greatest proofs that deep in our history something powerful had infiltrated our bloodlines. This sexual contact is heavily documented by the ancients and revealed in this book, but those who consider themselves learned will not believe it—rather trusting in a modern fable of evolution that these enormous skeletons strongly defy. Although bones are our greatest evidence of the history of such gigantic people, we also have some historical accounts from some rather credible sources.

Josephus mentions a giant who was prisoner to the king of Persia and was then recorded to be nearly eleven feet tall. His name was Eleazar. Vitelius recorded that this giant stood seven cubits tall (or 10 feet 2 inches) and was called a giant by reason of his greatness.[19]

In more contemporary times lived a giant who stood eleven feet six inches in height in the twelfth century during the reign of King Eugene II of

Scotland.[20] C.J.S. Thompson further cites that there is an account concerning an eleven foot tall giant named Aymon, who served as a bodyguard to Archduke Ferdinand. <u>A wooden image of this giant was preserved in the Castle of Ambras in the Tyrol</u>.[21]

The bones of giants are not all that remain of these remarkable people. As revealed earlier in this book, the footprints of an enormous man measured at 22 inches were found fossilized in the Paluxy River near Glenrose, Texas. Interestingly, the entire area is called Dinosaur Valley and contains prehistoric dinosaur skeletons and fossils in abundance. A dateless hoax or evidence of a pre-flood giant?

Other footprints have been discovered in more recent times, but not in solid rock. In the highlands of Tibet, huge footprints have been photographed in snow and dirt, some measuring up to 20 inches long.[22] Similar footprints in the Pacific Northwest have been found and photographed. The foot of one man named Robert Pershing Wadlow at age 22 stood eight-feet eleven inches and weighed 491 lbs. His foot size was an incredible 37AA![23]

Handprints also became a customary thing to record in later times. In the <u>Museum of the Royal College of Surgeons</u> is a cast of a hand measuring 11 inches that belonged to a man who lived in the early nineteenth century and stood seven feet eight inches tall. A man named Walter Parsons stood seven feet seven inches and served both King James I and King Charles I; <u>a true measure of his hand yet remaineth upon a piece of wainscot at Bentley Hall, by which it appears, that from the carpus to the end of the middle finger it was eleven inches long and the palm six inches broad</u>.[24]

Katherine Briggs in her *Encyclopedia of Fairies* remarks that some of those who were considered as fairies because of their size of abnormal appearance were actually <u>the remnants of a conquered people gone into hiding and yet creeping nervously around their conquerors</u>.[25] Considering Britian and Ireland's most ancient histories, we must assume that these conquered peoples were Formorians, Firbolgs of Danaanites. *The Annals of Ireland* by Duald Mac Firbis reflects this, revealing that traditions of fairies and strange creatures were actually <u>memories of an extinct race</u>.[26]

This connection with the past is greatly reflected in a British newspaper article printed over two hundred years ago that advertised a public display of <u>a young colossus, who, thought not sixteen, is seven feet four inches high... and must convince the world, that the ancient race of Britons is not extinct, but that we may hope to see a race of giant-like heroes</u>.[27]

Other remnants greatly feared from the bygone eras of entire colonies of giants were the monstrous hags like Grendel's mother in the lake ruins in Beowulf, and the dreaded Athach, Direach, and Black Annis. The traditions of the brutish women demonstrated that not all of the giants were male. In fact, James Paris de Plessis recorded in his book, *Short History of Human Prodigies, Dwarfs, etc.*, that in 1696 he met in London a giantess who stood seven feet high without her shoes, and mentions that she was well-developed, with a handsome countenance.[28]

We have taken brief glance at the relics left behind by the giants, but so far just among the inhabitants of the British Isles. The megalithic remains, geoglyphs, archaic legends and modern traditions and accounts, the prints, and even many skeletons and recorded accounts, have been cited. All of this has been gathered from one small corner of the world. In truth, a book ten times this size could not contain one-tenth of the evidences of giant civilizations long ago.

The many customs practiced by those who were affected by the ancestral relations that their predecessors maintained is already cited earlier in this book. It is the archaic ordinance of having four giants guard a city as protectors of the establishment, a practice also revealed by ancient texts such as the Bible and *Book of Jasher*, cited earlier, that was common among the Guardians long ago.

Another custom involves a festival usually focused around midsummer in Europe, and was celebrated with the viewing and burning of artificial giants made of wicker and other materials. The practice of constructing life-like giants was very popular among the Celts and Druids.[29]

In England the giants were a great processional feature in their celebrations. James Frazier, citing a 16th century writer, records in his book, *The Golden Bough*, that... in London, where to make the people wonder, are set forth great and uglie gyants, marching as if they were alive, and armed at all points... This 16th century writer is named Puttenham and he goes on to explain in his *Arte of English Poesie* (1589), that young boys inside the wooden giants worked instruments that enabled them to move the giants as if they were walking on their own.[30]

This feat of carpentry, the making of hollow giants, points back far into the nigh forgotten past of the British ancestors—the Trojans of Ionia. The Greeks constructed a giant wooden horse and filled it with soldiers and delivered it to the city of Troy as a token of truce. The Trojan Horse.

To Brutus and the early builders of London, then called New Troy, the Trojan Horse was the embodiment of treachery and defeat; but to the later Britons, the great wooden giants were symbolic of their forefathers greatest achievements—the conquering of Albion and its giants and the establishment of a new sea-faring Trojan empire that still remains a world power to this day.

><ins>...but they did not know the secret of the way things are, nor did they understand the things of old and they did not know what would come upon them, so they did not rescue themselves without the secret of the way things are.</ins> —*The Book of Secrets* (Dead Sea Scrolls)

Chapter Fifteen

Birth of the Great Lie

In the past fifty years the belief in life beyond the confines of earth has resurrected from the ancient traditions that held that gods traveled to earth from the heavens and strayed far from their own stars.

Contrary to popular UFO theory, the idea of alien intelligence is as old as the art of writing. The angelic Watchers that fathered the giants were deified and worshiped by the ancients as gods until the Creator imprisoned them in Tartarus for their blasphemy. Our negligence in understanding these most archaic beliefs has impaired our ability at truly unfolding history and comprehending the relics from these distant ages that we continually unearth.

The concept of flying as being completely modern has hindered the research of many strange and unusual artifacts excavated today. Preconceived notions about how human history has developed in technology and ability has been brainwashed into our history and archaeology students. The result of intense evolution propaganda has been the misclassification of physical relics and evidence of advanced technology excavated from often so-called prehistoric sites. Those who support the theory of evolution, which is supposed to be the organic and mental progression of a species by random mutations that benefit the strong, have forced themselves into a position where they cannot allow themselves to understand the implications of technological artifacts without compromising their apparent conjectures about human development.

Relics and historic evidence is found in the Babylonian texts called the Halkatha and the Sifr'ala of Chaldea, which cite the practice and techniques of aviation. Portions of these archaic writings appear to be flying manuals. The Sifr'ala dates back to more than 5000 years, possibly antediluvian.[1] The Hindu Samara Sutradhara (circa 1000 A.D.) contains intricate and precise instructions of aircraft design and maintenance, while the Ramayana describes perfectly today's version of a UFO.[2] A pre-Columbian gold trinket discovered in a grave resembles a delta-winged jet aircraft. Cockpit, tail wings, and rudders are definitive. Its uncanny resemblance to the F4 Phantom has made this artifact famous. Could this strange relic have something to do with Peru's mysterious geoglyphs?[3] Earlier in this book we discovered that ancient man associated the gods with celestial bodies and stars. Since men lived on the ground, it was their natural assumption that their gods lived far away in the skies and the bright heavens that appeared at night.

The golden plates of Ur read that gods in the form of men came down,[4] and a Sumerian inscription detailed in an earlier chapter declares, ...then came the flood, and after the flood, kingship came down from heaven once again.[5] The idea that physical gods descended to earth and appeared to ancient men is conveyed by both Biblical and secular sources. The Jewish noncanonical work entitled the *Book of Jubilees* states that he called his name Jared, for in his days the angels of the Lord descended on the earth, those so named the Watchers. (Jubilees 4:15)

This information reveals why the Hebrew translation of Jared's name is descent. It is also to be noted that the giants were called Nephilim, which means the fallen ones. James Lloyd in his Apocalypse Chronicles[6] newsletter recently printed a discovery by Zecharia Sitchin, stating that the early Babylonians called these giants Anunnaki, which means those who from heaven to earth came. Also detailed in the fascinating prophetic studies of the Apocalypse Chronicles, James Lloyd mentions the Anunna who appear in old Sumerian records and are described as gods of heaven and earth. He brings to attention the comparative structure of Anunnaki and Anunna to the Nephilim giants, called the Anakim by the Hebrews. This visible descent of physically present angels masquerading as gods is clearly referred to by the apostle Jude when he wrote

> ...the angels which kept not their first estate, but left their habitation. (Jude 6)

The Greek word used in the King James Version for first estate in this verse is arche, which chiefly means to be of certain rank, order, power, with an underlying connotation of proper time. What Jude was conveying was that these angels left their heavenly habitation and visited earth, fully knowing that when they appeared visually they would be regarded as gods, beings higher in rank and power than they were created to be.

Another hint as to the identity of the Anunnaki lies in the ancient art of metallurgy. Concerning this fascinating revelation, we will refer to volume II #4 of the Apocalypse Chronicles, issued by James Lloyd entitled, Where Angels Dare to Tread:

> "One theorist has submitted evidence that the Sumerian and subsequent Akkadian terms that describe their early metallurgical work are related to the term Anunnaki. The

Sumerian records specifically state that their knowledge of mining and metallurgy was given to them by the Anunnaki. While the term anu means heaven, the Sumerian word for tin was An.na, meaning heavenly metal. Anakum means pure tin as well as, "that which comes from or belongs to the Anunnaki."

Because the Sumerians' primary pursuit of mining was to produce bronze (they were, after all, in the Bronze age), and bronze is an alloy of tin and copper, there is some evidence that the word Anunnaki could actually refer to the term alloy, or mixed ones. The Nephilim would certainly be considered mixed.

Reflecting the ancient metallurgy of the Anunnaki, the works of Homer in his *Odyssey* and *Iliad* tell of Hephaistos, the god of forge fires and smiths, who was worshiped to a great extent in Athens. Hephaistos fathered a powerful race of arcane blacksmith gods called the Kabeiroi.[7] The Anunnaki were originally regarded as chthonic fertility deities, sexual beings acting as courtiers to the god of heaven. The Anunnaki answered only the great black dragon named Kur, and the underworld goddess Ere_kigal, both of whom are extensively detailed in the Sumerian text, *Inanna's Descent and the Death of Dumuzi*.

Although described frequently as a dragon, Kur is also in other texts depicted as a monstrous giant who abducted Inanna and forced her to abide at certain times in the underworld. The Anunnaki presided as seven fierce underworld judges, who stripped Inanna naked and sentenced her to die. The Anunnaki were related to another mysterious race of deities called the Igigi.[8]

The Anunnaki in Sumerian-Akkadian myth were created by the Supreme Being, An (or Anu). The meaning of An is sky, thus, to the ancients, the Anunnaki were from the sky. An had his center of worship in Uruk, the home of Gilgamesh. This creator god is detailed in the Enuma Elish text. The worship of An diminished after the Sumerians fell to Sargon the Great (circa 2300 B.C.).

The Anunnaki were provided a beautiful goddess to attend to their needs named A_nan. What capacity with which she served them is unclear, but it is evident that she was somehow linked to the wonderful products provided by the Anunnaki.[9] Being inventors and builders, the Anunnaki had no market for their inventions and innovations until mankind was formed.

The Anunnaki were more than likely Sumerian-Akkadian memories of the Nephilim. They were the incredibly intelligent giants after the flood. Their acute abilities in mining and metallurgy are seen long before the flood when the first program of sexual contacts between the sons of God and daughters of men occurred. Metallurgy is first described in the Scriptures before the flood with Tubal-cain, one of the sons of Lamech in Cain's lineage. Tubal-cain is called an instructor in Genesis 4:22. *Smith's Bible Dictionary* reads that Tubal-cain means iron in Hebrew, but its Arabic translation is Kain-smith. Tubal-cain must have learned how to mine ore, smelt, and forge, from sources far more industrious and knowledgeable than himself. The only other presence on earth capable of revealing these techniques were the disobedient sons of God called the Watchers.

Zosimus declared that the knowledge of metals, precious stones and scents dated back to the epoch mentioned furtively in the Genesis: 'The sons of God saw the daughters of men, that they were fair.'[10]

Kurt Seligmann in his book *The History of Magic and the Occult*, states that wise men long ago determined that the sons of God were fallen angels that must have been evil, as well as being great thinkers of old, much like Zosimus and Tertullian.

Zosimus wrote about a most ancient book called *Chema*, written by a mysterious alchemical master named Chemes. Zosimus wrote that the fallen angels had given lessons to the daughters of men with the aid of this book.[11] Chemes may be the biblical Chemosh, a Moabite god whose name means subduer. Chemosh had Babylonian origins like Nimrod, which means leopard-subduer, and so would Chemes if he was one of the first renowned metallurgists. The name Chemes today serves as the base word in alchemy.

In an old alchemical text, a priestess wrote that she acquired her knowledge from an angel named Amnael. The text claims her wisdom was received as reward for having sexual intercourse with Amnael.[12] Kurt Seligmann goes on to say, of alchemy and metallurgy, that they were considered a vain and cursed knowledge... connected with two great crimes: the intercourse of women with fallen angels, and Adam eating the forbidden fruit.[13]

It is very possible that Tubal-cain and others, during antediluvian times, gave these powerful angels their daughters in exchange for many wonderful secrets about the world's resources and other valuable information. In fact, the only industrious individuals mentioned in the Genesis text were in the lineage of Cain. Cain murdered Abel with a weapon. Cain's son Enoch had a city built in his name. Lamech was the first to have two wives. Jabal learned about cattle and migrating to better pastures, while his brother Jubal invented the harp and organ. The only inventor-builder mentioned in Adam/Seth's lineage was Noah, builder of the ark—the vessel by which the world as we know it was saved. The answer for this increase in knowledge lies in heaven. Cain's lineage received their information from the evil earth-bound angels, while Noah got his from God. As seen elsewhere in this book, the root word for demon is knowledge.

These angels were remembered by the people of India, who called them the Avatarati, or descenders. Arabian and Islamic writings as recorded in the Quran recall these embodied angels as the jinn, evil spirits that can take on physical form. Japanese Shinto tomes detail the descent of gods from the sky that married earth goddesses. This is found in the Japanese book, *Record of Ancient Things*. Mark Hitchcoch and Scott Overby also cite in their book, *Extraterrestrials...What on Earth is Going On?*, that in the Hindu book called the Bhagavad-Gita, there is written a passage about alien being from other worlds coming down to earth.[14] In the heavily documented and controversial book by Erich von Daniken called *Chariots of the Gods?*, we read:

> Sumerian, Assyrian, Babylonian, and Egyptian Cuneiform inscriptions constantly present the same picture: Gods came from the stars and went back to them.[15]

Mesoamerican beliefs also reflect ancient memories of gods that descended and taught the ancients. The fall of the Toltecs is blamed on a deity who came down and taught them harmful knowledges, named Titlacahuan. Some traditions still speak of a family of old being referred to as tricksters who falsely claimed to be gods, but were destroyed. The Ixil of Guatemala believed the ancients were angelic beings who were flooded. Later, god rained fire on them. The beings sent by God to execute these judgements were called Keepers.[16] Evidently, these beings were the Watchers, their angelic nature evident in that the Ixil regarded them as messengers of God. The translation of "angel" in Hebrew is messenger. Interestingly, the Aztecs hold that long ago the gods descended and made forests and flowers. And their stories involving starvation, women, and the ocean in these traditions all hint to the old accounts of the Watchers and their doings. The Aztecs even believed that music was first born in the sky and later brought to earth.[17]

When Paul and Barnabus healed a lame man in Lystra the people were astonished, proclaiming that the gods are come down to us in the likeness of men! These people called Paul and Barnabus Mercurius and Jupiter (see Acts 14:11-13).

Jupiter was the same as the Greek god Zeus, supreme of the gods (and regarded as Satan by early Christians). In early Hellenistic times, Zeus was worshiped as god of the underworld. Primitive worship included cannibalism and human sacrifice,[18] something Paul no doubt did not want to be associated with. In Revelation 2:13, Jesus refers to Pergamos as <u>Satan's seat</u>, where once stood a beautiful temple of Zeus.

If we take into consideration the Titan giants of lore and hundreds of stories involving their numerous deities, it becomes apparent to us today why their immediate reaction, in the presence of a "miracle," was to assume that Paul and Barnabus were personified gods. In fact, this belief was so impressed upon Greek and Roman society, that the town clerk of Ephesus told Paul that they were worshipers of <u>the image that fell from Jupiter</u> (see Acts 19:35).

Later, on the voyage to Rome for his appeal to Caesar, Paul became shipwrecked by a storm and landed on an island where a viper bit his hand. When the natives saw him discard the snake without harm, they <u>said he was a god</u> (see Acts 28:6).

Paul's situation is best summed up by Raymond E. Fowler in his book, *The Watchers*:

> <u>Legends abound from many parts of the world concerning contact with celestial beings who aided in man's development of civilizations. Such legends were the basis for the development of complex religious beliefs in the existence of gods from the sky.</u>[19]

These ancient superstitious tendencies to deify men, later, during the dark ages, developed into the medieval myths and fables of dryads, trolls, elves, and other fairies. Many of these beliefs contain reflections of Nephilim history. The Indo-European belief in fairies was very strong and associated with the hundreds of rock formations not yet adequately explained, and with the unique monuments spread out over the continent, left behind by the giants.

Many people long ago believed that these fairies were elemental spirits of earth, air, fire and water—the children of Mother Earth (Gaea of the Titans). These beautiful fairies could become hideous trolls and quietly enter a young girl's room under moonlight and take them away, or cause crib deaths, or to even sexually molest. For some historical accounts of children abducted by fairies hundreds of years ago, read *An Encyclopedia of Fairies* by Katharine Briggs, page 62; <u>Captives in Fairyland</u>.

Trolls derive from the Nordic beliefs in fairies. These creatures were associated with the underworld and stole small children and sometimes even swapped troll babies for human infants. Some trolls were giants that guarded passes or bridges.

> The motive assigned to fairies in northern countries is that of preserving and improving their race, on the one hand by carrying off human children to be brought up among the elves and to become united with them, and on the other hand by obtaining the mild fostering of human mothers for their own offspring.[20]

This profound insight is directly related to modern alien operations and is found in the *Science of Fairy Tales*, cited by Raymond E. Fowler.

Fairies were known to dance late at night in solitary places, in circular meadows secluded by trees, or in open fields where they frolicked in faerie rings. These circles were often found in the mornings embedded in crops by farmers and wayfarers. Strange lights, beautifully haunting music, and human disappearances characterized fairy activity in these mysterious rings. It was a common tradition to keep a safe distance from any reported fairy sites. Surprisingly detailed and consistent tales of human disappearances in fairy rings are found in many old Welsh legends and stories.[21] In England, Stonehenge and other similar rock rings were viewed as being fairy haunts long ago.

Darkly akin to the modern alien abduction theories are the old traditional beliefs that their thefts of human babies and older people is because mortal blood seems needed to replenish fairy stock.[22] Interestingly, fairies have been known to boast that their own babies were no longer as great and strong as in the old days.[23] They could only be referring to the giants.

Other sexually active spirits are the succubus and incubus recognized by the occultists today.[24] The succubus is actually very old, a campfire legend known all over the world by many names.

Almost every sixteenth-century book mentions the incubus.[25] These spirits incarnate, taking on the physical form of a beautiful female that lures men into sexual relations with them, until she tires of his company. At that time she will kill him by drinking the blood from his body. There is very little difference between succubi and vampires, which are better known to occultists as incubi. These are corporeal angels in the form of males who infiltrate people's bedrooms and lay with the female occupants while everyone else in the vicinity is bewitched into a deep slumber.

> St. Thomas Aquinas proposed that Satan once served first as a succubus (or female devil) to men, and then as an incubus to women... St. Thomas declared that children begotten in this way ought to be regarded as the children of the men whom Satan served as succubus. They would, however, be more cunning

than normal children on account of the demoniacal influence to which they were exposed in their pre-natal condition...

Dr. Paul Carus in his book, *The History of the Devil and the Idea of Evil*, continues, citing Matthaeus Paris, who mentions that within six months, one such incubus-baby developed all its teeth and attained the size of a boy of seven years, while his mother became consumptive and died.[26]

What an intriguing account—that a baby giant should be born from the union of a fallen angel and a human woman.

The beliefs in incubus spirits ultimately find their origin in the Bible, where the sons of God took the daughters of men and fathered the giants—great bestial men that later became evil spirits in the form of trolls, gargoyles, elves, goblins, and many other embodied demons. This change in the roles of the Nephilim in the kingdom of darkness was prophesied by Enoch to occur before the flood, as read in Enoch 15:9.

> ...the spirits of the giants shall be like clouds, which shall oppress, corrupt, fall, contend, and bruise upon the earth.

Ghosts, wraiths, spectres, and many other such incorporeal spirits known to haunt forlorn ruins and places where wickedness is, or has been practiced, find their origin with the giants. But the incubus and succubus beings, it seems, are none other than the Nephilim themselves, still eluding mankind and corrupting our blood with the continual interbreeding and creation of genetic hybrids.

> Stories and beliefs of sexual contact between inhumans and humans were popular in the Middle Ages. In this period we find a strong belief in the existence of male incubi and female succubi who forced human being to have sexual relations with them.[27]

Other modern occult beliefs are inspired by Nephilim history. Edward Bulwer-Lytton popularized a theory adapted by esotericists that a race of civilized giants dwell deep within the biospheric, subterranean cavern complexes of the Earth.

These giants are called the Vril-ya and are believed to one day emerge from their earthen cities and subdue the surface lands once again, where they lived long ago, before humans populated their domains. The late nineteenth century beliefs and the evidences put forth concerning the existence of these underworld giants is actually a blend of traditions, some biblical and others more pagan. The Formorians and Firbolg giants of Britain and Ireland were driven underground by the giant-kin, Philistine-related Tuatha de Danaan invaders. In turn, as we discovered earlier in chapter 11, (Albion...Isle of the Giants), the Trojan exiles under Corineus and Brutus vanquished many and forced the last of the giant remnants and Danaans into the mountains and caves, where they retreated underground. Even in the ancient Americas, native stories were told about lost races of giants and dwarves, mysterious beings that retreated underground once men wandered into their lands. The Yaque of Northwestern Mexico have long held that a race called the Surem, long ago vanished into the underworld.[28] The theory of the subterranean giants called the Vril-ya was put forth as a nineteenth-century explanation for the presence of the thousands of unexplained monuments and legends around the world. If Edward Bulwer-Lytton were still alive today, he would be astonished at just how close he's come to exposing some very ancient, guarded secrets previously unveiled in the texts of our Bibles.

The association of mysterious and often devilish phenomenon to specific geographical areas is not an old trend. In more recent times, the Bermuda Triangle has gained considerable popularity. It boasts of a lengthy history of vanishing vessels, bizarre localized storms, alleged time warps when ships or aircraft cannot account for missing hours, disturbing magnetic imbalances, UFO sightings, and vanishing aircraft. One of its better remembered victims was the Mary Celeste, a brigantine ship found floating empty in 1872. Nothing was missing that indicated piracy. The sails were in tatters, supplies and food intact, captain's log void of anything unusual. Until this day no one can explain the disappearance of those who were on board the Mary Celeste.

Another thoroughly documented mystery of the Bermuda Triangle is the disappearance of five U.S. torpedo bombers and a Martin Mariner Flying Boat in 1945. The sea was combed for signs of wreckage, but none were located. These planes and pilots vanished completely. And *since* 1945, as of this writing, over 325 planes and more than 1200 ships have crashed, sunk or completely vanished into the Bermuda Triangle.

Though we tend to scoff at the tales and legends that influenced our predecessors, there exists today even more ludicrous beliefs that our ancestors would have mocked us for having. Today, many of the myths we call "science" are no more accurate than the fables of old.

Science has deluded many people into believing that we evolved biologically from apes and other anthropoidic creatures that, in turn, had evolved from plasmic muck that had slimed its way onto the sands of prehistoric shores. Though a missing link has not been found to connect the thousands and thousands of years between the species of various animals, evolution is a snare that has caught many. It is a science that causes its victims to lose faith in God altogether, even denying His existence. Paul wisely warned us of these <u>sciences</u>:

> <u>...keep that which is committed to thy trust, avoiding profane and vain babblings, and oppositions of science falsely so called</u>. (I Timothy 6:20)

So many mysteries around the world today would be solved if the <u>oppositions of science</u> were not so overpowering. If scientists turned away from the fallacies of evolution and studied the *evidence* of giant activity in the past, then we would have a clearer understanding in our studies of the giants and gods of antiquity, the incredible architecture in Egypt and the Americas and Britain, and the strange, sky-facing earth drawings, among others. But instead of addressing the facts, we create alternate realities.

The fantasy, horror, and science fiction entertainment of today has beguiled the world into thinking that certain creatures and other worlds exist. We have turned to fables. Today, we are no more creative than our predecessors who dreamt up fantastic creatures and tales to explain away those occurrences which they could not understand. Today's trolls, elves, and fairies are not much different than those of the past.

We, as sophisticated modern people have returned to the past, seeking answers to the phenomenon that we cannot fathom. Those of the Middle and Dark Ages have peered into the woods, mountains, seas, and underworld for answers to these mysteries, but the ancients of more distant history looked to the heavens. Our primary denizens of today are technologically advanced extraterrestrials that UFO researchers claim are merely a species of intelligent life that is more <u>evolved</u> than our own, largely because of the current Darwinian-evolutionist paradigm. Not only do evolutionists try to deceive us about our origins, but they now claim we are not alone in this evolving universe. The trolls, dragons, imps, and dwarves have been replaced with aliens. Is there a difference?

Is it a mere coincidence that for the past five decades the entertainment media have bombarded us with alien abduction stories, UFO sightings, and alleged encounters of the third kind? Programs and movies such as <u>Battlestar Gallactica, Buck Rogers, The Last Starfighter</u>, the <u>Star Wars trilogy</u>, and numerous others, depict alien civilizations as being technologically superior and beyond our capacity to comprehend.

The latest successes by imaginative evolutionists are the various <u>Star Trek</u> movies and spin-offs that commonly show alien beings in different stages of evolutionary development. We also have the movies Independence Day, Starship Troopers and the made-for-TV hits like V and Invasion. Many stories and shows deal with worldwide kidnappings of huge populations of the worlds' people for the purpose of filling alien food storages, human slave camps on distant planets, extraterrestrial scienctific experiments on human subjects, and even the interbreeding of human captives with alien species. These imaginative ideas in entertainment today are no more than ancient reflections of what the angels did when they took the daughters of men.

The media are not the only source of locating these dark trends of the past. Many occultists boast of communicating with intelligent life in other solar systems using divination ad hypnosis. Witches have been known to confess that they had obtained special powers over others in their covens by consenting to sexual intercourse with incarnated spirits and demons, sometimes even aliens. The past twenty years have seen an alarming amount of women come forth from all walks of life and culture with stories about being abducted in their sleep by large-headed, little grey men with off-round eyes. These traumatic episodes leave these women paranoid, sometimes unable to account for missing time, and most women remember nothing of their experiences until they are abducted a second time. All of these accounts from thousands of women are the same. After their abductions their menstrual cycle is disrupted, but after a second abduction it continues normally. Clinical evidence gathered from many of these subjects has proven that embryonic fetuses were extracted.[29]

It is interesting that all of these stories are from women, thousands of cases that parallel each other even though these people have never met nor been influenced in any way. This confirms that their experiences were nothing more or less than forced sexual contact with extraterrestrials. The most astonishing and disturbing aspect of these testimonies is the physical description of these aliens. This description is more profound because of the thousands of variations in abduction accounts. No two abductions are the same. Some women were taken in their sleep. Others were on country roads, on ships, camping, far from home, and in many other places just as ordinary as the people abducted. But the unique link connecting these experiences is the physical description of these aliens which remains unchanged, no matter where the testimony comes from and in whatever language it is recorded in.

Thousands of historic and modern testimonies concerning extraterrestrial contact have witnesses describing alien beings as tall, blue-eyed, blond, humanlike entities that are usually accompanied by servile, fetus-like aliens much shorter.[30] This intriguing description is of modern Nephilim hybrids being genetically created by the fetus-like corporeal dark angels that are building a race of semi-giants, as they had done twice in biblical history—in the days of Noah, both before and after the flood. Blond hair, blue eyes and tall features are descriptive of the Egyptian racial portraits and reliefs in their temples, cited earlier in this book, depicting Sabeans, Amorites and Anakim giants, all partially descended from disobedient angels. These mysterious aliens, witnessed by thousands of people, are described by Raymond E. Fowler in *The Watchers* as tall, blond, robed, human-like entities.[31] Colin Wilson, in *From Atlantis to the Sphinx*, uncovered some stunning historical parallels concerning these racial characteristics. He found that the South American gods recognized as having brought civilization and learning to those cultures were named Quetzalcoatl, Viracocha and Kukulkan, gods that all had fair skin and blue eyes—as Osiris was represented in ancient Egyptian statues.[32] Interestingly, the gods Osiris and Orion (Nimrod) were regarded as being the same deity to the early Egyptians.[33] The Mayan civilization was cultivated long ago by a strange group of light-skinned, blue-eyed people that wore serpent emblems affixed to their heads called Viracochas.[34] In the mysterious city of Tiahuanaco, the god Viracocha is called Thunupa, the white god from the sea.[35] A seven-foot, life-sized statue of Viracocha clearly identifies this enigmatic god as being distinctly non-Indian, having a thin nose, round eyes and facial hair, the last being a characteristic that the Mayans definitely did not have.[36]

The Aztecs believed that long ago, gigantic white men who came from somewhere in the sky once visited them. The Spanish explorers and Conquistadors learned that these giants were called the race of the sons of the sun who instructed mankind in all kinds of arts and disappeared again.[37] This description calls to mind the Sumerian giant Gilgamesh, whose name means son of the sun, and the angelic Watchers that descended and taught men the secrets of God.

Concerning the strange physical characteristics of the mysterious Sumerians, Erich von Daniken proclaims that the figures and statues of these people appear to fit no racial group known on earth, having goggle eyes, domed foreheads, narrow lips, and generally long, straight noses,[38] traits cited earlier in this book that belong to the Amorite and Anakim giants and the large Aryan mummies in the Chinese Takla Makan desert. In *The Two Babylons*, by Alexander Hislop, we discover that the racial traits of gods and goddesses around the world from Babylonia, Egypt, India, Greece and Rome were of blue or grey-eyed, blond-haired entities with fair features.[39] Katherine Briggs, in *Encyclopedia of Fairies*, wrote that when fairies search for mortal children, a golden-haired child is in far more danger of being stolen than a dark one.[40]

These supposed extraterrestrials are depicted by the media as little dwarf-sized humanoids with large heads and oval eyes. This deception further promotes evolutionary thought because it is the form by which today's sexually corrupt angels appear to the women they abduct and molest. This universally-promoted description of a bulbous head and large eyes, with no mouth, conveys that this alien species has evolved beyond the need to verbally communicate and has a much larger brain, due to more intellectual development. This is plausible by the standards evolutionists have created for their mythical beliefs.

There is no doubt that the physical appearance of today's aliens has demonic origins. Many cultures around the world have believed in dwarves and little green or gray elves that inhabited the hollow world below, in the depths of the earth. A modern parallel to this ancient belief is that most UFO sightings report alien craft to be either entering or exiting from under the ground or the ocean. UFO's are seldom seen coming out of the sky, from high up. That is a media misconception because of the preconceived ideas of the origin of extraterrestrials.

Intriguingly, an ancient prophecy concerning this alien hybrid phenomenon was recorded over two thousand years ago. But because it is found in a book considered apocryphal, it has become ignored throughout the ages. In the Second book of Esdras of the Apocrypha is found an end-time prediction that says; the wild beasts shall change their places and a women shall bring forth monsters.[41]

Further evidence of alien activity in antiquity is found in Peru with the mysterious geoglyphic pictures mentioned earlier in this book. On this Nazca plateau is what appears to be an exact replica of today's version of E.T. The large head, thin neck, little body, and huge eyes without a mouth, perfectly mirrors the descriptions of "extraterrestrials" that conduct unusual and often sexually orientated experiments on abducted women. But this giant earthen artwork is dated from thousands of years ago, probably put together by the pre-Incan civilization that left behind so many large and sophisticated stone temples and monuments throughout the dense South American jungles. Other geoglyphs of alien-looking beings that fit modern E.T. descriptions gathered by researchers are discovered facing the arid sky in the Mojave Desert and South America.[42] Many Meso-American beliefs hold that short, gnome-like deities called rain dwarfs have for a long time kidnaped people. Other varieties of these gnomes were talked about in Panama and Brazil.[43]

The Tzeltal Indians of Chiapas, Mexico, believed in dwarflike entities called the ihk'al that could fly and randomly kidnaped women and force them to bear children.⁴⁴ This unusual tradition, like most legends, stems from an ultimate truth—from events that actually occurred to these remote people as the Watchers continued their genetic manipulations through the centuries, up to now. Perhaps someday, someone will unearth evidence that will reveal who the builders of the South American geoglyphs were and what their relationship was to the strange "E.T." artwork that was laid out for all in the sky to see.

Unfortunately, the main opposition to the existence of extraterrestrial activity and human abductions does not come from the evolutionary-minded scientific community, but from Christians who oppressively dismiss anything they do not understand. Anything they cannot force-fit into their notions of how biblical history is supposed to unfold is rejected. By misinterpreting Bible history concerning the sons of God and their physical taking of the daughters of men, believers today have trouble accepting the reality that God has given the fallen angels the authority to again execute their sexual machinations. This is a repetition of history that will be detailed in the next chapter. Scientists today hope to discover a captured alien specimen with these same physical descriptions because it would support evolution theory and would also, as a side effect, critically damage the faith of many Christians.

It is becoming more and more apparent that the spirit of antichrist is moving powerfully in our era toward brainwashing people into believing in an alien intelligence from the cosmos and the distinct possibility that these beings are of vastly incredible intelligence, putting the species of Homo sapiens much lower on the evolutionary scale. As an actor sets his stage and prepares his lines, so is Lucifer preparing the world for a subservient mentality as he did so long ago when the Watchers appeared. They ruled over mankind in the ancient civilizations of Sumer, Akkad and Babylonia when kingship once more descended from heaven.

The highest echelons of Christian theology and organization are directly influenced by the whims of Lucifer today, which is why modern theology tends to denounce the biblical account of the Nephilim. Satan is not pleased with his past failures and like any human strategist, does not desire to reveal his intentions to his opponents. Humanity. But the church of today and tomorrow needs to be made aware of what Lucifer is doing in preparation of the Messiah's return to earth and the apocalyptic battle that will ensue.

Today our seminaries brainwash the next generation of preachers and evangelists, teachers, and even theological scholars into believing that the Nephilim were merely wicked people, tyrants who overran the earth. This is a half-truth, akin to Christians believing that Jesus was and is the Son of God, but still disbelieving in a resurrection. The Bible calls them giants, a race God did not want on His planet. The Creator did not flood His planetary garden to kill a bunch of tyrants, but because the bloodlines were polluted and this corruption of the pure Adamic bloodline then brought forth the social decadence of the entire world. The Bible is very detailed in its descriptions of the giants and even of later peoples who still retained traces of angelic ancestry, but were not necessarily called giants. These descriptions are provided by the Bible writers to convey the unusualness in these people, proofs marking them as being of an accursed lineage. To us today, we know that these were genetic imbalances caused by nonhuman infiltration of our species.

Why is there such hostility toward those who believe in the biblical account of the Nephilim? Could it be generated by the agents of those who have directly interfered in the history of humanity... who cannot afford at this time to have the entire Christian world knowledgeable of their activities? With censorship's powerful hold on our seminaries and theological institutions of <u>controlled education</u>, we can better understand how we today know less about history than our predecessors.

Do angels have access to the heavens today as they once enjoyed? How far can they travel? Why is there no evidence of alien interstellar travel? If biblical angels are today's aliens, then what do they fly in? And in what realm do they now reside? The spiritual or material? It is interesting to discover that only <u>the angels that kept not their first estate</u> (Jude 6-7), those in the days of Noah, were imprisoned under <u>chains of darkness</u> and nothing at all is mentioned in the Scriptures about the demons who caused the second rise of the Nephilim, after the flood. Why weren't these disobedient angels confined as well? Could it be that they have been genetically tampering with humans since those distant times?

If these angels transferred themselves from the spiritual world to the physical world of earth to mate with human women, could they not assume another form if they chose to do so? Haven't many angels appeared in several various forms throughout Scripture and many other noncanonical texts? According to the book of Revelation, during the tribulation the evil angels will indeed be in an altered form, a hideous body which they will use to afflict the people of earth. This mysterious atrocity will be expounded upon later in this book.

If mankind could, in about fifty years of technology, reach the <u>moon</u>, how much more easily could fallen angels create UFO technology in five <u>thousand</u> years, especially since they are <u>greater in power and might</u> than ourselves? Man has not achieved our amazing feats alone, by ourselves. The incredible things that we have accomplished cannot be solely attributed to human ingenuity. We as humans have been <u>guided</u>, sometimes by the Creator and other times by those angelic beings that are continually in conflict with Him. The explosion of technology and knowledge is the direct result of our contact with the ancient Watchers. War and rebellion initially began in heaven but it continues on earth, and humanity hangs in the balance.

Controlled education has poisoned all but a small minority of people in all facets of life. In the case of Christian religion, this control has been exercised primarily through articles, commentaries, tracts, Bible study guides, and many other Christian press outlets penned by our modern scribes that have brainwashed our seminary students and future ministers into believing in the irrelevance of giants in Scripture—some even altering the meaning of <u>giants</u> to fit into entirely different and nonexistent contexts. For this and other reasons, Jesus said <u>beware of the scribes</u> (Luke 20:46). It seems he knew that theological writers, editors, and scholars <u>in his name</u> would distort history, and attack the veracity of his prophetic warnings concerning the end-times.

The depth of hypocrisy by these Christians is amazing. They unwaveringly accept the Biblical historicity of the virgin conception of Mary by the Holy Spirit, but openly deny that angels (once holy, but fallen) could have sexually united with human women. Apparently, today's biased Bible believers think it's a stretch on the imagination to accept that angels in antiquity physically appeared, but don't hesitate to proclaim that two angels <u>appearing</u> as men met Mary at the empty tomb of Jesus.

Enoch knew well of this phenomenon and in his writings we find that

> <u>Iniquity however, shall again be renewed, and consummated on earth. Every act of crime, and every act of oppression and impiety, shall be a second time embraced.</u> (Book of Enoch 90:6)

Epilogue

As in the Days of Noah

No other person in Old Testament antiquity is better remembered by believers and unbelievers alike than Noah. When his name is mentioned we instantly visualize the flood, the ark, and the end of the ancient world. Today he is the recognized father of hundred of millions of Christians, Muslims and Jews. But in the distant past, he was remembered by many pagan nations as well. For example with the Aztecs, the flood was inscribed upon the memories of their people as a global end to a previous age.

The Quichè traditions tell that at the beginning of their ancestry, the creator-spirits had several animals gather food that was mixed with water from the gods. With these the spirits created four male ancestors who were given four wives. In this way did eight people populate the world, but as they multiplied they became cold, so the god Tohil created fire. Unfortunately, this god only gave them fire once they submitted to offering him human sacrifices. The Sun (symbol of God) arose and the other gods were turned into stone, becoming idols along with the animals.[1] This "legend" is remarkable proof that the Mesoamericans were once Mesopotamians, having been "cut-off" from the east by flood, glacial melting and/or tectonic changes that resulted in the drastic elevation of the sea levels. The Quichè stories embody the flood and gathering of animals by Noah and his three sons who had four wives, also totaling eight people on the ark. The flood initiated rapid global cooling and a rapid Ice Age not consistent with uniformitarianism.

Nimrod began human sacrifice in the plain of Shinar to the Serpent of Fire, an idol likely representing the Phoenix. Often described as a fiery, planetary object, the Phoenix appears in the sky periodically, throughout history, and initiates cataclysmic events. The flood destroyed the pre-flood "gods," or giants, along with the animals, petrifying many into stone relics from antiquity.

According to Ron Wyatt, it was this glacial, post-diluvian epoch that wholly preserved the antediluvian nutrition of enriched vitamins and minerals. After the flood, only those lands on the equatorial plane were not encased in solid ice, in glaciers that stretched thousands of miles to the North and South Poles. Within these glacial walls were the frozen bodies of pre-flood animals and vegetation. Billions of quick-frozen specimens still edible were available for many decades after the deluge, as the glaciers slowly receded and meltwater formed thousands of lakes and small seas. This nutrition helped support post-flood longevity for a time—however, due to the absence of the vapor canopy/marine atmosphere, solar radiation quickened the aging process, where we find ourselves today.

Ron Wyatt further theorizes that it was quite possible that legendary cities such as Atlantis and others were real, having been ruined and abandoned as local flooding of lowland areas was caused by glacial melt-water.[2]

The North American Mandan Indians believed that earth began in water and darkness. Their civilization was never as advanced as the Mayans, but their beliefs that the beginning of the current world was by flood hints that there could be distant ties between the Mayan and Mandan people. Another native American people, the Maidu, believed that long ago the earth was covered in water. Land was repopulated by a few people who survived on a giant canoe.[3]

Both the Navajo and Hopi Indians from America's southwest believed in ages of history. According to their traditions, we are living in the fifth age and their ancestors survived the fourth age by escaping miraculously from mountain-sized waves that destroyed the world.

The Serbians of Europe remembered a valley paradise that their forebears dwelled in that was long ago flooded because of disobedience. The only survivor was Kranyatz, a giant who clung to a mountain peak until the waters abated.[4]

The Epic of Gilgamesh fragments, discovered at the site of Nineveh, provide us with what is most likely the oldest flood story known to man. The entire epic mirrors the Bible account said to have been written much later by Moses. Gilgamesh was a Sumerian hero and like Kranyatz of the Serbians, he was a giant.[5] Gilgamesh learned from Utnapishtim (Noah) why God flooded earth and that the Lord had told him to tear apart his house in the city of Shurrupak and build a boat with the wood.

What makes flood traditions so credible are the diverse elements added or deleted from the wealth of information already available in the Biblical account. The presence of giants and boats in some flood stories, while not present in others, conveys originality on the part of ancient historians, but consistency in the story being found worldwide. A good example of Biblical elements in pagan flood traditions is discovered in the historic lore of the Arctic-dwelling Siberian people. They believe that earth was initially only an enormous ocean beneath Yggdrasil, the Tree of Life that the Icelandic Vikings held so dear in their Norse memory.

The Japanese, too, believed in a floating world that harbored dark gods, demons, and monsters in its depths. In the Egyptian *Book of the Dead*, the god Atun declares that the world will sink into water <u>again</u>.[6]

As profound as his life was in distant history, Noah's story is even more incredible in <u>prophecy</u>. This fascinating man lived in a society infested with lawlessness, violence, and sexual relations with <u>demons</u>. Noah lived for six hundred years before the flood in a community in constant fear of marauding giants and powerful angels that forcefully <u>took</u> their daughters. In fact, Jesus promised that before his return to earth, the world would be in a social state similar to that of Noah's time. <u>And as it was in the days of Noah, so shall it be also in the days of the son of man.</u>

> <u>They did eat, they drank, they married wives, they were given in marriage, until the day that Noah entered into the ark, and the flood came, and destroyed them all.</u> (Luke 17:26-27)

In this disturbing passage Jesus reveals the pattern of cyclic history involving judgement. The flood was a global holocaust, however, it was a prophetic shade of a <u>greater</u> judgement to come—the Second Coming. What kind of judgement and for what reasons is more articulately revealed in another historic revelation spoken by Jesus.

> <u>Likewise also, as it was in the days of Lot, they did eat, they drank, they bought, they sold, they planted, they builded, But the same day that Lot went out of Sodom, it rained fire and brimstone from heaven, and destroyed them all. Even so shall it be when the son of man is revealed.</u> (Luke 17:28-30)

In this historic shadow of eschatology we discover that <u>fire</u> is associated to Christ's coming. God has promised that He would not flood the earth with <u>water</u>, but a fiery judgement is what we can expect in this next and final chapter. So intense was the lust and fervency to commit homosexual acts with others in the time of Lot, that the Sodomites attempted to molest two angels sent in to rescue Lot and his family. These violent men declined Lot's two virgin daughters, preferring the angelic visitors disguised as men. In response to this rampant lust, God melted Sodom and her sister city, Gomorrah.

This story illustrates how the wicked, at God's return to earth, will be physically burned, and then again, so it's later claimed, in the eternal flames of the lake of fire. Although Sodom and Gomorrah were made as eternal examples of the infernal rewards of wickedness, they are not the only cities to have suffered this type of fate. The city of Pompeii was completely destroyed by volcanic rock and fiery debris just as these earlier Canaanite cities were. Excavations have unearthed artifacts that have been withheld from public view because of their perversity. Archeologists have removed the ashes and unveiled this extinct culture, buried alive.[7]

The days of Noah were characterized by widespread societal evil, rebellion against God, violence, fear of giants, and of course, sexual relations with angels. The New Testament prophecies mirror these historic foreshadowings. Jesus foretold that evil would <u>increase</u> (Matthew 24:12), society would decline <u>morally</u> and ethically (Matthew 24:10), and there would be <u>flooding</u> (Luke 21:15), something Noah knew well. Timothy wrote that in the last days, <u>perilous times</u> would arise (2 Timothy 3:1) and that those who formerly followed the truth would <u>fall away</u>, preceding Christ's return. Paul wrote the same thing in 2 Thessalonians 2:3, and even recorded that a false sense of peace would lure the wicked into destruction (1 Thessalonians 5:2-3) right before the Second Coming. This revelation by Paul is significant because Jesus' overview of pre-flood and pre-apocalyptic Sodom and Gomorrah clearly states that society continued <u>marrying, building, and planting</u> as if they expected their lives to continue normally and they <u>ate, drank, bought, and sold</u>, thinking all was well and peaceful. America's high living standards today greatly reflect these ancient glimpses into the last days of antediluvian earth and last days of Sodom.

These dark times before and after the flood seem no different than what we are experiencing today. Entire cultures and communities are infested with man's evil imaginings, perverted doctrines, homosexuality, false gospels, witchcraft, covetness, deception, corruption, and debauchery. Just as the waves of the flood destroyed old earth, the tides of tribulation will afflict our world as well. But people are blind to this oncoming catastrophe. Lured by peace, many choose to disbelieve in cataclysms despite the powerful historical evidence.

The ongoing censorship of the Nephilim and ancient giants is occurring because the acknowledgement of their proven, historic existence connects to our very roots. Their existence gives powerful credibility to the veracity of ancient texts that claim that the human race has had extensive contact with some other higher intelligence in antiquity and that much of human history is a reflection of this strange and sometimes violent interaction. Though tainted by religionists, the biblical record is rife with evidence of this contact.

Parts of this book were written from a Judeo-Christian perspective so as to convey the true spirit of the biblical narratives and their modern interpretation by Nephilim researchers. The subject of the Nephilim goes far deeper than this work could convey. We still covered, although briefly, other cultures and belief systems in the ancient past that had contact with giants, but far more is known. They were here. To learn more profound secrets and knowledge about the Nephilim visit www.archaix.com. But tread carefully in the dark...

Reference Notes

Chapter One: Some Discoveries of Note
1. Archaeology: edited Paul G. Baun (Cambridge Univ. Press), p. 4-5.
2. Buber's Tanhuma Devarum 7 in Judaism, edited by Arthur Hertzberg p. 155, 156, George Braziller, NY 1962.
3. Secret Cities of Old South America p. 46.
4. The Greek Myths p. 685-686.
5. The History of the Christian Religion and Church During the First Three Centuries, p. 82.
6. Discovering Ancient Giants, p. 15.
7. Lost Cities and Ancient Mysteries of South America, p. 199.
8. Lost Cities of North and Central America, p. 468.
9. Discovering Ancient Giants, p. 20.
10. Discovering Ancient Giants, p. 20.
11. Discovering Ancient Giants, p. 21.
12. Discovering Ancient Giants, p. 48-49.
13. Lost Cities of Ancient Lemuria and the Pacific, p. 194.
14. Discovering Ancient Giants, p. 22, 67.
15. Lost Cities of Ancient Lemuria and the Pacific, p. 193.
16. Lost Cities and Ancient Mysteries of South America, p. 257.
17. Secret Cities of Old South America, p. 42.
18. Elder Gods in Antiquity, p. 288.
19. Chronicon on Podia, various examples.
20. Our Occult History, p. 38.
21. Ancient Man: Handbook of Puzzling Artifacts, p. 685-686.
22. Discovering Ancient Giants, p. 16, 88.
23. Lost Cities of North and Central America, p. 352.
24. Evolution Cruncher, p. 558.
25. Lost Race of the Giants, p. 15.
26. Discovering Ancient Giants, p. 25, 221.
27. Ancient Mysteries: James & Thorpe, p. 530.
28. Discovering Ancient Giants, p. 17.
29. Discovering Ancient Giants, p. 17.
30. Secret Cities of Old South America, p. 40.
31. Giants, Dwarfs and Other Oddities, p. 133.
32. Discovering Ancient Giants, p. 18.
33. Giants: A Reference Guide From History, the Bible and Recorded Legend, p. 84-85.
34. Giants, Dwarfs and Other Oddities, p. 175.
35. Celtic Myth and Legend: An A-Z of People and Places, p. 174.

36. Sargon the Magnificent, p. 140.
37. Lost Race of the Giants, p. 68.
38. Giants: A Reference Guide From History..., p. 85-86.
39. Giants: A Reference Guide From History..., p. 84.
40. Discovering Ancient Giants, p. 19, 31.
41. Legend Come to Life, p. 141.
42. Lost Cities of North and Central America, p. 352.
43. Secret Cities of Old South America, p. 293.
44. Mysteries of Time and Space, cited in Lost Cities of North and Central America, p. 576.
45. Lost Race of the Giants, p. 39.
46. Legend Come to Life, p. 74.
47. Ancient Giants Who Rules America, p. 303-305.
48. Elder Gods in Antiquity, p. 412.
49. Discovered! The Genesis Story of Creation, inside cover.
50. Footprints and the Stones of Time, p. 91.
51. Giants: A Reference Guide From History, p. 18.
52. Discovering Ancient Giants, p. 24.

Chapter Two: Origin of Nephilim Theory

1. The Golden Bough, p. 50, citing *The History of the Egyptian Religion, p. 105.*
2. Mythology of Mexico and Central America: Bierhorst, p. 146, 154.
3. The Book of Enoch: trans. Richard Lawrence, Introduction.
4. The Dead Sea Scrolls: Tales of the Patriarchs, p. 76-77.

Chapter Three: Antediluvian Giants and the Flood

1. Facts and Fictions Regarding Noah's Flood, p. 32.
2. The Dead Sea Scrolls; Tales of the Patriarchs, p. 76.
3. Extraterrestrials...What on Earth is Going On?, p. 162.
4. Encyclopedia of Gods: Over 2500 Deities of the World, Michael Jordan.
5. Antiquities of the Jews: Josephus, Book 1, 3:1-4, Book 5, 2:1-6.
6. The Dead Sea Scrolls: partial text, p. 331.
7. Chariots of the Gods?, p. 26.
8. Book of Wisdom, 14:6, cited in The Bible as It Was, James Kugel.
9. Antiquities of the Jews: Josephus, book I, 1:1-3.
10. The Bible As It Was, p. 58.
11. Chariots of the Gods?, p. 63.
12. The Mythology of Mexico and Central America, p. 137.
13. The Mythology of Mexico and Central America, p. 132.
14. The Mythology of Mexico and Central America, p. 146-147.
15. The Mythology of Mexico and Central America, p. 131, 137.
16. Epic of Gilgamesh: trans. N.K. Sanders, p. 108.
17. Noah's Flood: Ryan & Pitman, p. 198.
18. The Mythology of Mexico and Central America, p. 9.

19. The Mythology of Mexico and Central America, p. 9.
20. The Mythology of Mexico and Central America p. 132.
21. Antiquities of the Jews: Josephus, book I, 3:5-8.
22. Liber de Pallio: Tertullian, p. 1-2, 1033-34, cited in *Noah's Flood:* Norman Cohn, p. 73-74.
23. The Dead Sea Scrolls: Ages of the World, p. 238-239.
24. The Bible As It Was, p. 37.

Chapter Four: Post-Diluvian Giants

1. Sumerian King-List cited by N. K. Sanders, Epic of Gilgamesh, Introduction.
2. Noah's Flood: Cohen, p. 2.
3. Smith's Bible Dictionary, p. 271.
4. Encyclopedia of Gods: Jordan.
5. Illustrated Book of Myths: Phillip, p. 126.
6. After the Flood: William Cooper.
7. Encyclopedia of Gods: Jordan.
8. Encyclopedia of Gods: Jordan.
9. Illustrated Book of Myths: Phillip, p. 18-20.
10. Illustrated Book of Myths: Phillip, p. 20.
11. Encyclopedia of Gods: Jordan.
12. Encyclopedia of Gods: Jordan.
13. Illustrated Book of Myths: Phillips, p. 165, 174-175.
14. Doomsday: A View Through Time.
15. The Two Babylons, p. 31, 33-35.
16. Giants, dwarfs and Other Oddities, p. 25.
17. The Bible As It Was p. 111, citing Eusebius in Praeparatio, 9:18:2.
18. Giants, Dwarfs and Other Oddities, p. 181.
19. Giants, Dwarfs and Other Oddities, p. 20.
20. The Treasury of African Folklore, p. 550.
21. Giants, Dwarfs and Other Oddities, p. 129.

Chapter Five: Giants in the Promise Land

1. Antiquities of the Jews: Josephus, Book 3, 1, 4:1-4.
2. Antiquities of the Jews: Josephus, Book 6, 7:1-5.
3. Race in Ancient Egypt.
4. The Treasury of African Folklore, p. 570.
5. Antiquities of the Jews: Josephus, Book 4, 5:1-3.
6. Smith's Bible Dictionary, p. 84.
7. The Dead Sea Scrolls, p. 332-333.
8. Smith's Bible Dictionary, p. 124, citing Porter's *Five Years in Damascus.*

Chapter Six: Conquest of Canaan

1. The Mythology of Mexico and Central America, p. 132.
2. The Mythology of Mexico and Central America, p. 22.

3. The History of Magic and the Occult.
4. Apocalypse Chronicles, James Lloyd, Vol. II #2, pg. 1, citing Velikovsky's Worlds in Collision, p. 61, 155.
5. The Golden Bough, p. 24-25.
6. The Bible As History, p. 165.
7. The Bible As History, p. 130.
8. Giants, Dwarfs and Other Oddities, p. 130.
9. Race in Ancient Egypt, cited in The Bible As History, p. 181.
10. Antiquities of the Jews: Josephus, Book 6, 7:1-5.
11. Wyatt Archeological Research, Ron Wyatt, p. 106.
12. Discovered! Noah's Ark, p. 33.
13. Apocalypse Chronicles: James Lloyd, Vol. 5, #1, p. 3.
14. From Atlantis to the Sphinx, p. 269.

Chapter Seven: The Last Bible Giants

1. Deut. 1:28, Numb. 13:32, Gen. 6:4.
2. Judges 16:16-17.
3. Judges 16:18-21.
4. *Antiquities of the Jews*; Flavius Josephus, Book 6, 9:1-5.
5. *Antiquities of the Jews*; Flavius Josephus, Book 7, 4:1.
6. *Pseudo-Philo* 61, cited in *The Great and Distinguished Words of God*; El Publishing, pg. 263-264.
7. *Pseudo-Philo* 61, cited in *The Great and Distinguished Words of God*; El Publishing, pg. 263-264.
8. *Pseudo-Philo* 61, cited in *The Great and Distinguished Words of God*; El Publishing, pg. 263-264.
9. 1 Samuel 22:9-10, 18-19.
10. *Antiquities of the Jews*; Flavius Josephus, Book 7, 12:1-2.
11. *Antiquities of the Jews*; Flavius Josephus, Book 7, 12:1-2.
12. *Antiquities of the Jews*; Flavius Josephus, Book 7, 12:1-2.
13. *The Bible as History*; Werner Keller, pg. 43.
14. *The Bible as History*; Werner Keller, pg. 51.
15. Deut. 2:10.
16. *Antiquities of the Jews*; Flavius Josephus, Book 7, 12:4.
17. National Geographic Explorer Program on Abusir Excavation.
18. *Antiquities of the Jews*; Flavius Josephus, Book 5, 2:1-6.
19. *The Golden Bough*; James Frazer, pg. 24.
20. *Noah's Flood*; Norman Cohn, pg. 75.
21. *Born Different*; Frederick Drimmer, pg. 70.
22. Cited by Kurt Seligmann in *The History of Magic and the Occult*, pg. 30.
23. *Apocalypse of Baruch* 50:2-3.
24. *Jasher* 14:2.

Chapter Eight: Giants in Ancient Egypt

1. *The Great Pyramid... Prophecy in Stone*; Noah Hutchings, pg. 29.
2. *Dake Annotated Reference Bible*; Finnis Jennings Dake.
3. *From Atlantis to the Sphinx*; Colin Wilson, pg. 286.
4. *From Atlantis to the Sphinx*; Colin Wilson, pg. 93.
5. *Jasher* 2:6.
6. *Epic of Gilgamesh*; Translated by Maureen Kovacs, pg. 114.
7. *Epic of Gilgamesh*; Translated by Maureen Kovacs; Introduction.
8. *Ghost Lights and Other Encounters of the Unknown*; E. Randall Floyd, pg. 130.
9. *Jasher*, 3:10.
10. *Tracing Our Ancestors*, pg. 7.
11. *Antiquities of the Jews*; Flavius Josephus, Book 1, 3:1-4.
12. *Antiquities of the Jews*; Flavius Josephus, Book 1, 2:3.
13. *From Atlantis to the Sphinx*; Colin Wilson, pg. 83.
14. *From Atlantis to the Sphinx*; Colin Wilson, pg. 72.
15. *From Atlantis to the Sphinx*; Colin Wilson, pg. 60.
16. *From Atlantis to the Sphinx*; Colin Wilson, pg. 54.
17-22. Omitted.
23. *Antiquities of the Jews*; Flavius Josephus, Book 2, 9:1-7.
24. *Tracking our Ancestors*; Frederick Haberman.
25. *Jubilees* 8.
26. page 81.
27. *Jubilees*, 10.
28. *The Practical Bible Dictionary and Concordance*; pg. 118.
29. *Jasher* 31:43.
30. *Enoch* 7:10-11.

Chapter Nine: The Giant of Babylon

1. Cited by Alexander Hislop in *The Two Babylons*, pg. 240, Paschal Chronicle Vol. 1, pg. 50.
2. *The Bile As It Was*; James Kugel, pg. 12; Citing (Pseudo-) Eupolemus, cited in Eusebius, Praeparatio Evangelica 9:17:2-3.
3. *Antiquities of the Jews*; Flavius Josephus, Book 1, 4:1-3.
4. *The Bible As It Was*; James Kugel; pg. 126, citing Philo Questions and Answers, and pg. 127, citing Augustine of Hippo in The City of God, 16, 4.
5. Questions and Answers II:82, Philo of Alexandria.
6. *The Two Babylons*; Alexander Hislop, pgs. 32-34.
7. *Jasher* 7:30.
8. *The Two Babylons*; Alexander Hislop.
9. *Sibylline Oracles* 3:106-107, cited in *The Bible As It Was*, pg. 129; James Kugel.
10. Strong's Exhaustive Concordance (Archer, Horseman); *The Two Babylons*; Alexander Hislop, pgs. 37-38.
11. *Bulfinch's Mythology*; Edmund Fuller, pg. 102.

12. *Bulfinch's Mythology*; Edmund Fuller, pg. 164.
13. *Smith's Bible Dictionary*; pg. 226.
14. *The Two Babylons*; Alexander Hislop, pgs. 21, 63, 32, citing Pliny.
15. *The Two Babylons*; Alexander Hislop, pgs. 20-23.
16. *Illustrated Book of Myths*; Neil Philip, pg. 102.
17. *Illustrated Book of Myths*; Neil Philip, pg. 108-111.
18. *Doomsday...A View Through Time*; Russell Chandler.
19. *The Two Babylons*; Alexander Hislop, pg. 59.
20. *Encyclopedia of Gods*; Michael Jordan.
21. *The Two Babylons*; Alexander Hislop, pg. 229.
22. *The Two Babylons*; Alexander Hislop, pg. 298.
23. *The Great Pyramid... Prophecy in Stone*; Noah Hutchings, pg. 10.
24. *Smith's Bible Dictionary*, pgs. 26-27.
25. Cited by Michael Jordan *Encyclopedia of Gods*; Michael Jordan.
26. *Echoes of the Ancient Skies*; Dr. E.C. Krupp.
27. *Illustrated Book of Myths*; Neil Philip, pg. 173.
28. *Encyclopedia of Gods*; Michael Jordan.
29. *Encyclopedia of Gods*; Michael Jordan.
30. *Encyclopedia of Gods*; Michael Jordan.
31. *Encyclopedia of Gods*; Michael Jordan.
32. page 376.
33. *Born Different*; Frederick Drimmer, pg. 53.
34-37. Omitted.
38. *Encyclopedia of Gods*; Michael Jordan.
39. *Illustrated Book of Myths*; Neil Philip, pg. 47-48.
40. *Illustrated Book of Myths*; Neil Philip, pg. 134.
41. *Epic of Gilgamesh*; Maureen Kovacs; Introduction.
42. *Epic of Gilgamesh*; Maureen Kovacs; Introduction.
43. *Epic of Gilgamesh*; Maureen Kovacs; pg. 18.
44. *The Two Babylons*; Alexander Hislop, pgs. 114, 123-124, 217-218, 243.

Chapter Ten: The Giant Wars

1. *Jasher* 9:20.
2. *Jasher* 7:46.
3. *Jasher* 9:23.
4. *Apocalypse Chronicles*; James Lloyd, Vol. 5 #1, The Queen of Heaven and the Fallen Stars, pg. 1.
5. *The Bible as History*; Werner Keller, pg. 318.
6. *The History of Magic and the Occult*; Kurt Seligmann, pg. 8.
7. *The History of Magic and the Occult*; Kurt Seligmann, pg. 8.
8. Genesis 9:1.
9. Matthew 10:34-36.
10. *Jasher* 7:19-20.
11. *Jasher* 11:6.
12. *Tracing Our Ancestors*; Frederick Haberman.

13. *Tracing Our Ancestors*; Frederick Haberman, pg. 62.
14. *Epic of Gilgamesh*; N.K. Sandars.
15. *Epic of Gilgamesh*; N.K. Sandars, pg. 8.
16. *Epic of Gilgamesh*; N.K. Sandars, pg. 14.
17. *Epic of Gilgamesh*; N.K. Sandars, pg. 11.
18. *After the Flood*; William Cooper, pg. 188.
19. *The Bible as History*; Werner Keller, pg. 327-328.
20. *Jasher* 11:6.
21. Genesis 14:1.
22. *Epic of Gilgamesh*; Maureen Kovacs, pg. 15.
23. *Epic of Gilgamesh*; Maureen Kovacs, pg. 16.
24. *Epic of Gilgamesh*; N.K. Sandars, pg. 21.
25. *Epic of Gilgamesh*; Maureen Kovacs, pg. 2.
26. *Epic of Gilgamesh*; N.K. Sandars, pg. 7.
27. page 62.
28. page 59.
29. *The Bible as History*; Werner Keller, pg. 321.
30. *The Bible as History*; Werner Keller, pg. 32.
31. *The History of Magic and the Occult*; Kurt Seligmann, pg. 25.
32. *The Two Babylons*; Alexander Hislop, pgs. 141, 304-305.
33. *The Two Babylons*; Alexander Hislop, pgs. 51, 59.
34. page 195.
35. *After the Flood*; William Cooper, pg. 190.
36. *The Bible as History*; Werner Keller, pg. 318.
37. *The Bible as History*; Werner Keller, pg. 6.
38. *Jasher* 7:23.
39. *The Two Babylons*; Alexander Hislop, pg. 24.
40. *The Two Babylons*; Alexander Hislop, pg. 21-23, 40.
41. *The Two Babylons*; Alexander Hislop, pg. 23-25.
42. *After the Flood*; William Cooper, pg. 195.
43. *Epic of Gilgamesh*; N.K. Sandars, pg. 23.
44. *Jasher* 13:15.
45. *The Two Babylons*; Alexander Hislop, pg. 246.
46. *Genesis Commentary*; Peter Ruckman, pg. 354.
47. *Hebrew-Greek Key Study Bible*; Spiros Zodhiates.
48. *Genesis Commentary*; Peter Ruckman, pg. 353.
49. *The Two Babylons*; Alexander Hislop, pg. 69 citing *Cedrini Compendium*, Vol. I., pp. 29, 30.
50. *The Two Babylons*; Alexander Hislop, pg. 246.
51. *Jasher* 16:2.
52. Deuteronomy 2:20.
53. page 174.
54. page 141.
55. Deuteronomy 2.
56. *Genesis Commentary*; Peter Ruckman, pg. 346.

57. *Wyatt Archaeological Research*; Ron Wyatt, pg. 52.
58. *Genesis Commentary*; Peter Ruckman, pg. 353.
59. *Genesis Commentary*; Peter Ruckman, pg. 354.
60. *Smith's Bible Dictionary*, pg. 35.
61. *Antiquities of the Jews*; Flavius Josephus, Book I, 9:1.
62. Joshua 14:15, 15:13, 21:11.
63. *Jasher* 38:11.
64. *Giants, Dwarfs and Other Oddities*; C.J.S. Thompson M.B.E. pg. 136.
65. Genesis 15:16.
66. *Wyatt Archaeological Research*; Ron Wyatt, pg. 44, citing *The Early History of Israel*; Roland DeVaux; 1971, and *Biblical Archaeology Review*; June 1977.
67. *After the Flood*; William Cooper, pg. 172.
68. *After the Flood*; William Cooper, pg. 172.
69. *Wyatt Archaeological Research*; Ron Wyatt, pg. 44.
70. *Jasher* 12:68.
71. Joshua 10;13, 2 Sam. 1:18.
72. *Jasher* 27:2.
73. *The Two Babylons*; Alexander Hislop, pgs. 5-6, 21-22.

Chapter Eleven: Albion...Isle of the Giants
1. *Bulfinch's Mythology*; Edmund Fuller, pg. 14.
2. *Bulfinch's Mythology*; Edmund Fuller, pg. 282.
3. pages 178-179.
4. *Encyclopedia of Fairies*; Katherine Briggs, pg. 178.
5. *Apocalypse Chronicles*; James Lloyd, Vol. 5 #1, The Queen of Heaven and the Fallen Stars, pg. 2.
6. *Encyclopedia of Fairies*; Katherine Briggs, pg. 87.
7. *Encyclopedia of Fairies*; Katherine Briggs, pg. 405 (Motif A1659.11).
8. *Epic of Gilgamesh*; N.K. Sandars, pg. 120.
9. *Jasher* 12:52.
10. *Epic of Gilgamesh*; N.K. Sandars, pg. 103.
11. *Smith's Bible Dictionary* (Barbour), pg. 231.
12. *The Bible as History*; Werner Keller, pg. 57.
13. *Smith's Bible Dictionary* (Barbour), pg. 68.
14. pages 76, 108.
15. *Smith's Bible Dictionary* (Barbour), pg. 68.
16. *Practical Bible Dictionary and Concordance* (Barbour), pg. 35 and *Smith's Bible Dictionary*, pg. 94.
17. *Epic of Gilgamesh*; N.K. Sandars, pg. 16.
18. *Tracing Our Ancestors*; Frederick Haberman, pg. 8.
19. Number 21:33, Deut. 32:14, Isaiah 2:13, Zechariah 11:2.
20. *Encyclopedia of Fairies*; Katherine Briggs, pg. 313.
21. *Encyclopedia of Fairies*; Katherine Briggs, pg. 143.
22. *Genesis Commentary*; Peter Ruckman, pg. 282.

23. *Encyclopedia of Fairies*; Katherine Briggs, pg. 123.
24. *Tracing Our Ancestors*; Frederick Haberman, pg. 79.
25. *The Bible as History*; Werner Keller, pg. 151.
26. *The Bible as History*; Werner Keller, pg. 177.
27. *The Bible as History*; Werner Keller, pg. 86.
28. *The Bible as History*; Werner Keller, pg. 209.
29. *The Bible as History*; Werner Keller, pg. 209.
30. *The Bible as History*; Werner Keller, pg. 212.
31. page 179.
32. *Encyclopedia of Fairies*; Katherine Briggs, pg. 479 (Motif S262).
33. *Encyclopedia of Fairies*; Katherine Briggs, pg. 179.
34. *Encyclopedia of Fairies*; Katherine Briggs, pg. 8.
35. *Encyclopedia of Fairies*; Katherine Briggs, pgs. 8, 123.
36. *Encyclopedia of Fairies*; Katherine Briggs, pgs. 314-315.
37. *Encyclopedia of Fairies*; Katherine Briggs, pg. 400.
38. *Encyclopedia of Fairies*; Katherine Briggs, pg. 401.
39. *Encyclopedia of Fairies*; Katherine Briggs, pg. 148.
40. *Tracing Our Ancestors*; Frederick Haberman, pg. 118.
41. *Encyclopedia of Fairies*; Katherine Briggs, pg. 87.
42. *Encyclopedia of Fairies*; Katherine Briggs, pg. 253.
43. *Encyclopedia of Fairies*; Katherine Briggs, pg. 393.
44. Volume 1, Pg. 68.
45. Cited by Katherine Briggs in an *Encyclopedia of Fairies*; pgs. 90-91.
46. *After the Flood*; William Cooper, pgs. 222-223.
47. page 3.
48. *Tracing Our Ancestors*; Frederick Haberman, pg. 93.
49. *Tracing Our Ancestors*; Frederick Haberman, pg. 94.
50. *After the Flood*; William Cooper, pg. 202(Dodanim)-203.
51. *After the Flood*; William Cooper, pg. 199.
52. *After the Flood*; William Cooper, pg. 204.
53. page 204.
54. *Bulfinch's Mythology*; Edmund Fuller, pg. 206.
55. *Bulfinch's Mythology*; Edmund Fuller, pg. 284.
56. page 95.
57. *Tracing Our Ancestors*; Frederick Haberman, pg. 96.
58. *After the Flood*; William Cooper, pg. 223.
59. *Bulfinch's Mythology*; Edmund Fuller, pg. 283-284.
60. *Tracing Our Ancestors*; Frederick Haberman, pg. 96.
61. *Bulfinch's Mythology*; Edmund Fuller, pg. 188.
62. *Odyssey*, Book Nine; (Homer) New Coast and Poseidon's Son, Robert Fitzgerald.
63. *Bulfinch's Mythology*; Edmund Fuller, pg. 282.
64. *Giants, Dwarfs and Other Oddities*; C.J.S. Thompson, M.B.E., pg. 18.
65. *Giants, Dwarfs and Other Oddities*; C.J.S. Thompson, M.B.E., pg. 18-19
66. *Encyclopedia of Fairies*; Katherine Briggs, pg. 479 (Motif 6100.1).

67. *Odyssey*, (Homer) Book Seven, Gardens and Firelight, R. Fitzgerald.
68. *Odyssey*, (Homer) Book 9, New Coasts & Poseidon's Son, Robt Fitzgerald.
69. *Bulfinch's Mythology*; Edmund Fuller, pg. 284.
70. Cited by Frederick Haberman in *Tracing Our Ancestors*, pg. 78.
71. *Jasher* 90:29.
72. *Giants, Dwarfs and Other Oddities*; C.J.S. Thompson, M.B.E., pg. 138.
73. *Tracing Our Ancestors*; Frederick Haberman, pg. 97.
74. *Tracing Our Ancestors*; Frederick Haberman, pg. 97.
75. *Bulfinch's Mythology*; Edmund Fuller, pg. 284.
76. Cited by Katherine Briggs in an *Encyclopedia of Fairies*, pg. 102.
77. *Encyclopedia of Fairies*; Katherine Briggs, pgs. 75-76.
78. *Encyclopedia of Fairies*; Katherine Briggs, pgs. 206-207.
79. *Encyclopedia of Fairies*; Katherine Briggs, pg. 123, citing Jane Wilde's *Ancient Legends of Ireland*.
80. *Encyclopedia of Fairies*; Katherine Briggs, pg. 58.
81. *Encyclopedia of Fairies*; Katherine Briggs, pg. 24.
82. *The Enchanted World...Night Creatures* (Time Life), pg. 21.
83. *The Enchanted World...Night Creatures* (Time Life).
84. page 35.
85. *The Bible as History*; Werner Keller, pg. 191.
86. pages 92-93.
87. Genesis 15:16.
88. *Encyclopedia of Fairies*; Katherine Briggs, pg. 175.

Chapter 12: Epics of the Giants

1. Beowulf; Burton Raffel, citation from Robert Creed in the Afterward, pg. 128.
2. Beowulf; Burton Raffel, Introduction, ix.
3. *Epic of Gilgamesh*; N.K. Sandars, pgs. 46-47.
4. Beowulf; Bruton Raffel, lines 104-114.
5. *Enoch* 15:8.
6. *Encyclopedia of Fairies*; Katherine Briggs, pg. 298-299.
7. *The History of the Devil and the Idea of Evil*; Dr. Paul Carus, pg. 250.
8. Beowulf; Bruton Raffel, lines 419-421.
9. Beowulf; Bruton Raffel, lines 883-885.
10. *After the Flood*; William Cooper, pg. 229.
11. Beowulf; Bruton Raffel, lines 1264-1266.
12. *The History of the Devil and the Idea of Evil*; Dr. Paul Carus, pg. 250.
13. *The Enchanted World...Night Creatures*; Time Life Books, pg. 7, Perilous Paths Through the Dark.
14. Beowulf; Bruton Raffel, lines 1545-1547.
15. Beowulf; Bruton Raffel, lines 1557-1561.
16. Beowulf; Bruton Raffel, line 1666.
17. Beowulf; Bruton Raffel, lines 2135-2136.
18. Beowulf; Bruton Raffel, lines 1613-1616.

Reference Notes 211

19. *Enoch* 66:14.
20. Beowulf; poem, line 732.
21. Beowulf; poem, line 449.
22. Beowulf; poem, line 165.
23. Beowulf; poem, line 2090.
24. Beowulf; poem, line 2088.
25. Beowulf; poem, line 1267.
26. Beowulf; poem, line 595.
27. Beowulf; poem, line 426.
28. Beowulf; poem, lines 1345-1352.
29. Beowulf; poem, line 1647.
30. Beowulf; poem, line 1662.
31. Beowulf; poem, line 1677-1681.
32. Beowulf; lines 1694-1696, Burton Raffel.
33. *Tales From Ovid*; Ted Hughes, pgs. 10-12.
34. *Tales From Ovid*; Ted Hughes, pgs. 13-14.
35. Joshua 11:21-22.
36. *Gods and Fighting Men*; Lady Gregory, cited in Katherine Briggs, *Encyclopedia of Fairies*, pg. 87.
37. Beowulf; poem, line 1267.
38. *Epic of Gilgamesh*; Maureen Kovacs.
39. *Epic of Gilgamesh*; Maureen Kovacs; First tablet notes.
40. *The Golden Bough*; James Frazer, pg. 50, footnote #4 on *The History of Egyptian Religion*.
41. *The History of the Devil and the Idea of Evil*; Dr. Paul Carus, pg. 3.
42. *Epic of Gilgamesh*; N.K. Sandars.
43. *Epic of Gilgamesh*; N.K. Sandars.

Chapter 13: Relics of the Gods
1. *Chariots of the Gods?*; Erich von Daniken, pg. 20.
2. *The Mythology of Mexico and Central America*; J. Bierhorst, pgs. 8, 50.
3. *The Mythology of Mexico and Central America*; John Bierhorst, pg. 22.
4. *The Mythology of Mexico and Central America*; John Bierhorst, pg. 22.
5. *The Mythology of Mexico and Central America*; John Bierhorst, pg. 164.
6. *The Mythology of Mexico and Central America*; J. Bierhorst, pgs. 79-80.
7. *The Mythology of Mexico and Central America*; John Bierhorst, pg. 154.
8. *Echoes of the Ancient Skies*; Dr. E.C. Krupp.
9. *After the Flood*; William Cooper.
10. *Maps of the Ancient Sea Kings...Advanced Civilizations in the Ice Age*; Charles Hapgood, cited by Richard Noone in *5/5/2000 Ice: The Ultimate Disaster*.
11. *The Atlas of Archaeology*; Mick Aston & Tim Taylor, pg. 55.
12. *Facts and Fictions Regarding Noah's Flood*; Charles Weismann, citing *Makers of Civilization* by Prof. Waddell, pg. 27.
13. *Tracing Our Ancestors*; Frederick Haberman.

14. *Noah's Flood*; William Ryan & Walter Pitman, pg. 24.
15. *Noah's Flood*; William Ryan & Walter Pitman, pgs. 203-204.
16. *Mysterious Places*; edited by Jennifer Westwood, pg. 172.
17. *Feats and Wisdom of the Ancients*; Library of Curious Facts, Time Life Books, pg. 133.
18. *Mysterious Places*; edited by Jennifer Westwood, pg. 226.
19. *Encyclopedia of Gods*; Michael Jordan.
20. *The Mythology of Mexico and Central America*; John Bierhorst, pg. 172.
21. *The Mythology of Mexico and Central America*; John Bierhorst, pg. 172.
22. *Feats and Wisdom of the Ancients*; Library of Curious Facts, Time Life Books, pgs. 77-78.
23. *Mystic Places*; Time Life Books, pg. 82.
24. *Mystic Places*; Time Life Books, pg. 82.
25. *Mysterious Places*; edited by Jennifer Westwood, pg. 46.
26. page 100.
27. *Mysterious Places*; edited by Jennifer Westwood, pg. 12.
28. *Encyclopedia of Fairies*; Katherine Briggs, pg. 227.
29. *The Holy Quran*; Presidency of Islamic Researches, IFTA, pg. 417, note 1040.
30. Quran, *Surah 7, Ayat 69.*
31. Quran, *Surah 7, Ayat 9.*
32. *The Holy Quran*; Presidency of Islamic Researches, IFTA, pg. 1161, note 3459.
33. *Merriam Webster's Collegiate Dictionary.*
34. *The Great Pyramid... Prophecy in Stone*; Noah Hutchings, pg. 10.
35. *Wyatt Archaeological Research*; Ron Wyatt, pg. 4.
36. *Antiquities of the Jews*; Flavius Josephus, Book 5, 2:1-6.

Chapter 14: The Bones of Giants

1. Cited on Foreword and translations in Michael Crichton's *Eaters of the Dead*, a fictional account that begins at the <u>end</u> of the historical Fadlan Manuscript (pg. 41).
2. Wyatt Archeological Research, Ron Wyatt.
3. *The Vikings and America*; Erik Wahlgren, pg. 32.
4. *Discovered: The Genesis Story of Creation*; pg. inside and front cover, W.A.R.
5. *Antiquities of the Jews*; Flavius Josephus, Book 5, 2:1-6.
6. *Bigfoot*; Mary Blount Christian, pg. 23.
7. *Feats and Wisdom of the Ancients*; Time Life Books, pg. 133.
8. *Mysterious Places*; edited by Jennifer Westwood, pg. 12.
9. *Giants, Dwarfs and Other Oddities*; C.J.S. Thompson, M.B.E., pg. 175.
10. *Giants, Dwarfs and Other Oddities*; C.J.S. Thompson, M.B.E., pg. 133.
11. *Chariots of the Gods?*; Erich von Daniken, pgs. 34-35.
12. *Giants, Dwarfs and Other Oddities*; C.J.S. Thompson, M.B.E., pg. 132.
13. *Born Different*; Frederick Drimmer, pg. 70.

14. *Giants, Dwarfs and Other Oddities*; C.J.S. Thompson, M.B.E., pg. 140.
15. *Giants, Dwarfs and Other Oddities*; C.J.S. Thompson, M.B.E., pg. 142.
16. *Born Different*; Frederick Drimmer, pg. 50.
17. *Giants, Dwarfs and Other Oddities*; C.J.S. Thompson, M.B.E., pg. 164.
18. *Giants, Dwarfs and Other Oddities*; C.J.S. Thompson, M.B.E., pg. 168.
19. *Giants, Dwarfs and Other Oddities*; C.J.S. Thompson, M.B.E., pg. 132.
20. *Giants, Dwarfs and Other Oddities*; C.J.S. Thompson, M.B.E., pg. 133.
21. *Giants, Dwarfs and Other Oddities*; C.J.S. Thompson, M.B.E., pg. 142.
22. *Bigfoot...Man, Monster or Myth?*; Carrie Carmichael.
23. *Born Different*; Frederick Drimmer, pg. 50.
24. *Giants, Dwarfs and Other Oddities*; C.J.S. Thompson, M.B.E., pgs. 177, 144.
25. *Encyclopedia of Fairies*; Katherine Briggs, pg. 135.
26. Cited in *Encyclopedia of Fairies*; Katherine Briggs, pg. 28.
27. *Giants, Dwarfs and Other Oddities*; C.J.S. Thompson, M.B.E., pg. 161.
28. *Giants, Dwarfs and Other Oddities*; C.J.S. Thompson, M.B.E., pg. 149.
29. *The Golden Bough*; James Frazer, pg. 280.
30. *The Golden Bough*; James Frazer, citing Puttenham's *Arte of English Poesie* (1589); pg. 128.

Chapter 15: Birth of the Great Lie

1. *Feats and Wisdom of the Ancients...* Library of Curious Facts: Time Life Books, pg. 28.
2. *Feats and Wisdom of the Ancients...* Library of Curious Facts: Time Life Books, pg. 29.
3. *Feats and Wisdom of the Ancients...* Library of Curious Facts: Time Life Books, pg. 30.
4. *Chariots of the Gods?*; Erich von Daniken, pgs. 24, 106.
5. Sumerian King-List cited in the Introduction to the *Epic of Gilgamesh*, translated by N.K. Sandars.
6. *Apocalypse Chronicles*; James Lloyd, Vol. 3, #2, Planet X and the Power of the Heavens.
7. *Encyclopedia of Gods*; Michael Jordan.
8. *Encyclopedia of Gods*; Michael Jordan.
9. *Encyclopedia of Gods*; Michael Jordan.
10. *The History of Magic and the Occult*; Kurt Seligmann, pg. 79.
11. *The History of Magic and the Occult*; Kurt Seligmann, pgs. 79-80.
12. *The History of Magic and the Occult*; Kurt Seligmann, pg. 80.
13. *The History of Magic and the Occult*; Kurt Seligmann, pg. 127.
14. *Extraterrestrials...What on Earth is Going On?*; Mark Hitchcock and Scot Overby; pg. 91.
15. *Chariots of the Gods?*; Erich von Daniken, pg. 56.
16. *The Mythology of Mexico and Central America*; John Bierhorst, pgs. 164, 178, 179.

17. *The Mythology of Mexico and Central America*; John Bierhorst, pgs. 146-147.
18. *Encyclopedia of the Gods*; Michael Jordan.
19. *The Watchers*; Raymond E. Fowler, pg. 205.
20. *The Science of Fairy Tales*; Edwin Sidney (1848-1927) Hartland, cited in *The Watchers* by Raymond Fowler, pg. 212.
21. *Encyclopedia of Fairies*; Katherine Briggs, pgs. 88-89.
22. *Encyclopedia of Fairies*; Katherine Briggs, pg. 96.
23. *Encyclopedia of Fairies*; Katherine Briggs, pg. 142.
24. *Encyclopedia of Fairies*; Katherine Briggs, pg. 232.
25. *Encyclopedia of Fairies*; Katherine Briggs, pg. 232.
26. *The History of the Devil and the Idea of Evil*; Dr. Paul Carus, pg. 286.
27. *The Watchers*; Raymond E. Fowler, pg. 211.
28. *The Mythology of Mexico and Central America*; John Bierhorst, pg. 101.
29. *The Threat*; David Jacobs.
30. *The Watchers*; Raymond E. Fowler, pg. 224.
31. *The Watchers*; Raymond E. Fowler, pg. 229.
32. *From Atlantis to the Sphinx*; Colin Wilson, pgs. 20-21.
33. *From Atlantis to the Sphinx*; Colin Wilson, pg. 82.
34. *From Atlantis to the Sphinx*; Colin Wilson, pg. 135.
35. *From Atlantis to the Sphinx*; Colin Wilson, pg. 147.
36. *From Atlantis to the Sphinx*; Colin Wilson, pg. 147.
37. *Chariots of the Gods?*; Erich von Daniken, pg. 93.
38. *Chariots of the Gods?*; Erich von Daniken, pg. 27.
39. *The Two Babylons*; Alexander Hislop, pgs. 85-86.
40. *The Two Babylons*; Alexander Hislop, pg. 195.
41. 2 *Esdras* 5:8, cited in *Giants, Dwarfs and Other Oddities* by C.J.S. Thompson M.B.E., pg. 18.
42. *Mystic Places*; Time Life Books, pgs. 133-134.
43. *The Mythology of Mexico and Central America*; J. Bierhorst, pg. 172.
44. *The Watchers*; Raymond E. Fowler, pg. 209, citing John Keel's research of anthropologist Brian Stross.

Epilogue: As in the Days of Noah

1. *The Mythology of Mexico and Central America*; J. Bierhorst, pgs. 179-80.
2. *Wyatt Archaeological Research: Discoveries Volume*; Ron Wyatt, Discovered Creation, pg. 28.
3. *Illustrated Book of Myths*; Neil Philip, pgs. 74-75.
4. *Illustrated Book of Myths*; Neil Philip, pg. 49.
5. Gilgamesh is included among the giants in the Dead Sea text called the *Book of Giants*.
6. *Doomsday...A View Through Time*; Russell Chandler.
7. *Doomsday...A View Through Time*; Russell Chandler, pg. 114.

Bibliography

5/5/2000; Ice; The Ultimate Disaster; Richard Noone (Three Rivers Press)
Abominable Snowmen: Legend Come to Life; Ivan T. Sanderson (Cosimo Classics)
The Aeneid; Virgil (Penguin Books)
After the Flood; William Cooper (New Wine Press) 1995.
Ancient Giants Who Ruled America; Richard J. Dewhurst (Bear & Co.)
Ancient Legends of Ireland; Lady Wilde Jane; (Ward & Downey, Downey, London, 1887)
Ancient Man: Handbook of Puzzling Artifacts: William Corliss (Sourcebook Project)
Ancient Mysteries: Peter James & Nick Thorpe (Ballantine Books)
The Antiquities of the Jews; Flavius Josephus, translated (1736), by William Whiston, (Hendrickson Publishers, 1987)
The Apocalypse Chronicles; James Lloyd (Christian Media)
Apocalypse of Baruch (Destiny Pub.)
Archaeology: edited Paul G. Baun (Cambridge Univ.)
Arte of English Poesie, Puttenham
The Atlas of Archaeology; Mick Aston & Tim Taylor (D.K. Pub.)
Beowulf; Burton Raffel (Mentor Books)
The Bible as History; Werner Keller (Bantam Books)
The Bible As It Was; James L. Kugel (The Belnap Press of Harvard Univ. Press, Cambridge, Mass. London, England) 1997
Bigfoot; Mary Blount Christian; (Crestwood House)
Bigfoot...Man, Monster or Myth?; Carrie Carmichael; (Raintree Steck Vaughn)
The Book of Enoch; trans. by Richard Laurence LL.D (Artisan Pub.)
The Book of Jasher; (Artisan Pub.)
The Book of Jubilees; Wintermute, O.S.; Translator
Born Different; Frederick Drimmer (Atheneum)
Bulfinch's Mythology; Modern Abridgement by Edmund Fuller (Dell Pub.)
Celtic Myth and Legend: An A-Z of People and Places; Mike Dixon-Kennedy (Cassell Illustrated)
Chariots of the Gods?; Erich von Daniken (Berkley Books, NY)
The City of God; Augustine of Hippo
De Borussiae Antiquitibus; Erasmus Desiderius Stella (1466?-1536)
The Dead Sea Scrolls; Michael Wise, Martin Abegg & Edward Cook (Harper San Francisco)
Dialogue with Trypho; Justin Martin
The Dictionary of Misinformation; Tom Burnam (Harper and Row, Pub)
Discovered: Noah's Ark!; Ron Wyatt (Wyatt Archaeological Research)
Discovered! The Genesis Story of Creation; Ron Wyatt (Wyatt Archeological Research)

Discovering Ancient Giants: William Hinson (Seaburn Books) 2013.
Doomsday... A View Through Time; Russell Chandler (Servant Ministries)
Echoes of the Ancient Skies...The Astronomy of Lost Civilization by Dr. E.C. Krupp (Harper & Row Pub., NY)
Elder Gods in Antiquity: M. Don Schorn (Ozark Mountain Pub) 2008.
The Enchanted World...Night Creatures (Time Life Books)
An Encyclopedia of Fairies; Hobgoblins, Brownies, Bogies, and Other Supernatural Creatures; Katherine Briggs (Pantheon Books)
Encyclopedia of Gods; Michael Jordan (Facts-on-File, Inc.)
Epic of Gilgamesh; Maureen Gallery Kovacs: (Stanford Univ. Press, Stanford, CA.)
The Epic of Gilgamesh; N.K. Sandars (Penguin Books)
*Evolution Cruncher (*now titled *Evolution Handbook)*: Vance Farrell (Evolution Facts, Inc.)
Expository Bible Encyclopedia; A.R. Fausset (Zondervan)
Extraterrestrials...What on Earth is Going On?; Scot Overby & Mark Hitchcock (Hearthstone Press)
Facts and Fictions Regarding Noah's Flood; Charles A. Weisman (Weisman Pub.)
Feats and Wisdom of the Ancients...Library of Curious and Unusual Facts (Time Life Books, Alexandria, VA)
Footprints and the Stones of Time: Dr. Carl Baugh & Clifford Wilson (Creation Research Institute)
From Atlantis to the Sphinx; Colin Wilson (From International Publishing Corporation)
Ghost Lights and Other Encounters of the Unknown; E. Randall Floyd (August House Pub, Inc.)
Giants: A Reference Guide From History, the Bible and Recorded Legend: Charles DeLoach (Scarecrow Press
Giants, Dwarfs and Other Oddities: C.J.S. Thompson (Citadel Press) 1989
Gods and Fighting Men; Lady Gregory (John Murray, London)
The Gold of Exodus; Howard Blum (Simon & Schuster)
The Golden Bough; James Frazier (1854-1941) (Gramercy Books)
The Great and Distinguished Words of God; El Publishing, Arlington, TX
The Great Pyramid...Prophecy in Stone; Noah Hutchings (Hearthstone Press)
Halley's Bible Handbook (Zondervan)
The Handwriting of God, Grant Jeffrey (Frontier Research)
Hebrew-Greek Key Study Bible (KJV) Spiros Zodhiates (AMG Pub.)
Historia Regum Britannaie; Geoffrey of Monmouth (1100-1154 A.D.). a.k.a.
History of the Kings of Britain, Edited by W.W. Comfort Dent, London, 1914.
Histories, Herodotus
The History of Magic and the Occult; Kurt Seligmann (Gramercy)
The History of the Christian Religion and Church During the First Three Centuries: Augustus Neander (Book Tree reprint)

The History of the Devil and the Idea of Evil; Dr. Paul Carus (Gramercy)
The Holy Quran (Presidency of Islamic Researches, IFTA)
Iliad; Homer (Barnes & Noble, Inc.)
Illustrated Book of Myths; Neil Philip (Dorling Kindersley)
Judaism: edited Arthur Hertzberg (George Braziller NY) 1962.
Lost Cities and Ancient Mysteries of South America: David Hatcher Childress (Adventures Unlimited)
Lost Cities of Ancient Lemuria and the Pacific: David Hatcher Childress (Adventures Unlimited)
Lost Cities of North and Central America: David Hatcher Childress (Adventures Unlimited)
Lost Race of the Giants: Patrick Chouinard (Bear & Co.)
Maps of the Ancient Sea Kings: Advanced Civilizations in the Ice Age; Charles Hapgood (Turnstone)
Merriam Webster's Collegiate Dictionary
Mysterious Places: edited by Jennifer Westwood (Galahad Books)
Mystic Places; Time Life Books
The Mythology of Mexico and Central America; John Bierhorst (William Morrow and Company, Inc. New York)
National Geographic Explorer program on Abusir Excavation
Nineveh and Its Remains; Sir Henry Layard; (1853)
Noah's Flood; Norman Cohn (Yale Univ. Press: New Haven & London)
Noah's Flood; William Ryan & Walter Pitman (Simon & Schuster)
Noah's Flood, Joshua's Long Day and Lucifer's Fall...What Really Happened?; Ralph Woodrow (Ralph Woodrow Evangelistic Ass.)
The Odyssey; Homer, trans. by Robert Fitzgerald (Doubleday Anchor)
The Old Testament Pseudepigrapha; James H. Charlesworth, (Doubleday & Company), 1983, N.Y.
Our Occult History: Jim Marrs (William Morrow) 2013.
Petra; E. Raymond (Artisan Pub.)
Philo of Alexandria; Questions & Answers
Plato...Five Great Dialogues; Edited by Louise Ropes Loomis (Grammercy)
Popular Tales of the West Highlands; J.F. Campbell, 4 Vol. New Edition (Alexander Gardner, Paisley and London, 1890-93)
The Practical Bible Dictionary and Concordance (Barbour)
Praeparatio Evangelica; Eusebius
Prose Edda; Snorri Sturluson (1200 A.D.)
Race in Ancient Egypt (may be confused with Life in Ancient Egypt by Adolf Erman)
The Rephaim; Miss Fanny Corbeaux
Sargon the Magnificent; Mrs. Syndey Bristowe (Association of Covenant)
The Science of Fairy Tales; C.S. Hartland (Walter Scott, London, 1891)
Secret Cities of Old South America: Harold T. Wilkins (Adventures Unlimited)
Secrets of Time; Stephen Jones (God's Kingdom Ministries)

Serpent in the Sky... High Wisdom of Ancient Egypt; John Anthony West (Wildwood)
The Signature of God; Grant Jeffrey (Frontier Research)
Smith's Bible Dictionary (Barbour)
Serpent in the Sky...High Wisdom of Ancient Egypt; John Anthony West (Wildwood)
Some Kati Myths and Hymns; G. Morgenstierne; (cited in *Encyclopedia of Gods* by Michael Jordan)
Space Travelers and the Genesis of the Human Form: Joan d'Arc (Book Tree)
The Stones Cry Out; Bonnie Gaunt (Bonnie Gaunt)
Strong's Exhaustive Concordance (World Pub.)
Tales From Ovid; Ted Hughes (Farrar Straus Giroux)
The Threat; David Jacobs (Simon & Schuster)
Tracing Our Ancestors; Frederick Haberman (Covenant Pub., London)
A Treasure of African Folklore; Harold Courlandour (Marlowe & Company)
The Two Babylons; Alexander Hislop; (Loizeaux Brothers, Neptune, N.J.)
The Vikings and America; Erik Wahlgren; (Thames and Hudson)
The Watchers; Raymond Fowler (Bantam)
Worlds in Collision; Immanuel Velikovsky (Victor Gollancz, 1950)

Other Works by Jason Breshears

The Lost Scriptures of Giza (paperback, hard cover & kindle)
Centuries after a cataclysmic depopulation of the world, mankind sought to replicate the one great monument that survived from the previous age. Pyramids were erected everywhere as colonies of survivors thrived, but none have matched the Great Pyramid of Giza in size and meaning. Its secrets are now uncovered and explored in this important groundbreaking book. This book also reveals:
• Ancient traditions of the pyramid found in an extinct language.
• An ancient body of teachings holding that Enoch was the architect of the Giza monuments before the Great Flood.
• New discoveries of the amazing teachings and ministry of Abraham at the Great Pyramid in Egypt.
• A secret body of obscure scriptures in the Bible that refer to the Great Pyramid.
• Ancient knowledge that the Great Pyramid complex was long ago beneath the Mediterranean Sea.
• Ancient Egyptian accounts of the discovery of the Great Pyramid, with Egyptian based memories of Abraham visiting the Giza site.
• Secret traditions regarding the Sphinx and why it appears older than the pyramids – but is not.
• Historical records showing that the Great Pyramid was built to preserve knowledge and survive through a planetary cataclysm

When the Sun Darkens (paperback, hard cover & kindle)
Numerous times throughout Earth's history there have been major cataclysmic events. These events have resulted in large-scale climactic changes, mythological stories of floods and visitations from the skies, and sometimes the complete extinction of life. The major planetary body that has caused much of this carnage has been referred to by many names. Jason Breshears has termed it Phoenix, based on his research into the distant past and what it was usually called by witnesses. By piecing together ancient documents from the most reputable sources available, we have, in this book, the most extensive and accurate rendering of the cycle of the Phoenix, including when it will come again. Some of us, according to the author, will live to see its return. Beyond the foundational scientific evidence, the author ties in various Bible prophecies that relate directly to it. Many books exist on this subject, but few have broken new ground like this one, due to the extensive research involved.

Note from the Author: After years of researching into chronological and calendrical systems from around the world I made a single profound discovery not found in ANY published books EVER. Over thirty ancient destructions and eyewitness accounts specifically dated and confirmed by multiple recorders from widely separated civilizations left us writings today that DATE the appearance of a vast red object approaching earth and passes, leaving earthquakes, volcanic ruin, floods and a red mud, rain and/or reddish dust blanketing our atmosphere. These findings, coupled with what ancient writers mentioned of the very old legends of the Phoenix, led me to write *When the Sun Darkens*, published by Book Tree of San Diego in 2009. My discoveries did not end with the publication of this work, but so much new materials came into my possession that I had to write *Nostradamus and the Planets of Apocalypse*.

Nostradamus and the Planets of Apocalypse (paper, hc & kindle)
This book maps out the entire historical chronology of planetary cataclysms starting in 4309 BC, covering the cyclical return of Nibiru, the planet Phoenix, and more. It also reveals the code for understanding the prophecies of Nostradamus, showing when they have occurred in the past, or when they will occur in the future. It takes the work of Mario Reading, who first broke the code, and shows how it perfectly applies to all of Breshears' previously made cataclysmic predictions for the years 2040 and 2046. Mr. Reading made mistakes in interpreting some quatrains for the years 2001-2012 that did not involve his code, so his work has been largely dismissed. Breshears brings Reading's work back to life with stunning clarity, and takes it one step further in our understanding of prophetic events. Also covers the predictions of Mother Shipton, who was not only a contemporary to Nostradamus, but made the exact predictions Breshears and Nostradamus made concerning two large scale global catastrophes that will occur six years apart. Despite the many predictions of others, the year 2012 passed with no worldwide cataclysmic events because, according to the author, they were never interpreted or explained correctly, until now. The author remains unmatched in his in-depth research regarding historical and geological cycles, which in turn allows him to accurately map major planetary events, past and future, many of which are outlined in this book.

Anunnaki Homeworld (paperback, hard cover)
The Anunnaki is a legendary race that appears in the oldest documents preserved by mankind. They are said to inhabit an outermost planet that orbits our sun in an extremely elliptical orbit. Each time this planet gets near to the earth it creates planetary cataclysms. Many researchers claim it will be returning soon. The work of Zecharia Sitchin, author of the Earth Chronicles series of books, focuses on the Anunnaki and their previous visits. Many have asked Sitchin, "When will this planet return?" He never gave an exact date, but said it was more than halfway back. Jason Breshears gives an exact year, and does so confidently, due to his extensive research. He delves not only

into historical records, as Sitchin had done, but also uses scientific cycles and mathematical formulas that relate to our concepts of planetary time and orbits. The historical records, chronologically presented by Breshears, help in identifying cyclical patterns. He also employs advanced geometry, interprets complex crop circle patterns, and uses biblical prophecy in support of some of the astronomical events he has predicted. He does not cover much on the mythical aspects of the Anunnaki gods themselves, but focuses more on the actual sciences that can predict their return. Ancient stories and carefully documented proof are two different things. For these reasons, this book is highly recommended.

This work restores what our scholars have lost. The *truth* about our planet's past and future. This author's prior work, *When the Sun Darkens*, concerned the history and 2040 AD return of planet Phoenix, a fragmenting and uninhabited world having little bearing on this present thesis. The fact is herein demonstrated that there is indeed a *second* wandering planet that occasionally visits our inner solar system, a gigantic, broken and presently *populated* world that is now fast approaching Earth and will arrive at 2046 AD. This planet is NIBIRU, and its orbital history completely forged the unfolding of human events.

This is the "Anunnaki Homeworld" and its return was a constant fear of the ancients. The most magnificent architectural wonders from the Old World, the Great Pyramid and Stonehenge, as well as the earth's most archaic dating systems, all remain as mute witnesses of the presence and orbital chronology of this alien planet. Even the modern misinterpreted Mayan Long-Count system, when *accurately interpreted, as will be shown herein, was a sophisticated countdown to the exact date of the return of NIBIRU* and its Anunnaki occupants in 2046 AD. The popularized year of 2012 AD was never the end of the Mayan system, and this will be conclusively proven in this book.

The pyramid was not a tomb. Stonehenge was not a temple. This book, written three years before 2012 and released in 2011, *proves* that it is not mathematically possible for 2012 AD to be the end of the Mayan Long-Count calendar. These are the assumptions of men trained to think one-dimensionally, those blind to the silent atavistic patterns appearing mysteriously in our grain fields that beckon us to search deeper into the messages of universal geometry. We are being warned, and these warnings concern 2046 AD.

Whatever preternatural forces are at work behind these amazing crop formations, it is abundantly clear that the exact same formula is employed in interpreting the three-dimensional calendrical geometry of Stonehenge I and II, and also the method for understanding the *calendrical messages of crop patterns*. READER BEWARE... what the masses believe and what this thesis demonstrates cannot both be true.

Return of the Fallen Ones: Nephilim Histories, the Antediluvian Worldm Anunnaki Chronology and the Coming Cataclysm (paperback, hard cover) In ancient times there are stories of the gods who appeared on Earth and brought knowledge and civilization to mankind. The oldest stories were from ancient Sumer and these gods were called the Anunnaki, or Nephilim, also known as the Fallen Ones. They were considered fallen after co-mingling with the daughters of men, so their realm became the Earth rather than the "heaven" from which they came. Their offspring were said to be giants and these myths and legends are found throughout the world. The author spent years of study to reveal an accurate, chronological history of these ancient beings, unveiling in this book a calendar of their events more accurate than anything previously known. This book presents vast research on worldwide myths, records of earth changes documented from cultures worldwide, and the author's immense work on planetary cycles to predict the return of these fallen ones, and the chaos and catastrophe that always came with them. The author was in a situation that, for many years, left him alone to study these things more completely than most anyone could imagine. As a result, the information being shared in this book should be studied seriously by those interested in these subjects. It is considered a masterpiece of investigation filled with new finds, new concepts and a totally new understanding of human antiquity.

Awaken the Immortal Within (paperback, hard cover & kindle)
There's a ton of self-help books at every trash dump in every major city. You've seen them, read them and they didn't work. There's a reason for this. A single fact about how we view the world around us that remains unmentioned by these authors.
This explosive book shows exactly what mental practice was employed by the author that fundamentally CHANGED EVERYTHING in his life. From inside a prison cell with no resources, no money, very limited access to anything he needed, he changed a single thing about how he perceived the world around him and suddenly received help from the most unusual places, secured four publishing contracts as a convicted felon still in prison, received not one, but THREE paroles after 26 years and was released at 43 years old. He had been out of prison for only 59 days and released four more books on Amazon, with a California publisher about to release another of his nonfiction works. This man herein shares with you a secret that OPENED EVERY POSSIBILITY in his life, forever altering the dynamics of his existence for his benefit. He claims that he is not special in any way, that ANYONE can do what he did and declares that what he reveals in this book will PROVE IT. Note from the Author: All my life I thought myself independent from the masses, a rogue, tough guy making my own way. How deceived I was. After decades of living the wrong way, in a passive state of reactive impulses, I was shocked into being STILL. For the first time in my life I observed what was occurring around me, what had been transpiring all around each

one of us our entire life. I WOKE UP and this simple act CHANGED MY FREQUENCY. No longer in resonance with the negative, and requiring NO EFFORT ON MY PART, I broke through the condition of bondage and entered a realm where EVERY DAY things go my way. Now, no one nor any thing stands as a barrier between me and the things I seek to do and experience. So profound is this change that I often infect those I'm in closest contact to and they too enjoy the benefits, profiting by my knowledge and contact. Do not deny yourself that which is rightfully yours. Start LIVING. What I will show you can be found nowhere else. Accept this singular tenet and your world will change. You will become a concentration of vast creative potential, an auric field saturated with all of the knowledge and power acquired in life ready to be drawn upon at will, a vortex that pulls people and favored circumstances to you through the illusionary barriers of time-space. Nothing can be beyond the reach of your will. No boundaries exist because all is connected. Your power will be magnified in patience and trust, knowing that events, circumstances and things are instantly moved by your thoughts, aligning toward you by repetitively thinking in the positive... desired results are drawn more and more into your life through daily streams of thought and expectation. As your daily behavior reflects these thoughts, what you want begins manifesting in your life. The holospheric Oversoul will both obey the master or afflict the slave; the master has all he wants and builds his own life, the slave remains adrift in a chaotic sea of thought-constructs belonging to others.

About Jason Breshears

Jason M. Breshears has authored 17 books and several articles, 10 works available on Amazon. His research bibliography is currently over 1200 nonfiction books read and data mined during a 25 year period, approximately 320,000 pages from many rare works as old as four hundred years, including translations of texts dating as far back as four thousand years. His core conclusions, discoveries and observations are available on archaix.com. As a pen & ink illustrator and graphic artist, many of his book covers and artwork are done by himself. Breshears is one of the only researchers in the world who specializes in ancient chronological systems, focusing on global antiquities from 4309 BCE to 522 CE. Many of his historical discoveries cannot be found in any other works. For this reason he was awarded with multiple publishing contracts with Book Tree in San Diego.
Breshears started Ophis in 2017, a consultation service that uses PREPS, or Pattern-Recognition Event Prediction Software, that he developed for personal and business applications. Ophis development emerged naturally out of his extensive studies on time-space anomalies and complex calendar systems of ancient technolithic civilizations.

Personal Note from Jason: I'm witty with a dark sense of humor; my pendulum swings between gladiator and goofball. I value smartasses. A free spirit, humor is my ally, I embrace my deviance, finding solace among the shadows. I recognize that I see the world around me through a lens different than my peers. A pirate philosopher playing both sinister and sacred, I honor no God—my spirituality is measured in my actions toward others. I'm implacable in my beliefs until overwhelmed with new information, love meatballs but dislike spaghetti, scrape the good stuff out of tacos and subway sandwiches and the toppings off of pizza. Life's too short for shells and crusts. I sing in the shower, drink my coffee black, love short-haired dogs and I'm hoping heaven has grilled-cheese sandwiches. I'm all-American, a patriot who has studied and admired the history of this great nation and I'm upset with the morons who are ruining it. My friends are few, but genuine. In a world that thrives on artificiality I take care to identify friends from fictions. In summary, I've never been accused of being normal.

My Philosophy: Though all men are created equal, they do not remain that way. In this age males are many but men are few. But there are some of us that rise above the rest and have the right to represent our gender as a whole... men of peace with capacity for war, we who speak what others are afraid to say, the apex of both the sacred and the profane. I am one of these men, just as evil as I am holy, separated by sin but bound to God, a student and teacher from the occult to Christianity. Poets and philosophers, visionaries and Vikings, we few have a divine right to claim that we are men... all others are merely males. The following are my beliefs, the architecture of my personality:

* "The man of principle never forgets what he is, because of what others are." —Baltasar Gracian
* "The real voyage of discovery consists not in seeking new lands, but in seeing with new eyes." —Marcel Proust
* "I am something more than I suppose myself to be, and perhaps all those perfections which I attribute to God are in some way potentially in me." —Rene Descartes
* "A man's worth is not measured by his accomplishments, but in what he strives to accomplish." —Cicero, 1st cent. BCE
* LIVING is the purpose of life.
* "A person who sees what he wants to see, regardless of what appears, will some day experience in the outer what he so faithfully sees within." —Ernest Holmes, 1919.

www.archaix.com Learn more about new discoveries in archeology, ancient texts, traditions, etymology and observations concerning the ancient world, the Nephilim, intruder planets, the cycles of historic world-shattering cataclysms, amazing World Chronology Charts, secrets about the Great Pyramid complex, and other surprising research painstakingly uncovered that the Establishment censors from public view.

www.ingramcontent.com/pod-product-compliance
Lightning Source LLC
Chambersburg PA
CBHW042131160426
43199CB00021B/2879